45189,

# ANIMATION
## From Script To Screen

ALSO BY SHAMUS CULHANE

*Talking Animals and Other People* (an autobiography)

# ANIMATION

## From Script To Screen

## Shamus Culhane

**Columbus Books**
**London**

Copyright © 1988 Shamus Culhane

First published in Great Britain in 1989 by
Columbus Books Limited,
19-23 Ludgate Hill, London EC4M 7PD

*Designed by Karin Batten*

**British Library Cataloguing-in-Publication Data**

Culhane, Shamus.
    Animation from script to screen.
    1. Cinematography, Animation, Manuals
    I. Title.
    778.5'347

ISBN 0-86287-959-0

*This book is dedicated to Winsor McCay, Walt Disney, Norman McLaren, and the other bright minds who have brought the art of animation this far.*

# Contents ~~~~~~~~~~

# List of Illustrations ~~~~~~~~~~~

# Acknowledgments

With gratitude and thanks to the people who have helped and encouraged me to write this book: A Da, Arthur Babbitt, Frédéric Bàck, Edward Bakst, Dante Barbetta, Jeanine Basile, Cosmo Anzilotti, Dick Rauh, David Smith, Robert Edmonds, William Hurtz, Walter Lantz, Wayne Becker, Don Duga, Howard Beckerman, Frank Capra, Susan Catmull of P-I-X-A-L, Gene Deitch, Les Drew, David Ehrlich, Al Eugster, Elvena M. Green, Arthur Heineman, Faith Hubley, Leslie Cabarga, Lou Bunin, Cliff Roberts, Emily Hubley, Derek Lamb, Janet Perlman, The Fax Company, Paul Julian, John Lamb and Gary Beydler of Animation Controls, Caroline Leaf, Norman McLaren, Gil Miret, Cardie and Charles Mortimer of Westfall Productions, Inc., The National Film Board of Canada, Michael Sporn, Takako Oshita and Seinosuke Arata of Hiroshima 87, Ishu Patel, Jaques Drouin, Kaj Pindal, Michael Porsch, Børge Ring, Morton Schindel of Weston Woods Studio, John Schnall, Alexander Schure, Chancellor of The New York Institute of Technology, Louis Schure, head of Computer Graphics Laboratory, Senji Seya, Jim Lindner of The Fantastic Animation Machine, Yan M. Shanchung, Alvy Ray Smith, Gayle Thomas, Betty Edwards, author of *Drawing on the Right Side of the Brain,* my editor Ruth Cavin, my publisher Tom Dunne, and my wife Juana, who, more than she realizes, was a great help in writing this book.

I hasten to add that I am not writing this book solely for cartoonists. As you will find out, there are many filmmakers who are what is snobbishly called "fine" artists. There is as much reason to call them "animators" as there is to describe the makers of children's television programs and theatrical short subjects that way.

This book is not a shortcut to proficiency. I see it as part of a curriculum. There is no way that I could, in a single book, encapsulate the many facets of learning that must be examined and understood before one can create a meaningful animated film. I consider this book to be the hub of a number of books, which I list here, and which will not only give the student the methodology of animation but the history of the profession as well.

## Book List

### History

Adamson, Joe. *Tex Avery: King of Cartoons.* Teaneck, New Jersey: Film Fan Monthly, 1975.

Cabarga, Leslie. *The Fleischer Story.* New York: Nostalgia Press, 1976.

Canemaker, John. *The Animated Raggedy Ann & Andy.* New York: Bobbs-Merrill Co., 1970.

Culhane, Shamus. *Talking Animals and Other People.* New York: St. Martin's Press, 1986.

Finch, Christopher. *The Art of Walt Disney.* New York: Harry N. Abrams, Inc., 1973.

Maltin, Leonard. *Of Mice and Magic.* New York: McGraw-Hill Book Company, 1980.

Peary, Gerald and Danny. *The American Animated Cartoon.* New York: E. P. Dutton, 1980.

Russett, Robert and Starr, Cecile. *Experimental Animation.* New York: Van Nostrand Reinhold, 1976.

Schickel, Richard. *The Disney Version.* New York: Simon & Schuster, 1968.

Thomas, Frank and Johnston, Ollie. *Disney Animation: The Illusion of Life.* New York: Abbeville Press, 1981.

### Instructional

Blair, Preston. *Animation.* Tustin, California: Foster Art Service.

Culhane, John. *Special Effects in the Movies.* New York: Ballantine Books, 1981.

Da Silva, Raul. *Making Money in Film and Video.* New York: Prentice Hall Press, 1986.

―――. *The World of Animation.* Rochester, New York: Eastman Kodak Co., 1979.

Edwards, Betty. *Drawing on the Artist Within.* New York: Simon & Schuster, 1986.

―――. *Drawing on the Right Side of the Brain.* Los Angeles. J. P. Tarcher, 1979.

Eisenstein, Sergei. *Film Form.* New York: Harcourt Brace Jovanovitch, 1942.

―――. *Film Sense.* New York: Harcourt Brace Jovanovitch, 1942.

―――. *Immoral Memories.* Boston: Houghton Mifflin Co., 1983.

Graham, Donald W. *Composing Pictures.* New York: Van Nostrand Reinhold, 1970.

Muybridge, Edweard. *Complete Human and Animal Motion.* New York: Dover Books, 1987.

Nicolaides, Kimon. *The Natural Way to Draw.* Boston: Houghton Mifflin Co., 1941.

Nizhny, Vladimir. *Lessons with Eisenstein.* New York: De Capo Press, 1979.

## Books on Writing

Field, Syd. *The Screen Writer's Workbook.* New York: Dell Publishing Co., 1984.

Nash & Oakey. *The Screen Writer's Handbook.* New York: Barnes & Noble, 1974.

Ziegler, Isabelle. *The Creative Writer's Handbook.* New York: Barnes & Noble, 1974.

## Art Analysis

Culhane, John. *Fantasia.* New York: Harry N. Abrams, Inc., 1983.

Malraux, André. *The Psychology of Art: Museum Without Walls, The Creative Act,* and *Twilight of the Absolute* (3 volumes). Princeton: Princeton University Press, 1978.

## Computer Animation

Kerlow & Rosebush, *Computer Graphics.* New York: Van Nostrand Reinhold, 1986.

## Evaluating the Bibliography

Some books on the list are a necessary part of your learning process. Others are on the list because, I believe, they give you a well-rounded picture of the art form and of animation as a business.

These are the books you should have:

*The World of Animation,* because it contains much valuable information, including how to build your own camera stand.

*The Natural Way to Draw.* This may be the best book on drawing ever written. You will learn how to do accurate quick sketches, but best of all is the writer's personal attitude about being an artist.

*Drawing on the Right Side of the Brain* is a real breakthrough on the subject of creativity. It puts into succinct English the theories of creativity that have been taught since ancient times but never put into scientific terms.

*Animation,* by Preston Blair, is a wonderful exercise book by a top-flight animator.

*Composing Pictures* is invaluable for the novice layout or background artist. It was written by one of the greatest art teachers of our country. Even animators and directors should possess it.

*Complete Human and Animal Motion* is a book every animator should have and study assiduously.

*The Screen Writer's Workbook* is full of practical information for the novice writer, but should also be read by those who plan to become directors.

*Computer Graphics* will sprain your head because it is full of words that cannot be found in the dictionary, at least not yet. Try to read it anyway.

*Special Effects in the Movies* will give you some ideas about the use of the optical printer and other processes.

The rest of the books, while not really necessary to the curriculum, are all fascinating and provocative. In addition, I have a few divertisements of my own, which I will unfold in subsequent chapters.

A great deal in these books and the others I have mentioned will be useful to even the most conservative artist, but the reader knows where my heart is. I want to have us all experience the bacchantic joy of drawing with the right side of the brain.

It may surprise you that in this book I use a number of very old animated films to illustrate ideas. This is done for several reasons. One, for the most part, the pictures are readily available in 16 mm film and video cassettes. This is not true of very modern animated films. Two, many of these pictures are the best possible examples because they were made at a time when there was a lavish use of drawings to attain life quality in the animation. Three, fine animation does not get dated.

It is difficult to realize that by present-day standards, Walt Disney was a primitive in that his films were made using the cel system. It is true he did switch from inking cels to using cels produced on a copier made especially for the purpose by Xerox, but his painting department still has to compile several sets of color charts, one for each cel level.

It is easy for the painters to make mistakes and paint a character with the wrong cel level. This results in a vexatious color jump on the screen.

Using computerized equipment, the colorist has no such problem because no cels are involved. Not only that, computer coloring is at least five times faster than using a paintbrush.

Even with these advantages, it will be a long time before the use of cels dies out—probably many years. So in this book, we are going to have to parallel instructions, both for cel animation and the computer.

Long before you have completed reading the books and finishing the exercises that are involved, you will have made some experimental films. I promise that they are not going to be the usual fumbling attempts of amateurs, with the lack of pace and the helter-skelter editing that is common among beginners. I am a teacher, not an instructor. Therefore, you will not learn how to do something before you have understood *why* you are doing it.

There are many ways of using the curriculum I am offering you. It depends on your maturity, your intelligence, and the intensity of your drive to become a skilled filmmaker. The length of time it takes doesn't really matter. You can only learn up to your capacity at the moment. A few years from now, your personality will be more mature and you probably will be able to cull more information from these same books than you did the first go-round.

Some of these books will be read once; others will be your lifelong companions, to be read and used again and again for the rest of your professional life. What is exciting to me as a teacher is the possibility that I may teach somebody who will take the animation medium into a great leap forward. Notice that I do not mention studios. Groups of people do not form the van of a new movement. New movements are led by individuals who have passions and ideas of which their fellow workers aren't even aware until they are finally revealed. So compelling are these new vistas that old methods and customs learned by painful study are happily abandoned in favor of new points of view.

The process of self-education should be a richly rewarding experience. It is not some Herculean task, no Augean stables to clean out. You learn at your own speed; no need to stuff yourself like a Strasbourg goose to meet a test. Some of these books will interest you more than others. Realize that this will change as the years go by because your tastes will undergo many modifications.

I hope this form of self-education will make you resilient and full of intellectual curiosity, ready to drop hard-won knowledge if the art of animation takes on new forms, new theories. Don't prize what you already know; prize your capacity to take in and use new information. There is nothing more pathetic than an artist whose work habits are so constricting that a new school of thought leaves him or her stranded like a beached whale. Age is not a factor. Grim Natwick, creator of Betty Boop, did some fine animation at eighty-six. I have scolded animators in their thirties for being old-fashioned.

The best insurance for a long, happy, and successful career is not a set of cast-iron work habits. It is a sound knowledge of the principles of animation, which enable the artist to rise to any new mode of thinking or new process, mechanical or aesthetic, of filmmaking.

If you, the reader, are a talented person, I hope you bow in thankfulness to whatever forces of nature you worship, because you are one of the chosen. Think of the incredible number of people who are born, live, and die without ever experiencing the exaltation of a creative act. Respect your good fortune and nurture your talent.

One thing I can guarantee, if you enter the animation profession, you will not have a prosaic life. Just imagine the millions of people who get up in the morning and spend all day typing invoices, turning nuts, waiting on tables, directing traffic, and drudging through hundreds of other commonplace jobs.

You, on the other hand, will enter an enchanted world every morning, a world of the imagination, where bad-tempered ducks squawk at mice, crazy woodpeckers cavort, and elephants will fly if you want them to.

If you like to travel and work in different countries, you may. I have worked in New York, Miami, Hollywood, Toronto, Montreal, London, and Milan. I can guarantee that you will never be bored. There is one proviso: You will not be bored if you are one of the leaders of the profession. As in any other business, there is plenty of hackwork, dreary beyond belief. Luckily, there are plenty of hack artists available who can do this kind of work without suffering a qualm.

This brings me to the problem of competition. It is my observation that over 90 percent of any group of workers are unwilling to improve their abilities by study—unless it happens during working hours and the boss supplies the means.

When I worked for Walter Lantz, directing his films, we had about fifty people on the staff. Three of us were studying after work; I was going to Chouinard's Art Institute one night a week and poring over *The Natural Way to Draw* several other nights.

Two of the studio's best animators, Emery Hawkins and Pat Matthews were also studying Nicolaides. We were the only people on the entire staff who were students! Lack of interest in the profession, lack of energy both physical and psychic, and laziness left forty-seven people out of the competition. I believe this was also about the average in the other studios.

The exception was the Disney studio, where most of the creative members of the staff studied at night and on weekends. This was ironical because they were already the best-educated artists in the profession.

So, for the ambitious neophyte, these figures should be reassuring: The competition consists of less than 10 percent of the entire animation profession.

I had a brief stint of teaching at The School of Visual Arts. Here I encountered some youngsters who rebelled at the idea of producing a film in an orderly fashion, that is, making a storyboard, model sheets, bar sheets, and so on. They stared me impatiently. "Look man, like, I don't need all that crap about exposure sheets and all that. Just lemme fool around with the camera. I wanna be, you know, like, free."

I finally realized that what these young people were rejecting was really the cutey-cute characters of the 1930s, the violence in the animation of the 1940s and 1950s, and the adulation of the superhero in the 1970s and 1980s. I can see why these themes are not acceptable to the young people of our time, but production methods should not be dumped along with the content. It's throwing out the baby with the bathwater.

We, in our time, after a faltering start, are beginning to use what may

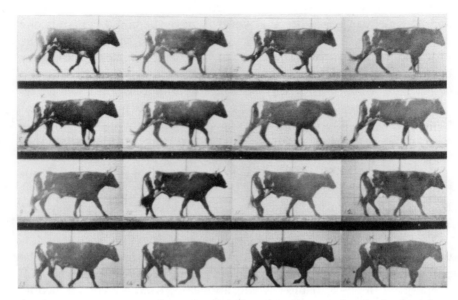

Although Edweard Muybridge compiled his action photographs of animals and humans more than a century ago, they are still the best source of information for the animation of various walks and runs.

be the greatest medium for artists ever devised, computerized animation. No other medium for creativity has such a sublime admixture of controlled time, movement, drawing, painting, speech, and music.

Join me in the excitement of knowing that we are part of a select group of people whose membership goes back into prehistory. We are one with the artists who drew the bison in the caves of Altamira, designed the patterns of the rocks at Stonehenge, made the wondrous sculptures in the portals of the cathedral at Chartres, and created the portraits and religious paintings of the Renaissance.

Let me give you a tip, the result of long observation and much practice. You are about to get an education in a very emotional and complex profession. Don't go about the learning process as if it were your Wednesday-night bridge game. Bring some passion into it; feel how exciting it is to be an artist, and how marvelous that you are going to expand your talent to its maximum over a period of many years, not in a haphazard way but with good tools, sound advice, and, above all, hard work.

The more you know about every aspect of filmmaking, the more you are equipped to go forward, "Like, you know man . . . free."

*Note:* At the back of the book is a glossary of terms particular to animated filmmaking. The first time each of these terms is used in the text, it is italicized, as a signal that the definition may be found in the glossary.

# 1

# How an Animated Film Is Produced

Animating a film is very much like making a flip book, where you flip the pages and the figures on them seem to move. The closer the various parts of the character are to the position in the previous drawing, the slower the action will appear to be; the wider the spacing between parts, the faster the action.

The pages of a flip book are bound, to ensure registry. The animator maintains registry by working on paper that has punched holes, designed to fit on pegs fastened to a drawing board. In the center of the board is a pane of glass, and under it is a light box. The paper is thin enough so that when the bottom light is on, the animator can see the animation on four or five sheets of paper. That way, the position of the animation on the next drawing can be gauged.

To save unnecessary work, very often the various parts of a character are split up. For example, if the figure stands in one place for a long time, the animator may elect to make a separate drawing of the feet, instead of tracing them on drawing after drawing.

The same is true of other areas. If at one point only the head is moving, the body may be drawn separately. So now there are two levels, the feet and the body, which the camera operator will not

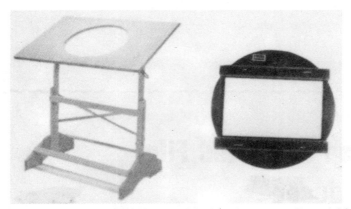

Fax Company's animator's drafting table, with disc cutout; 12- and 16-field animation disc, Acme or Oxberry pegs.

change. If the arms are moving, the animator may draw the feet and the body on one drawing, leaving the head on one level and the arms on another.

When one drawing of a part of the body is held for a time while other parts are moving on different levels, the camera operator needs careful instructions from the animator. A form called an exposure sheet has been developed over the years. (See illustration on page 108.)

In commercial animation studios the animator draws the key movements of a given action, numbers the drawings, and annotates them on the exposure sheet. The work then goes to the assistant animator, who follows the instructions on the exposure sheet, adding more drawings. The scene is then passed to the second assistant. At this point there will be only one or two drawings to be made in between those that have been made by the other two artists. For this reason the second assistant is called an "inbetweener."

The next step is called a pencil test. The drawings are photographed under an animation camera. (See illustration above.) The table under the camera is equipped with the same kind of pegs and bottom light that the animation crew works with.

The camera is rigged to shoot one exposure at a time, and can slide up and down the column to make long shots, close-ups, and trucks.

The resulting footage is shown in a projection room, and reviewed by the animator, the story crew, and the director. It is at this point that major corrections or additions are made. The revised animation is reshot and screened once again. If the work is approved, all the draw-ings are transferred to punched acetate sheets the same size as the drawing paper. The transfer is made either by tracing each drawing in ink, or by a Xerox machine especially designed for this purpose.

The *acetates,* called *"cels,"* are then colored, using opaque paint. One complication is that while the transparent cels themselves seem to be colorless, they actually have a slight tone. Very often as many as four or five cels are used to make up a single exposure, so the paint has to be carefully graded to offset the color built up in the cels as the sheets accumulate. A character that was on the bottom level of a five-cel scene, and for technical reasons has to be moved to the top level, cannot be colored with the same palette for both sets of draw-ings. The cels on the bottom level have to be painted with lighter values than the ones on the top level, otherwise there will be a very perceptible color jump.

While this painting is going on, *backgrounds* are made for every scene, according to the sketches of the *layout* artist. The paper used is the same size as the cels and, like them, is equipped with peg holes. The backgrounds may be done in any medium—oil, watercolor, colored pencil, pastels, cutout bits of colored paper. Since the cels are transpar-ent, when they are combined with a background, the whole assemblage looks like one complete picture.

Before photographing, the camera operator fastens the background art securely to the camera's table, because it is not going to be removed until the scene is finished. Then, following the animator's instructions on the exposure sheet, the first combination of cels is placed on the background, and the indicated number of exposures are made.

This group of cels is then stripped off the pegs and another set placed down. This operation continues until all the cels have been photo-graphed.

At this point, the sound track may consist of as many as a dozen separate reels. Perhaps several have music that was recorded prior to the start of production; others may be sound effects. *Dialogue* may be on several tracks. After the color photography has been done and approved by the director, all these sound tracks are combined on one track.

The sound track and the color negative are sent to a laboratory and a combined track and animation print is struck off. If this print is satisfactory, the production is complete.

That, in a nutshell is how an animated film is produced. Of course,
I have omitted many of the less-important stages, such as checking,
because I want to make this explanation easy for the novice to grasp.
We'll deal with the details as we go from one department to the next
in the following text.

# 2

# Job Options in a Cel-System Studio

Following is a compendium of the various kinds of jobs in a studio that is still using the cel system:

**DIRECTOR**   He or she works with the story department on new ideas; supervises the development of the stories; approves character sketches; directs recording of dialogue and music; creates the *bar sheets;* works with the layout person; hands out work to the animators; supervises the pencil test and orders *retakes;* oversees the painting of the backgrounds; checks the *rushes;* and okays the final photography and the *answer print.* The director also has the power to suggest hiring and firing to the producer.

**ASSISTANT DIRECTOR**   The assistant director keeps all records of the filmmaking process; writes up exposure sheets from the bar sheets; keeps the tally of good and bad takes at recordings; handles the tape recorder in *sweatbox* sessions; and lightens the director's load by taking on as many details of the directorial process as possible.

**WRITER**   He or she creates plots and *gags* for established characters and devises new characters; works closely with the director and *storyboard* artists; confers with director during sweatbox sessions, looking for additional gags; and stands ready to make revisions if the original material isn't working in animation. Some writers can write lyrics for original music written by the studio music composer.

**STORYBOARD ARTIST**    The storyboard artist works with story department, drawing essential sketches for an interpretation of the story in graphic terms. He or she must be a good cartoonist with the ability to make funny poses; and has to have some knowledge of basic background material such as landscapes and architecture.

**CHARACTER DESIGNER**    He or she must have a large vocabulary of proportions for characters and many different drawing styles. It is vital that the designs must lend themselves to good acting and are capable of being animated. In most cases, the characters must look good in more than one view.

**LAYOUT ARTIST**    The layout artist must be an excellent cartoonist, capable of following the basic designs of established characters and making humorous poses of them. He or she needs the ability to do research on costumes, architecture, and landscapes. It is essential to have a sound knowledge of perspective and composition; and also to be conversant with the technical needs of the animator and the camera operator.

**ANIMATOR**    He or she must have versatility in animating various styles of characters, especially in a studio where the product is television spots. The animator needs to know a great deal about acting theory and practice; fine draftsmanship is essential, as is the ability to make funny drawings and actions. He or she must have total knowledge of the camera in order to write comprehensive camera instructions. The animator should have some executive ability in order to supervise the assistant animator and *inbetweener.*

**ASSISTANT ANIMATOR**    His or her chief function is to add to the rough drawings made by the animator, leaving one or two inbetweens throughout for the inbetweener (see below), and to prepare the scenes for pencil testing. After approval by the director, the

'PEEP', 'QUACK' AND 'CHIRP' ——>
DOING THE SPIDERWALK

Drawing from *Peep and the Big Wide World,* a National Film Board of Canada production. Animated and directed by Kaj Pindal. The drawings are pasted together and put on a reel-like film, then recorded directly on videotape. The colors are added by computer.

assistant cleans up the *roughs* and checks the exposure sheets for errors; and computes *pan* moves before turning the work over to the inbetweener. As the assistant gains expertise, the animator gives him or her small bits of animation to do. Gradually this amount is increased, until the assistant animates small scenes, then more important shots, finally graduating into a full-fledged animator.

**INBETWEENER**    The assistant animator's assistant is given simple tasks, usually doing single inbetweens, gradually working up to three, then five inbetweens. There are very few artists who have chosen to make inbetweening a profession; they usually aspire to become assistants and eventually animators.

**PLANNER**   This job is in effect one where each scene, after it is cleaned up, is subject to a scrutiny to see whether it is possible to combine drawings on the same cel when the scene is being inked or Xeroxed, thus saving the expense of superfluous cels and making the scene easier and quicker to photograph. The work needs a person with a strong sense of order and a sound knowledge of the camera.

**BACKGROUND ARTIST**   A great facility in many kinds of media is needed for this work. Watercolor, acrylics, oils, pastel, and cutout papers are the materials usually used to make backgrounds. Many layout artists draw with very few details, expecting the background artist to supply them, and he or she must be ready to do so. Most background artists are satisfied to make this job a permanent one. Very often the artist is not a cartoonist but a person with an extensive classical art education.

Character design for *The Night the Animals Talked*. Drawings by Shamus Culhane.

**INKER**   It is not necessary to be a talented artist to become an inker. Neatness and a firm, careful hand are the main requirements. The work is normally done by women who make inking a career; very few men elect to become inkers because the job, under present conditions, is a blind alley.

**XEROX OPERATOR**   Again, this is not a job requiring any artistic ability. It is the same kind of work that is performed in any office—in effect, another dead end.

**CHECKER**   Some inkers may qualify for this job, but there are few checkers needed in a studio. What the work entails is a complete dry run on the cels and background to see whether there are any mistakes in the painting; the animation must be matched to the background to see if it is in registry; if, for example, a part of a character goes behind an object. Checkers have to be painstakingly neat and tidy, to the point of obsessiveness, because missing a

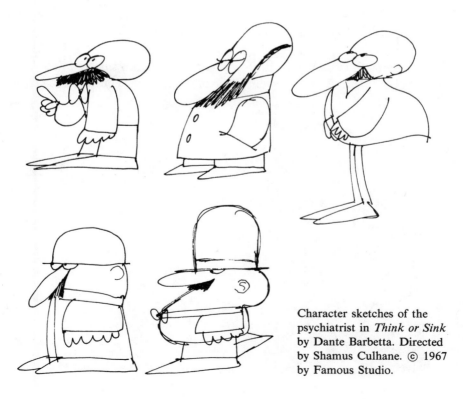

Character sketches of the psychiatrist in *Think or Sink* by Dante Barbetta. Directed by Shamus Culhane. © 1967 by Famous Studio.

mistake means that the scene will be photographed in color, and a work print ordered at considerable expense, before the error is caught by the editor or the director in sweatbox.

**CAMERA OPERATOR**    The camera operator must have a sound knowledge of all aspects of animation-camera photography, as well as a grasp of all the intricacies of laboratory work, both black-and-white and color. It is necessary to know how to keep the equipment in good running order. Above all, consummate patience is needed, because a good part of photographing animation is by rote, just like any other machine work.

**EDITOR**    Unlike this editor's live-action counterpart, the animation editor is robbed of the opportunity to select shots and put together a film. Instead, the main function is to assemble tracks and reels according to the bar sheet, attend recording sessions, and keep all the reels in *sync.* Compared to live-action editing, it is an unrewarding job.

## Moving from Creative to Technical Work

As you can see, there are a number of jobs in a studio that require skill rather than talent. There is a sharp line of demarcation between the two

Gil Miret's design for the two thieves in *The Opera Caper.*
© 1967 by Famous Studio.

kinds of work, and, except for the job of assistant director, no way for a skilled worker to cross over into the more creative functions. In that one position, it is possible for a person untalented as an artist but gifted in other ways, to go from a skilled but relatively dull job in the studio to work as a director's assistant.

Directors have to work at a very intense pace. They have only so much energy to expend every day, and naturally they do not want to expend it on record keeping or any other noncreative work. The more the assistant can take over responsibilities, the more valuable he or she becomes. The job can be fascinating—listening to the creative people solving problems by talking and drawing; watching a picture emerge from the first stammered conjecture in a preliminary story meeting to the laughter and applause at the sneak preview; knowing better than anybody else how all the aspects of the filmmaking process were shepherded by the director, and the small victories and defeats along the way.

# 3

## Tapping into Your Creativity

There are several books in the bibliography that are going to be required reading. I expect that at some point you will want to own them all, but a few will be worth studying over a period of many years.

First and most important is Nicolaides's book, *The Natural Way to Draw,* which is probably the best book on drawing that was ever written. The series of exercises he has created are ideal for learning how to draw an accurate rough sketch. Without this facility, it will be very difficult to learn to make high-speed roughs, which means that some of my teaching methods will be impossible to absorb.

Perhaps you think that you draw a pretty fair rough and do not need practice. I would like you to begin a course of exercises on drawing one-minute roughs for one hour every day. Keep all your drawings, date them, and at the end of a month compare your latest drawings with the first ones. You will be amazed!

By the end of the second month of daily exercises, you should be able to sketch a working drawing in twenty to thirty seconds. Ignore the contour drawings and the drawings made without looking at the paper. Later, for your own education, this kind of exercise can be added to your schedule. But concentrate on these lightning-fast sketches for the next few years.

The value of being able to draw high-speed roughs was brought home to me when I began my research into creativity.

As soon as I started to become an animator, I was puzzled by a strange phenomenon. I would go to work in the morning and have a marvelous few hours drawing with almost no effort. Then I would go to lunch and return to find that the magic touch was gone. All afternoon, I plied my eraser as often as my pencil, only to throw out the whole afternoon's work at five o'clock.

Sometimes the reverse was true: After hours of struggling, I would seem to shift into gear and drawing was fun and games again. It worried me because there was such a vast difference between my bad drawings and my good ones.

I was working at Fleischer studio at the time, and I seemed to be the only person who worried about these wild swings between mediocrity and expertise. After my contract expired, I worked as a director for several years, first at Iwerks studio, then at Van Beuren's. But I still was interested in animation, and I realized that there was much to learn beyond the rudiments I had picked up at Fleischer's, so I applied for and got a job at Disney's.

The standards of drawing there were so high that, even at my best, I felt I wasn't good enough—and I was right. So I was in a panic when I hit a streak of bad drawings. Poor work was a sure way to end up out of a job. What to do?

I was convinced that animator's block was something psychological, so I started looking for books about creativity. Most of them were pompous bits of jargonese. Then I questioned my fellow workers at the studio to the point of becoming a nuisance, all to no avail. Everyone I talked to, even stars such as Tytla and Ferguson, freely admitted that there were times when they couldn't draw without incredible effort. And there were other times when the drawings seem to flow from their pencils with no struggle.

The remedies they suggested were unsatisfactory. Freddie Moore recommended switching from pencil to crayon. Tytla just bulled his way through the day, then threw the results away the next morning. Everybody agreed that animator's block existed, but nobody had the remotest explanation for it. Yet I was sure that if it was such a universal affliction, there must be some principle that was being used or abused.

I stumbled into the answer quite by accident, or unconscious intuition, as a result of doing all this thinking and reading about creativity. I had been at Disney's almost two years and I always was on the verge of being fired. Instead, Disney shifted me from animation to drawing storyboards, which I detested. Finally, I was assigned to work with Bill Roberts, one of three Pluto specialists. The others were Norman Ferguson and Fred Moore. Under Roberts's strict guidance, my drawing improved.

Eventually, I got my big chance. There was a sequence about Pluto and a crab in *Hawaiian Holiday,* which would normally have gone to one of the Pluto specialists, but they were all busy on *Snow White.* So I was given the assignment.

Instead of starting to work on the animation as soon as I was given the storyboard sketches and the layouts, I fell into a languid mood. It felt like a kind of daydream, not thinking about the work at all. This was in sharp contrast to the intense anxiety I had felt when I heard about the assignment.

I wasted a whole day in this fashion. By five o'clock, all I had to show for my time was a page of inch-high sketches of Pluto in poses that were an improvement on the storyboard drawings—about a dozen drawings in all.

Even these were not made with any concentration. They were more like doodles. The next day was a repeat performance, or the lack of it. Once again, I scrawled a few inch-high drawings of Pluto and some sketches of the crab. By the third day, I should have become anxious. If Ben Sharpsteen, the director, happened to drop into my room to see what I was doing, he would have been appalled. I had three pages of tiny drawings. That was all. But it was as if I was waiting for some inner message, some resolution in my psyche that would start me off.

Midmorning of the fourth day, I was suddenly galvanized. I was used to drawing rather quickly, except when I was suffering from animator's block, but I never drew with this speed. I never stopped to number drawings; gave only a cursory glance at the exposure sheets; and forgot about spacing charts.

My only purpose was to pour out this information about the action, and it was like a giant flood. I made no effort to control it. If a drawing didn't suit me, I ripped it off the pegs and threw it on the floor as I reached for a fresh sheet.

None of the roughs were completed drawings. Some were just an eyeball; others were finished bodies, except for the head. It was a kind of shorthand. Thanks to Bill Roberts's rigorous training, no matter how fast I drew, the drawings did not lose proportion or size. That first day, I must have drawn over a hundred sketches. The next day was the same. I seemed to be able to retain this relaxed but intense mood even when it was interrupted by lunchtime or the end of the business day.

An example of rough
animation by Shamus
Culhane. The drawing took
approximately six seconds.

Little additional actions, not on the storyboard, began to appear of
their own volition. The crab became a personality instead of just a
prop—a kind of crustacean Eddie G. Robinson. I had the sensation that
I was at once the performer and the audience, watching with objectivity
the antics of a baffled Pluto and a belligerent crab, yet feeling their
emotions as I drew.

In less than a week, the entire sequence was roughed out . . . about
seven hundred drawings. I realized that I had one strict rule: I never
stopped drawing for any of the usual reasons for interrupting the work,
that is, studying the exposure sheets, erasing mistakes, or checking the
*model sheets.*

I never even stopped to see why a drawing was discarded. The
important thing was to keep going on my pell-mell roughing out. I
never once used an eraser. A drawing was either right or I threw it
away, even though it may have needed only a minor correction. Nothing must stop this rush of drawings and ideas. Somehow I recognized
unconsciously that these mechanical things—fiddling with drawings,
stopping to write numbers, even looking closely at the exposure
sheets—were all factors that would break this miraculous flow of information.

That's what the roughs were—not so much sketches as information.
Nobody else could have possibly used them to make cleaned-up drawings because they were mostly reminders that at a certain point in the
roughing-out process, I *felt* a certain way. I was feeling the action of
Pluto as he snarled at the crab, or the crab as he shoved his hat forward,
preparing to stalk over to the dog. So these doodles of snarling mouths,
scurrying claws, and drooping tails were more memory joggers than
drawings.

A group of kittens are an ideal subject for quick sketch. Drawings by Shamus Culhane.

I had been such an unknown quantity as a neophyte animator that I had not been given an assistant, so I was going to do all my own *cleanups.* Now that the entire sequence was roughed out, I started the process of numbering the drawings and going about the prosaic business of making out the exposure sheets. It took me over six weeks to clean up what had gushed forth like a geyser in five days.

As the various scenes began to appear in the *pencil-test reel,* Walt and the storymen realized that I had added a new dimension to the crab, so they added little touches of their own.

Whenever I made these additions, I went back to my original scribbles, and, using a few drawings just before the new action, I would resume drawing at top speed. I did even new actions that involved a few feet in this way. Then I would go through the clean-up process and revise the exposure sheet.

Al Eugster's version of Minnie, Mickey, and Donald Duck, Woolie Reitherman and Frenchy de Trémaudan's animation of Goofy, and my Pluto and the crab sequence had such vitality that it was obvious we had created a superior cartoon. This was affirmed at the Venice Film Festival the following year. *Hawaiian Holiday* won an award as the best short subject of the year.

Looking back over this astonishing experience (unlike anything that had ever happened to me as an artist), I began to analyze the details of the whole event.

## Drawing with the Right Side of the Brain

It seemed that I had divided my animation into two very separate stages. The first was this daydream stage, which had culminated in a burst of energy. It was obvious that the most important feature of drawing at top speed at this stage was that I was purposely not allowing myself time to think. Contemplation and introspection had no place in this stage of creativity.

In the second stage, there were no impulsive moves; conscious thinking was my main effort. I was now totally involved in interpreting those drawings I had dashed out. I looked long and hard at each scribble, trying to recall the sensation I was having at the time I drew that particular pose.

So I had stumbled on a method of creativity, completely divided into two separate and distinct functions, and, like oil and water, they didn't mix.

I was anxious to try this exhilarating experience on my next picture, but it turned out to be impossible. I was given the "Heigh-ho" sequence in *Snow White,* where the dwarfs march home. The work was loaded with technicalities. Each dwarf had his own style of walking, yet they all had to march in unison without gaining or losing ground—all this in perspective shots, back views, scenes with giant shadows of the dwarfs. There was no place for breakneck drawing in any of these shots.

In the interim, I went back to my obsessional reading about creativity. Oddly enough, I found hints about the separation of thinking and feeling in the creative act in the writings of such diverse personages as Dr. Sam Johnson, Joan Miró, Aldous Huxley, Pablo Picasso, and Rollo May. I can't recall the title of one interesting book, a book devoted to theories about the function of the brain. In it, the author wrote dryly, "Contrary to our puritan ethos, the brain functions most efficiently when it is in, what we call disparagingly, a daydream."

Of course, in my enthusiasm, I wanted to tell everybody about my wonderful discovery. I met instant resistance. Norman Ferguson came in one day to congratulate me on my Seven Dwarfs marching. He called it "a real nifty piece of work." I started to tell him about this high-speed technique, but Fergie froze up and left abruptly. Suddenly I realized that I had been talking to the one man in the studio who had been using this technique all along.

He was doing the high-speed scribbles but he had John Lounsbery to clean them up. He rarely ventured out of the "feeling" stage except for writing numbers on the drawings and filling out exposure sheets. So when I started talking to Ferguson about high-speed drawings, it was like telling a golfer that I noticed that he always wagged his club three times before taking a swing. People have been killed for less.

I did notice that from time to time, while I watched, an animator would begin to pour out drawings with no effort, but at some point he would interrupt himself to erase a drawing. I restrained myself from telling him that he had just cut off his flow of creativity. I was right, but he probably would have thought that I was mad.

Unfortunately for my zeal, the rest of my friends reacted pretty much like Fergie. Nobody wanted to discuss their work habits. However, I am stubborn, so since 1938 I have expounded on this technique to new assistants, animators, audiences at lectures, and new pupils—with no luck whatsoever.

Rollo May thinks that this is because people have an aversion to getting into what seems to be a mild trance, where there is a heightening of the senses. People want to feel that they are in control, so they avoid the experience. Whatever the reason, the fact is that for all these years, I have yet to get a disciple.

## The Two Sides of the Brain

Suddenly I came upon a book written by a drawing teacher, *Drawing on the Right Side of the Brain* by Betty Edwards. We have a lot in common. We both have been intensely curious about the fact that some people easily learn to draw, while others struggle with at best a very poor result.

Edwards's research led to studies that were carried out at the California Institute of Technology by Roger W. Sperry and a group of fellow scientists. In brief, they were finding that, unlike Gaul, the brain is divided into two parts.

The left side of the brain is logical. It remembers phone numbers,

Tom Nelson
August 8, 1978

Tom Nelson
September 3, 1978

Lyman Evans
April 2, 1978

Lyman Evans
May 8, 1978

The best argument for the use of the theory that the right side of the brain is the creative side is seen in these four drawings, with their incredible improvement within the space of a few weeks. © Betty Edwards, *Drawing on the Right Side of the Brain,* courtesy of the author.

birth dates, arithmetic, and the location of one's hat rack. It is the strict enforcer. Given a chance, it will shut down the function of the right side and take over. When creativity is called for, the right side, in effect, has to fool the left side into backing off and stop from trying to take charge.

The high-speed drawing technique is going at such a pace that there is no time for reflection and contemplation. As long as there is no stopping, the right side of the brain is in charge, but one bit of thinking about an eraser, or the need for a number on a drawing, and the left side grabs the opportunity and shunts the right side out of the way.

Now to a nice clean-cut young artist armed with a Pink Pearl eraser, a quire of paper, and an exposure sheet, it must seem like the height of folly to give up these controls and allow something to happen without restrictions or "control."

In reality, by hanging on stubbornly to that eraser, the chance to be most creative is lost. The left side of the brain is so orderly and resistant to flights of fancy that, in comparison to the right side, it is a great bore. It is only on the right side that two or more wild fancies meet and form a synthesis—some incredible result that would never come about by conscious effort.

Understand me, it is possible to be an artist all your life, operate with the left side of your brain with only minimal use of the right, and, if you have enough latent talent, manage to turn out acceptable work. My guess is that what we call hack work is often achieved that way.

I realize that there are two kinds of personalities. One, like mine, has the mischevious curiosity of a monkey, wants to know how everything works and why. The other personality is less secure, doesn't want to know how the mind works, because, like the golfer's need to make three little strokes, it's more comfortable to play the game by rote.

## Seeing Instead of Looking

The right side is strictly intuitive, willing to forgo reason and logic, and, unlike the left side, able to tap into what I call, for want of a better term, the memory bank. The memory bank is a part of the process of *seeing,* rather than *looking.* For example, two people are idly watching a very old man walk down the street. One watches the man, regards him as a symbol of decrepitude, and dismisses him with no further need for information. The other person sees the painful straining of the pelvis, the panting mouth, and the dragging feet shuffling along the pavement. The man is not a beggar; he is wearing what used to be a fine coat, and rising from the collar is a worldly wise face. A battered Borsalino is slanted over a pair of merry eyes. So much for seeing as opposed to looking.

I am convinced that all great artists, including animators, have the ability to *see,* and it is being exercised every waking minute. Not that any of this information is stored on a conscious level, but it is there when it is needed.

Now that I am aware that I have this facility, it amuses me to catch myself storing information. This man laughs like a donkey brays; look at the movement on the fat arse of that woman—it's like a piece of machinery; what a funny way to hold a cigarette, with the lighted end pointed toward the palm. I am convinced that this kind of information storing goes on all day, unless one is doing what we call "thinking."

I consider Betty Edwards's book a must for any student of animation. The most astonishing feature of her findings is the fact that there seems to be no prolonged struggle for proficiency. On the other hand, does this not parallel my own jump from crowd-shot mavin to Pluto specialist? Walt Disney put it succinctly when he was talking to me about my work: "I never saw anybody improve so goddamn fast."

I heartily recommend that the reader buy not only *Drawing on the Right Side of the Brain* but also Edwards's newest book on the subject, *Drawing on the Artist Within.* Kimon Nicolaides and Betty Edwards have a lot in common. I suggest that you use his high-speed drawing exercises in conjunction with her approach to using the right side of the brain.

Let me stress that I am not aiming these books solely at the animators. I feel that anybody in the creative area of filmmaking should do these exercises. *The Natural Way to Draw* can be useful for character designers, storyboard artists, and even writers. How much easier it is for a writer to explain an idea to the director with even a crude rough sketch, instead of trying to do it all verbally.

For the moment, use your own hand as a model; later you will be drawing characters. Start right now with the exercises, and please note that sixty minutes of drawing every day is better than a seven-hour session once a week—far better. Working one day a week gives your unconscious a chance to build up a resistance to new work habits; a once-a-week schedule leads to falling back on your old ways of thinking, just as surely as with a patient going to psychotherapy.

# 4

# Life Quality Versus Stylized Animation

The pioneer producers of animated films, Bray, Barré, Nolan, Lantz, Terry, and La Cava all thought of the animated cartoon as a moving comic strip. Even Disney's early films, including Mickey Mouse, were no better. The drawings had no weight, sag, or squash. None of them made any effort to conceal the fact that these were moving *drawings*.

A notable exception to this particular point of view was the animation by Winsor McCay, who created Gertie the Dinosaur. Gertie was

Winsor McKay's Gertie the Dinosaur became a vaudeville star. This drawing is from McKay's first film, made in 1909. The Museum of Modern Art Film Archive.

so lifelike that he took her into vaudeville, making his appearance dressed as an animal trainer. Seemingly in response to his commands, accented by the cracking of his whip, the dinosaur would do various tricks. Gertie looked so real that many people thought McCay must have traced a movie of a large lizard.

McCay had done nothing of the kind. He merely used his skill as a draftsman with a well-developed sense of showmanship.

The other exception to the comic-strip point of view was Max Fleischer. He and his brother Dave invented a machine called a *rotoscope,* which made it possible to trace a live-action movie exposure by exposure. With these tracings as a base, an animator could develop very lifelike actions.

The Fleischer brothers created a rotoscoped character called Koko the Clown, who popped out of Max's inkwell at the start of every film, made a pest of himself in Max's office, and dove into the inkwell to finish the film.

While McCay had only one assistant, a fellow who traced the backgrounds on each drawing, leaving the creative work for McCay, the Fleischers had no such scruples. They hired a staff of artists who, by guess and by God, taught themselves animation. They learned the rudiments very quickly because they had the help of the tracings of the live actor, usually Dave Fleischer.

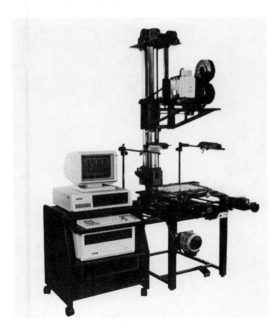

Lynx Robotics' motion control system. Fax Company's senior stand.

## Disney Introduces Cartoon Characters Who Act

So McCay and the Fleischers were the only people who tried to get away from the comic-strip influence, until Disney started a quiet revolution in his studio. He began to point out that the audience would really like some acting, instead of pie-in-the-face humor. The storymen came up with *Three Little Pigs* and *The Grasshopper and the Ants* in the early 1930s, and by the time *The Country Cousin* was produced in 1936, the Disney studio had no rivals. Warners and MGM set off in pursuit, but it was a long chase.

Max Fleischer dismissed the Disney approach as "too arty," and settled for Betty Boop and Popeye. Van Beuren and Terry just added sound to the dreary cartoons they had been making, and Screen Gems followed their lead rather than Disney's.

Animators were notoriously peripatetic, gaily hopping from Hollywood to New York as the mood seized them. Not, however, the Disney animators. So the technical methods of drawing lifelike action remained pretty much a trade secret until the Disney strike in 1941. Then many of the younger but highly talented youngsters left Disney's, never to return. And in leaving Disney, they also brashly departed from the Disney standard of life quality in their films. Two veteran directors, Frank Tashlin and Chuck Jones, urged them on.

The result was that the youngsters came full circle, back to the days when it was no secret that animated cartoons consisted of drawings. UPA, which started with a hard core of young ex-Disney artists, startled and delighted the public with high-style design and animation and offbeat stories to match.

*Noah's Animals,* a Shamus Culhane production for Westfall Productions, Inc. Backgrounds by Irra Duga.

*The Man in the Window* by Shinji Seya. A man in prison finds that freedom can be found within.

Character design for a television spot. An example of a stylized figure. Shamus Culhane Productions, Inc.

## How the Two Styles Differ

So, from the middle 1940s to the present time, the two points of view have maintained themselves on fairly equal terms. In this book, I am going to stress the necessity of learning both forms of animation, with the accent on the technical aspects of life-quality animation—not that it is a better technique or point of view, but merely because the technical problems of producing this kind of animation are more difficult than making stylized cartoons, which have no need to maintain the same volume in the characters: Nobody cares in stylized cartoons whether the characters have weight or not; squashing and stretching may or may not be used. Everything is more casual, yet more imaginative, because of the lack of a set of rules about physics, the laws of mass, and gravity and momentum.

Simulated or not, these same laws do apply to life-quality animation and are, therefore, restrictive, to an extent.

We will concentrate on life-quality animation for the same reason that it is better first to learn to drive a manual-shift car. Then you can easily find out how to drive an automatic within a few minutes. On the other hand, a driver who has learned first on an automatic shift will experience some trouble in switching. So it is that a good animator of life-quality animation can adjust easily to high-style drawing and action in a few minutes. However, the opposite is not true. Very few of the principles of high-style animation would help an animator struggling with his first scene of life-quality action.

## The Learning Plan

This is how we are going to go about your education: Throughout this book, you will find a series of exercises—in animation, writing, or layout drawing. Don't skip an exercise because it may not interest you. In a studio, you do not get choices about what you will or will not do. Get used to the idea. Do not do exercises out of context, either. They have been designed to add to your information in a methodical way.

The chapters have been designed to take you through every phase of production. Even if you believe that your sole ambition is to do layouts, pay attention to all the phases of filmmaking. When you understand the difficulties of all the other jobs in a studio, you will be better prepared to work as a part of a production team. The tunnel vision of a rabid specialist is no asset to the group; besides, what a good feeling to be multiskilled, able to step in and help in departments other than your own when an emergency arises.

One thing I want you to learn is the fact that the wastebasket is your best friend; to do something over because you are not satisfied is not a defeat, but a victory. Be your own harshest critic, unsparing in your analysis of your work and ready to junk it at the slightest suspicion that you could do better.

That way, you are competing with less than 10 percent of the profession, whatever your category. You will have a never-ending battle with yourself to keep on improving your results. It will never stop, but gradually as you gain some recognition, the process will have some rewards.

Most of us who have gone through the mill at Disney's are never satisfied with our work. One can be intellectually very pleased with oneself about an outstanding piece of work . . . at least people may say it is outstanding. You will find, however, as you look at the work on the screen or in the *cutting room* that you have a vague sense that it might have been better. The smug feeling of accomplishment will never be yours.

Animating the way I am going to teach you is an emotionally draining process, seemingly all work and no play. That is not strictly true. There is a fierce joy in the quick-sketch process, exhausting as it is; and during the cleaning up, it is amusing to try to solve the mystery of some of the shorthand that happened during that violent outburst of energy. You will undoubtedly suffer; learning is no happy experience in the beginning, but in time, one finds that creativity evokes exhilaration.

## Your Actors

I feel that it is wiser to have you learn to draw three characters very well, instead of feeding you a multitude of drawing styles. The important factor is that you learn how to put the characters through their paces, solving animation problems and becoming facile in the quick-sketch process.

So here are three characters, very different from each other in size, weight, and proportion. Their temperaments are different, too, which will influence the way they are animated.

**Fatty** is the muscle man of the group. He is slow-witted, cheerful, and willing to help. He moves with a kind of ponderous agility, so there is a good deal of stretch and squash in his animation.

**Skinny** is a high-strung, jerky, awkward guy who is a mass of nerves. He is uncoordinated and walks with a kind of shamble, elbows out, pigeon-toed, head stuck out in front, so that he resembles a stork or ibis. Usually cheerful, he is easily frightened.

**Tiny** is the pet, and he knows that he is cute, but not to the point of being obnoxious. He realizes that much of the time he is the most entertaining person in the group. He has a bouncy walk, bursting with energy and well-being.

These are your actors, and you will have to learn to draw them so well that their proportions are second nature; any pose you think of, you must draw with facility, so that it isn't what the pose *is* so much as *why* is it being drawn—what emotion is being expressed.

A model sheet of Tiny. Even the hat has to carry out the line of action.

*Exercise: Quick Sketches*

Right now the most important task ahead of you is the quick-sketch exercises. I expect you to draw for one hour at least five days a week. Buy lots of paper and pencils because you are going to draw a complete character each minute of the hour. Use a soft pencil and have a handful of sharpened pencils ready to substitute when the first pencil's point is worn down.

In order to avoid doing an exercise in scribbling pointlessly, take one character a day and use a theme, such as fright, hearty laughter, running, walking, jumping. At first, you will be hard put to dream up more than a few poses, and I don't say that you will ever be able to think of sixty, but don't confine yourself to full-face sketches. There is the rear view, profile, and three-quarter to consider, also the sitting instead of standing.

Work at top speed. Above all, never stop to erase! Work with a big stack of paper on the pegs, as much as they will hold. Do two or three drawings on the same sheet of paper, rip it off, and dispose of the drawing rapidly. This is no time to try to put each piece of paper in some neat niche. Try drawing the figure in what seems to be a medium shot, about four inches high for Fatty, and the others in proportion.

Do not be tempted to stop drawing or to slow down in order to toy with some interesting view of a hand. If you want to correct or improve some aspect of a drawing, do it on your own time, after the quick-sketch session is over.

At first, you probably will not make any drawings of value. After a time you will want to save some particular sketches. Build up a *morgue,* and after a few months, as your skills improve, you will start weeding out many of the drawings. What looked good at the end of the first month will seem pretty poor stuff at the end of six months of sketching.

Just to vary the tactile senses, try switching to red or blue crayon pencils. Sometimes this will enable you to suddenly draw much better, which means that you have eluded that left side of the brain and its need to control.

What will happen is that as you grow accustomed to rapid sketching, you will find you will be able to put in more detail. Try very hard to confine yourself to that one-minute-per-sketch routine. If possible, buy a stopwatch, or if that is too expensive, use your wristwatch. Place it where you can see it on your drawing table, not on your wrist because that will make you stop drawing to look.

In this model sheet of Fatty, note that there is squash and stretch in the mass of the face, just as there is in the body.

Don't be discouraged by your first efforts if they are clumsy and out of proportion. If you have tried one pose and it was a failure, try it again and again. It is not necessary to make a new pose for each sketch. Before you start drawing, set yourself some problems: What is the theme going to be? Which character this time? Are you drawing one character more often than the others? Which one have you been avoiding? Make a point of drawing him for the next three days.

A model sheet of Skinny. This is what a pencil test looks like. Notice that fine
details can be read very easily in negative form.

## Overcoming Bad Habits

There is a psychological factor to overcome. People have a tendency to do whatever comes easiest, avoiding difficult problems. It is going to be your role to understand this tendency and to circumvent it as often as it crops up. You cannot learn if all you do is what you have already mastered.

If you are having trouble with concepts, use comic strips, comic magazines, and books as sources of poses. Then translate the pose into one of our three characters. But don't use part of our sketch hour poring over this kind of material. Do it on your own time.

I have no objection to you first reading this book, as well as *The Natural Way to Draw* and *Drawing on the Right Side of the Brain,* in its entirety. Just don't start doing any of the exercises out of context. What we are working up to is a portfolio of drawings and a pencil-test reel of short bits of animation.

# 5

## Writing for Animation

The power of the animation medium is never more impressively revealed than in contemplating the many kinds of scripts that can be written for it.

Aside from the films that come readily to mind—the short subject made for the motion picture audience, the half-hour special, and Saturday-morning kid shows—there is animation used in medical films, physics, arithmetic, history, and biology, as well as many animated explanations of processes of machinery and chemistry. The medium is also useful for expounding abstract ideas, and was widely used in propaganda films during World War II.

### What Animation Can't Do

A professional writer for animation has to be able to think in graphic terms. However, there are definite limitations. While animation seems to be limited only by the imagination of the writer, there are barriers. Acting in animation is still on a very crude level. We have no Oliviers or Chaplins among our cartoon characters, so there would be no point in writing an animated film that places the burden of subtle acting on the animator. This goal may never be reached; in spite of the efforts of the staff at the Disney studio (and they have included some of the best draftsmen in the profession), very subtle acting may never be possible to attain in this medium. The sequence that stirred the most empathy in the audience of *Snow White* was the grief of the Seven Dwarfs as they stood around the bier of Snow White. That was animated in 1937, and no sequence in subsequent pictures has come even close, so I am inclined to think that animators trying to stir an audience by emulating our top live actors are chasing a will-o'-the-wisp.

In my opinion, the best use of animation is when it caricatures, not imitates, real life. The dance of the Chinese mushrooms in *Fantasia,* Pinocchio's stumbling efforts in Stromboli's puppet show, Pluto's pantomime as animated by Norman Ferguson, Mr. Magoo's nearsighted fumbling, the explosive tempers of Donald Duck and Yosemite Sam, and the crisp insolence of the unflappable Bugs Bunny are all near enough to real people to delight the audience. Nothing could be gained by painfully rotoscoping some actors to attempt to simulate live-action versions of these characters. Every art form has its peripheries, and I believe that animation has a definite limitation in its exploitation of animals and human beings.

When the animator, as performer, is allowed to put his own interpretation on a given character, it is a personal artistic effort. When he or she is saddled with a rotoscope version of the animation, the issues are muddled. It is two artistic efforts in an unhappy marriage of very distinctly different art forms.

## Staying True to Character

Disregarding educational films and other categories, and focusing on entertainment animation, when working with established characters, that is, personalities well known to the public, it is imperative to find out the confines of the character structure.

For example, according to Chuck Jones, there are definite house rules for even so loose a story structure as the Road Runner series. The Coyote never hurts the Road Runner; usually the Coyote's schemes to catch the Road Runner blow up in his face. These situations are never reversed.

Pluto was never depicted as having more intelligence than the average dog, and Mr. Magoo, the nearsighted star at UPA, never saw anything clearly, no matter how big it was.

So if believability in the characters is one of the components of your story line, it will be necessary to equip them with certain attributes in emotional structure, as well as definite physical appearance. If a proposed gag goes beyond these peripheries, it should be junked. Save it for another film.

## The Rise of the Cartoon Writer

In the early days of commercial animation, story discussions were held after work in an atmosphere redolent of cheap cigars, cigarette smoke, and bootleg whiskey. After a few hours of discussion, the three or four animators involved had pieced together a series of roughly outlined situations and several gags, enough for a story. There was no attempt to draw any of the ideas. The story conference was strictly on a verbal level. Nor were there any professional story writers. The animators were expected to create their own stories.

Each animator was assigned a part of the story, with the understanding that he would start his sequence in such a way that it would hook up with the previous and following sequences. In between these two specifications, he was free to animate whatever he pleased, as long as the action was vaguely related to whatever theme they had chosen in the story meeting.

It wasn't until the early 1930s that Disney, Fleischer, and Iwerks set up groups of men (usually ex-animators) whose sole function was to write stories. Then there was an attempt to create cartoons with real plots, with definite beginnings, middles, and endings, rather than a barely related string of gags.

## Graphic "Scripts": The Storyboard

For a time, scripts were typed live-action style, but soon it was obvious that this produced complications. For example, the script might indicate that a character entered a scene in a funny way. What kind of funny way? Often a written description of a gag proved to be unfunny when it was translated into animation.

So the storymen (there were no women in the story departments in those days) began to draw rough sketches of the salient scenes and gags, gradually adding more and more drawings, until it became customary to draw the entire story. In order to have them easily seen by the whole

FOOTSTEPS OVER TITLE.

CUT TO MR. SPOON WALKING
DOWN HALLWAY.

VOICE OVER— MY NAME IS
NESBITT SPOON. YOU MIGHT
SAY I'M AN AVERAGE
KIND OF A PERSON.

—TODAY WAS AN
AVERAGE KIND OF A
DAY,

EXCEPT I LEFT THE
OFFICE EARLY TO
VISIT MY DOCTOR.
(PRESSES BUZZER)

A storyboard for *Why Me?* by Janet Perlman. This National Film Board of
Canada cartoon was unusual in that the subject was death.

writing team, the sketches were tacked or pasted on a wall. Then
someone got the bright idea of putting them up on large pieces of
beaverboard. This had several advantages: It was easy to mount the

sketches with thumbtacks and the entire board and drawings could be moved to another room for a full-scale presentation.

Written descriptions were held to a minimum. They usually consisted of the dialogue that applied to a particular drawing or some basic camera instruction, such as fade in or out, or *dissolve*. If any idea couldn't hold up graphically, it was promptly discarded; this was a lot cheaper than waiting until it was unsuccessfully animated.

Now making a storyboard is such a universal practice in filmmaking that it has become customary in live-action pictures, as well. In animation it doesn't matter whether the subject is a ten-second television spot or a half-hour special; a storyboard should be drawn. Never work solely from a written script.

Unless there is some business reason, such as having to impress the client, it is not necessary to draw a background for each sketch. When there is a change of locale, it is advisable to draw it, and even to indicate a color scheme. Then, for subsequent sketches, merely draw the characters quite roughly.

## Two Kinds of Stories

Of course, the $64,000 question is: Where and how do you start to create a story? Broadly speaking, there are two kinds of stories; the kind that have a beginning, middle, and end, and pictures such as the Road Runner, which are merely strings of gags.

Naturally, the latter are by far the easier pictures to create because of the absence of plot. Some writers specialize in gag writing; others concentrate on situations that generate humor. Themes can be found in current news. A gag in a current magazine, a joke you hear, some offbeat conversation with a very drunken person you meet at a cocktail party, or a scene you witness on the street may spark an idea. If you want to be a writer, start thinking as a writer; begin to *see* rather than look. Once you have made this adjustment to being a seeing person, the ideas will pour in. File them in your memory bank; also get into the habit of keeping a log of gags or themes that seem to be useful, even if they don't apply to anything you are working on at present.

## Developing Your Story

It is rare that an idea for a story springs full-blown like Athena from Zeus's forehead. Usually, the story starts with some gag that is set up

what can happen? Is there a flag? Can he become enmeshed in it? Does the pole start to break? Who saves him—Fatty or Skinny? How? What available prop or props can be used to rescue him? Does the face of the clock open, revealing the works? Does a large spring snap out, ensnaring Skinny in its coils? Does a pail fall on Fatty's head so that he staggers on the brink of falling into the street?

Can Skinny have a fight with a figure that emerges from a door in the clock tower, ready to strike the hour? Does the figure strike Skinny instead? Do they have a duel, with Skinny wielding his mop like a sword against the other figure equipped with a mace, a halberd, a gigantic club . . . what other weapon? Is the figure a knight in armor, a friar? What other bizarre kind of character? Does another character join in from a door on the other side of the clock? Do Tiny and Fatty come to Skinny's rescue? If not, why not? If they do, can they win? How?

How does this script end? Does the trio win? How does the film start?

### Exercise: Write a Story

Draw and write this kind of story for a five-minute short subject for theatrical release. Start off with a premise. I have given the locale and the possible characters. Now flesh out these factors into a story. Don't start until you have figured out the ending. You may change it later, but I want you to be able to write down the story idea in three sentences at most. Don't think up a limp idea for the ending so that you can go on to write the meat of the picture because it sounds like more fun than thinking up an ending. Don't cheat and disregard it in favor of thinking up some juicy gags.

Remember that you wouldn't be allowed to do that in a studio, and I want to have you work as if you were working in a very strict story department. You're going to be working on this project a long time, probably more than six months. Work hard. This is one of your samples, so sweat and stew until you have done the best possible job. Don't forget the daily quick-sketch hour. Now you can make them fruitful hours by drawing the characters in a clock-cleaning situation.

One of the factors in creating a story is research. So go to your local library and find different styles of clocks, old and modern. Are you going to use gargoyles? Look at some medieval types and make Photostats to take home. Get stats of figures that strike the hour on clocks, such as the famous ones on the tower in Prague. Look over books on medieval weapons. Think graphically. If you want to be a writer and tell yourself that you can't draw, I say nonsense. Keep trying. A writer who can draw even the most primitive figures is more valuable in a studio than somebody who cannot draw at all.

How do all these zany ideas come about? We know that "thinking hard" is an invitation for the left side of the brain to take over, in which case you will only think of gags that have been done before. What you need to do now is try to become an audience for your brain's right side.

Remember, there are eventually going to be many audiences for your film. Try to think of yourself in a lazy, relaxed way as part of such an audience. What would you love to see on the screen? Which character appeals to you most? What would you have him do? Without straining, let him do it. Keep yourself loose the rest of the day, inviting vagrant thoughts about the clock cleaning. Don't try to sweat it out. It may be several days before you come up with your first gag using this method. I can only tell you that it works.

Go over in your mind the list of possible props, and the environment, the architecture, the clothes the characters are wearing. What's the most screwy character that comes to mind as the bell ringer? Just let it come without straining. Start writing a list and keep a file of graphics as you accumulate them.

Remember always to consider the personality structure of every character. How he or she reacts to a given situation is what your story is about. Aristotle in his *Poetics* was wrong when he said that character is subsidiary to the action. Every personality lives in a private world, which is shared with nobody. The set of values that comprise this character is what interests the audience. The nearer they are to real life, the more the audience is entertained. Characters react to a situation, not the other way around. So much for Aristotle.

## Legal Protection for Your Work

Since this story is going to be an important part of your samples, it is going to go through many hands before you land a job or an assignment. How do you protect it? It is no longer necessary to go through the business of copyrighting.

One approach is to make a copy and send it to yourself registered mail. Leave it unopened against a time when you have to prove that you drew the script before a certain date. Another method is to register it at the Writers Guild of America, West, 9038 Melrose Avenue, Los

Angeles, CA 90069. They will register scripts for television, and plays, treatments, and concepts for television series.

## Selling Your Story: Agents

It is almost a hopeless idea to send a script directly to a prospective client. Get an agent; an agent is a professional door opener. Try to get a Hollywood or Beverly Hills agent; they are right on the firing line every day. It doesn't matter whether you live in Chillicothe or Scabrous Hills, Oklahoma, because you are not the one doing the selling.

Agents are a lot more than salesmen; they are also advisors and counselors. Remember, they have their fingers on the pulse of the market. If your agent suggests revisions in your property, pay attention. Take the advice, even if you are inclined to like your own version better. We all do that, but the professional is willing to change material when it is expedient to do so. That doesn't mean that you have to be a Milquetoast about it. Defend your reasons for writing what you did, but realize that if your arguments do not sway your agent, you would be wise to do it over, and do it without sulking.

Get used to the fact that you will spend a good deal of your working life making revisions. That is the nature of the writing business, so accept it without rancor. You will have to do it anyhow, so why not take it in good spirits? Nobody is deliberately trying to put you through the wringer out of malice, so don't get paranoid. There are too many other more important things to do, such as earning a living from your writing skills.

It is perfectly permissible to approach a number of agents at the same time. Write a résumé giving your background as a writer. Include such facts as having won prizes when you were still in school. Prepare a list of the material you have to show, whether completed or not, and ask for the agent's release form. Sign it and return it with the material you want to show.

Thomas Wolfe took his first book to Max Perkins in a small steamer trunk. In these days when most publishing houses are unimportant minions of gigantic conglomerates, Mr. Wolfe would probably not be allowed in the freight elevator with his burden. Be sure your material is clean, neat, and professional-looking. Mail it flat, not folded or rolled up. Put scripts in covers but do not have the pages stapled into a permanent binding. Observe the margin requirements for the area of entertainment you are trying to enter. If the baby spilled strawberry jam on the first page, even if you manage to wipe most of it off, do it over.

If you can't get an agent, realize that you are in hot water. Many studios will not even look at a script unless it goes through channels, that is, a registered agent. Of course, if you are in Hollywood, you could take a chance and drop in on Hanna-Barbera, or some other studio, and try for an appointment to show your wares. But it's a long shot.

It might be better to look over your material and start improving it. Remember that every agent is looking for some new talent to augment his or her income. If you were turned down many times, it means that in the opinion of the sales part of the business, you wouldn't be profitable. Take heed. Either quit altogether or buckle down to the grim business of sharpening your skills.

## The Writers Guild

If you have sold a television or movie script or a story line, or have had thirteen weeks of employment as a writer for a signatory to the Writers Guild contract, you *have* to make application to join the Guild. It is not a matter of your choice; the application is mandatory. But you can't just walk into the front office of the Writers Guild and tell them you want to be a member. You must have done one of the preceding things in order to qualify.

## If You're Not a Writer

So far it is obvious that this whole chapter has been devoted to people who want to become professional writers. How about the rest of you? Most of the very best directors can also animate very well, or they can lay out a film, paint a background, or write a entire script unassisted.

Some can do all of these things. The more you all are aware of the problems of everybody else's job, the better you'll be in your own. So whether your goal is to be a character designer or whatever, struggle through this five-minute script, and don't skimp on the storyboard.

You will be surprised at the amount you will learn. It may take you several months to complete a story. What of it? If you were in school trying for a Ph.D., you'd be glad to put in the time. Don't stint on these exercises. Remember you are assembling a portfolio. A number of associated projects will be more impressive than a dozen attempts at one branch of filmmaking.

For prospective writers, the only solution to your problems is writing, writing, writing. At this point in your career, in addition to your one hour of quick-sketch exercise and this five-minute short, you might consider writing about a dozen television spots. Start with a twenty-second, then a thirty-second, finally a full minute.

## Professionalism

Allow me to digress for a moment. Does this sound like a lot of work? It is, but your future is in the balance. For youngsters just starting to think of a career, who probably have full-time work, I consider that fifteen hours a week is the absolute minimum for preparing to pursue any job in an animation studio. There is the problem of energy, both physical and psychic. You cannot hope to do all this work and have the same social life as your peers. You will need enough rest so that you do not approach your studies in a state of exhaustion.

Sometimes when I was interviewing people for a job, I would ask how much study they were doing on a regular basis. A surprising number said none. When asked how they expected to learn, the answer was usually that they expected to pick up experience on company time. They had other interests—bowling, movies and television, and, of course, the opposite sex.

I would then launch into my favorite lecture about the cost of frittering away these precious formative years in idle entertainment while the competition was going to art school or reading a book similar to this one. The point is that it is not enough to have talent; it has to be exercised, which means that it must be pushed beyond its comfortable limits—not just once in a while but on a steady basis. That is the meaning of this book. It is not for dilettantes.

I have mentioned physical energy being frittered away. There is also psychic energy to be considered. Are you cultivating intellectual curiosity? Are you glad when you find some information about your subject that you had not known? Or does it frighten you that you didn't know? Can you plunge into this fairly long film with enthusiasm?

### Exercise: Television Commercials

To get back to the writing of television *commercials:* Give yourself a problem by examining newspaper or magazine advertisements. Pick out the lines of copy that are the salient facts about a product. For a twenty-second spot—you probably will not have screen time for more than that—your graphics are going to be little more than a demonstration of the product. Use one or more of the three characters.

You will be surprised how the extra ten seconds in a thirty-second spot make such a difference in your story approach. Now you can add a line of copy that may not be directly hard sell.

It is possible to order story sketch pads from a local art store or send away for them at F&B Ceco or Arthur Brown (their addresses, and others, are in the Appendix of this book). If you prefer to make your own, use typing paper and draw a five-by-seven-inch field. Type "scene no." and "drawing no." under the field. Leave space for copy and, where necessary, a description of the action not covered in the drawing, such as "sink glitters."

After having to cram action and dialogue into twenty and thirty seconds, a one-minute spot is going to seem interminable. There is time for fairly complicated acting. However, don't forget that the purpose of a television spot is to sell, so don't stray from the subject matter. There are spots on the air so self-consciously clever that one wonders what they are selling.

While an offstage voice is perfectly acceptable, having the characters speak carries more impact. Having more than one character talking gives the sound track more color.

Speaking of color, do add color to the drawings, either crayon or Magic Marker. The drawing does not have to be meticulous, and it is not necessary to use a complicated color scheme. Don't try to use watercolor because it will wrinkle the paper.

Most animated television commercials are designed to move along at a brisk pace. Fifteen scenes in a one-minute spot would not be unusual. Unlike films made for the theatrical screen, television specials and commercials should use extreme long shots sparingly. The small size of the screen makes for a poor result. The scenes often appear weak, whereas on a big screen in a theater, the long shot often gives a feeling of grandeur and vast space.

## A Story Is Made Up of Sequences

In creating stories for motion pictures think in terms of the film being composed of sequences that, put together, make a story. You will find that your plot for the five-minute film will fall naturally into sequences.

The figures emerging from the clock tower to toll the time and the subsequent involvement with one or more of the main characters would be a sequence. Another sequence might be one of the characters on a flagpole. Realize that each sequence must have a high point, something funny has to happen either in the dialogue or graphically. If the story goes along too long without some humor, the audience's attention span will not endure. Look for ways to embellish a gag. Remember you are dealing with actors, not just figures who are walking through a story.

Suppose you have a problem of having to lift a very heavy safe, and it is up to the elves to do it. You decide that Fatty is eventually going to pick it up, and his weight, combined with the safe, makes the floor give way. Now he could just grab the safe, lift it up, and go through the floor . . . end of gag.

Instead, how about the other elves? Suppose Tiny eagerly puts his arms around the safe and tugs futilely. Skinny then picks him up by the collar and puts him to one side. Then *he* tugs and hauls at the safe but doesn't get anywhere either. Fatty steps up and taps him on the shoulder, motions for him to get out of the way. He does, and Fatty pushes up his sleeves to the elbow, stretches his arms to flex his muscles, bends over, and with a mighty heave picks up the safe. He is wearing a broad grin of triumph that changes to a look of dismay as the floor starts to creak. Then he suddenly vanishes with the safe through a hole in the floor.

Quite a difference in viewpoint, isn't it? The characters are doing some acting instead of walking through the situation in a perfunctory manner.


## Building an Animation Library

Everybody in the animation business should make it a practice to tape animated cartoons and eventually to have a morgue of pictures taken from the air. One devotee I know got up at six o'clock every morning to tape a series of cartoons that were not appearing later in the day.

Whatever your goal, these films are worth your study, and the work of several writers, directors, and layout people are going to be especially valuable. Frank Tashlin, a gifted writer/director, worked at the Schlesinger Studio and Screen Gems. Chuck Jones, Friz Freleng, and Bob Clampett directed at Warner's. Maurice Noble, an outstanding layout artist, worked with Jones for years. Paul Julian was Freleng's background artist. The team of Hanna and Barbera directed many beautifully paced Tom and Jerry cartoons at MGM.

Any layouts and backgrounds from Disney's are fine examples of filmmaking. The work of the Kinney brothers, Jack as director and Dick as writer, in a series of how-to-do-it films featuring Goofy was far removed from the usual Disney mode because it was satirical.

Three Disney animators, Babbitt, Tytla, and Ferguson should be studied carefully because they were the men responsible for the switch in animation from slapstick to modern comedy.

Tedd Pierce, Bugs Hardaway, Mike Maltese, and Tex Avery created some of the funniest characters in animation history. They worked at Warner Brothers. Avery was a director, as well, and his zany style of humor gave the Disney staff some stiff competition. He was more restless than the other Warner directors. Tex worked at Walter Lantz's and MGM, too, but his best work in my opinion was done at Warner's. His brash version of Bugs Bunny with his saucy "What's up, Doc?" became world-famous. The Warner writers had a breezy style that was far removed from Disney's more restrained brand of humor. Then, too, the directors at the Disney Studio were under the close supervision of Walt himself, while the Warner directors had complete freedom of expression.

Aspiring writers should study the way the Warner characters were handled in comparison to the way the writers in MGM and Disney wrote for their characters. Animation should be studied by running various isolated actions over and over until the principles of animation that were used are understood, that is, stretch and squash, anticipation, secondary action, gestures during dialogue, and *mouth action.*

Another source of education for the writer are the works of humorists from Rabelais to Mark Twain and Anatole France, right down to Russell Baker and George Herriman.

Study the story situations and acting of great comics such as Charlie Chaplin, Harry Langdon, and deadpan Buster Keaton and Harold Lloyd for their individualistic treatment of kinetic gags. Try to see animation film festivals for the very latest approaches to story: Caroline Leaf's Eskimo myths, Børge Ring's *Anna and Bella,* Faith Hubley's *Cosmic Eye.* They are all on subjects that would never have been attempted a few decades ago.

Layout and background artists should weigh the difference between the academic approach to composition and painting as exemplified by MGM, Disney, and most of the Warner shorts and the adventurous freewheeling designing of John Hubley and the other artists at UPA.

Do not accept the work of these people as gospel. Examine the films critically. What could you have done to improve some aspect of the pictures? Jot down your opinions in a notebook, or make sketches of ideas that you consider to be improvements on what you have been studying.

## Bakshi's *Fritz the Cat:* A Breakthrough

One filmmaker worth studying in a negative sense is Ralph Bakshi. In a profession full of colorful characters, Bakshi is almost in a class by himself. A New York street kid with a minimum of formal education, he succeeded in making the first X-rated animated cartoon, *Fritz the Cat.*

While the bulk of the film has been taken from three stories in Robert Crumb's underground comic strip, it is Bakshi's interpretation of the material that supplies the shocker. Nobody had previously dared to veer from the Victorian primness of the standards set at the very beginnings of the profession.

More than any other studio, Disney's was a model of the Victorian mode. Nobody, by any stretch of the imagination, could see Snow White going off into the sunset with her Prince and visualize them making "the beast with two backs."

Bakshi defied the Victorian restrictions. His sexual themes were raw, crude, and casual as a quick lay in the back room of a Brownsville poolroom. As the picture progressed, it seemed to have become autobiographical, and Bakshi in various interviews has admitted that it was a form of catharsis. Even that phase of the picture is a first.

The negative aspects just about cover every aspect of filmmaking. Bakshi has no real sense of continuity or pace, so there are big holes in his story line and the picture progresses in fits and starts. His dialogue tracks are often muffled and inaudible. His composition of crowd shots must have Sergei Eisenstein turning over in his grave, as if he were on a barbecue spit.

Look long and hard. You are watching the work of a man who had a message but lacked the intellectual means to put it on film. Even so, *Fritz The Cat,* because of its content, is a powerhouse of a film, and Ralph Bakshi has earned himself a place in animation history.

## A Lesson for Scriptwriters

Another film worthy of study for its mistakes is *Raggedy Ann and Andy*, a feature animated cartoon that was a $4 million bomb. In this case, some superb animation of the Camel with the Wrinkled Knees by veteran animator Art Babbitt, the Greedy by Emery Hawkins, and Raggedy Ann by Tissa David could not lift this film from the doldrums.

The writers, unacquainted with the medium, fell victim to the fallacy that is shared by the public, that is, animated cartoons are written for the children in the audience. Quite the opposite is true. I have never known a group producing films for theatrical release who wrote anything but films for adults. This film, however, was designed for the age level of children who would be cajoled after seeing the film into buying the Raggedy Ann and Andy dolls. The result is a mechanically coy, self-conscious script that was deadly dull, in spite of the charm of the characters that Johnny Gruelle had designed for his books.

Some of the sequences seem to have remained overlength because of the fact that they were so well animated. The Greedy sequence could have been cut by half because the plot was not developing after the character and his appetites were explained.

To compound the errors, Joe Raposo, a very gifted composer under normal conditions, created sixteen (count them, 16!!!) songs, wall-to-wall music, so that if any adults in the audience were awake after the first five minutes of blearily watching the action, the soporific effect of all these songs was bound to put them into Slumberland.

Dick Williams, whose track record on short subjects, titles, and television spots is unsurpassed, proved to be unable to handle such a potpourri of mistakes of judgment. As a director on feature films, he has yet to prove himself, because on Raggedy Ann he made his own share of errors.

This film shows that the best talent and $4 million does not guarantee success. Sound judgment and the ability of the director to handle the talent are more important.

To confound their critics, both Bakshi and Williams recently turned their talents to new ventures with remarkable results. Bakshi has managed to circumvent the horde of ad agency mavins, broadcast superbrains, and toy-making retardates who have turned most of Saturday morning television into a morass of half-hour-long commercials.

He has created a series of animated shows called *Mighty Mouse; the*

*New Adventures.* The new Mighty Mouse is a parody of the original character, and the films are, in a self-conscious way, similar to the Warner Brothers' cartoons of the fifties. The frenzied action and inside jokes are an echo of the work of directors like Bob Clampett and Tex Avery.

Naturally Bakshi's detractors among the television and advertising executives wish he would go away, because he certainly has steadfastly refused to go along with the soporific pap that has been served up on children's Saturday morning programs these many years. In this venture Bakshi commands the attention of every serious student of animation.

After the Raggedy Ann debacle, Dick Williams returned to his dual role as director/producer of some of the most acclaimed television spots being produced, and as part-time director of the feature cartoon he has been working on for about sixteen years. The film, currently called *The Cobbler and the Thief,* has been solely financed by the profits from Williams's television spots.

When he was offered the opportunity to direct the animation in *Who Framed Roger Rabbit,* Williams jumped at it. The result is that this feature is easily the best use of combined animation and live action to date. By using turning edges instead of the conventional flat color areas, Williams achieved a more satisfactory visual amalgam of the two media. It may be a long time before the high standards of this film are surpassed. The picture should be seen four or five times in order to study and understand the various effects Williams has produced.

I believe the lesson that can be learned from these two men is that one should never be daunted by failures, great or small. Have faith in your talents.

## Cassettes and Films

In addition to taping cartoons from the air, there are an increasing number of cassettes for sale that are exclusively animated cartoons. Even the Disney Studio is selling cassettes of some of its most important pictures.

Unfortunately, the films of our younger stars in the profession are not so easily accessible. One exception is the title film of *Mystery!* hosted by Vincent Price. This television title was animated by Derek Lamb from a series of drawings done by Edward Gorey in his psuedo-

Edwardian style. Tape that and study Lamb's sensitive use of stylized animation, which conforms to Gorey's manner of drawing. The title is a combination of two extraordinary talents, which makes the film a small but important masterpiece.

The forerunner of this kind of animation was directed by Chuck Jones at Warner Brothers in 1942. *The Dover Boys* was a definite break with the Disney tradition of making the characters look like little live people. It was simply a film of high-style drawings that were spoofing a series of books about the Rover Boys. These were a trio of unbelievably goody-goody youths, and the series was aimed at improving the minds and manners of the eight- to 12-year-old readers by relating the adventures of these unbelievably noble teenagers, Dick, Tom, and Sam, who were continually being harassed by an unbelievably wicked Dan Baxter. The conduct of the three boys was in the classic Victorian mode and made hilarious material for the movie audiences of the more cynical and anti-Victorian 1940s.

Although there is a span of about forty years between *The Dover Boys*

Derek Lamb created the basic idea for the title, then looked through all the books that Gorey had illustrated and selected a cast of characters from them.

and *Mystery!*'s title art, it would be worthwhile to acquire both cartoons in order to study the use of satire, not only in the stories but in the animation of the characters. Both Derek Lamb and Chuck Jones were very aware of the comic possibilities in the action, as well as the design of the films.

In addition to cassettes, there are 16 mm films, and many firms are in the business of renting them. In most cases, their catalogues seem to specialize in some era of animation and usually concentrate on the theatrical animation of a few studios. However, a few rent the work of independent filmmakers and should not be ignored.

A professional animation writer must be conversant with all manner of styles, from Gene Deitch's *Tom Terrific* (which was a line drawing with no color, working over a plain-colored card background) to Caroline Leaf's sand animation.

## Graphic Suggestions for the Written Script

The first tentative steps in creating an animated film should at the same time start to zero in on the appearance of the picture. This can't be done without a wide knowledge of the possibilities. The writer should have some suggestions for the storyboard artist, and between them they should have some ideas to present to the director before the story has progressed very far.

What about our clock cleaners? Would a light airy treatment, like a Dufy rendering, do the best possible job on the clock tower? Would Dubuffet's childlike but sophisticated style suit the film better? Should the colors stay within the linear area or spill over slightly? What about cutout paper instead of painting the backgrounds?

While the choices seem endless, it isn't so. The drawing of the three characters quickly narrows down the style selection. They are not highly stylized, so the backgrounds are going to have to be somewhat conventional.

When you see a film for the first time, you are a part of the audience. The second time, you are a professional writer looking at somebody else's material; by the third and fourth times, you are in a position to really evaluate the structure of the work. After that, you can afford to start thinking of better ways to have written certain parts of the film.

In the United States, commercial animation, that is, animated films for motion pictures and television, are, for the most part, fairly conventional in subject matter and drawing style. This is not true of foreign animation. The pictures there are much more individualistic. Study the work of Alexandre Alexieff, Peter Foldes, Bruno Bozzetto, Jiří Trnka, Emile Cohl, Gene Deitch, George Dunning, Oskar Fischinger, Bob Godfrey, Yoji Kuri, Len Lye, Norman McLaren, Børge Ring, Dick Williams, Derek Lamb, Caroline Leaf, Frédéric Bàck, and Kaj Pindal.

To get back to our clock cleaners. Have you thought about the weather as a factor—snow, ice, a lightning bolt, wind? How is the mechanism of the clock wound up? Does it have weights on chains like a grandfather's clock? Is there an enormous key? Don't strain to think of your film, rather let some of it come to you in reveries, right before you go to sleep. In effect, let it catch you unawares.

Above all, do not go around enthusiastically telling all who will listen some gags from your proposed plot. You can talk yourself right out of your story. Keep it to yourself until you have a completed storyboard. Maybe this sounds like strange advice. What happens is that every time you recount a part of your story, you expend some of your psychic energy. After a while, the gags sound rather tired. If you keep it up, suddenly you will be bored by the whole subject. You will have exhausted your psychic energy in looking for compliments from your friends and family. Wait for the kudos until you can proudly show a completed job. Then you will have earned the praise. Even in a studio, it is better to confine your discussions of a picture to other writers, the storyboard artist, and the director. They are directly involved in your work. Animators who run into you in the hall are not.

## Rules and Restrictions

In these parlous times, the only area of free thinking in commercial animation is feature films. Everywhere else, in television specials, the Saturday-morning shows, and commercials, the advertising agencies and the networks lay a heavy hand on the creative processes. They have more constrictions and restrictions than the Inquisitorial rack and these are no less painful. So be prepared to have to cope with mindless rules and even more mindless people. If anybody claims that an advertising agency is a font of creativity, I have only to point out that, from the very beginning, radio, for example, has been organized and managed by agencies. During this entire time not *one* important American writer of radio programs has appeared on the scene!

with the mechanics of a prop, you may be missing a chance for a great gag.

Let me stress once again that only the right side of your brain is creative. It doesn't work when you are doing what we call "thinking." That's a left-side function. For example, after you have made your scribbled lists, you may want to put them into some kind of order, that is, all architectural features together, all cleaning materials grouped. The left side is very expert at making this kind of comparison; the right side is probably incapable of doing such a job. Keep the two functions separate. Remember that you cannot be creative while being critical of the results.

## Typing the Script

When it is time to type a script, remember that there is an accepted form for the spacing of the top and bottom of the pages, and where to use upper and lower case. Put the title at the top of each page on a line with the page number. All dialogue and camera instructions should be in upper case for easy reading. The name of the character involved must be at the head of every bit of dialogue, even if it consists of one word. (See the following sample page.)

Don't try to become a surrogate director. Keep your camera instructions sparse, and be sure you know what you are asking for. Don't call for an OVER-THE-SHOULDER SHOT OF THE ENTIRE BRITISH FLEET IN A C.U.

Make your set descriptions succinct. The same is true for details such as clothes. If it is sunset, and time is important to the story, spell it out, but don't load your script with verbiage.

As soon as possible get your script photocopied and put the copy in a safe place, preferably not under the same roof as the original. Scripts get lost or burned up. T. E. Lawrence left his original manuscript for *The Seven Pillars of Wisdom* in a London taxi. It was never found and there was no copy.

It may look fancy, but do not use a permanent binder on your script. Use a cover that does not need holes in the paper for rings, either. The pages of your script are going to be subject to a lot of wear and tear. Notes will be scribbled, pages omitted, and lines excised. Keep it loose!

THE SEVEN DORFS

Snow White LEANS OVER to Prince looking FLIRTATIOUS.

> Snow White
>
> NOW, HOW ABOUT THAT THERE BIG SE-
> CRET?

> Prince
>
> WELL, IT'S ABOUT YOU AN' THE WICKET—

They are PETRIFIED as the Queen calls OFFSTAGE. Then the
Prince DUCKS BEHIND the mirror, and Snow White starts
DUSTING FURIOUSLY.

> Queen
>
> SNOW WHITE, IS YOU ALL FINISHED UP?

> Snow White
>
> YES MA'AM, WICKET QUEEN. IT'S ALL
> DUSTED.

The Queen RUNS HER FINGER across the mirror and looks
SATISFIED.

> Queen
>
> THAT'S BETTER. NOW GO OFF AND CLEAN
> UP THE GOLD AND SILVER DISHES AND
> STUFF.

> Snow White
>
> AFTER THAT COULD I GO? . . .

Queen (INTERRUPTS)

NO, YOU CAN'T. AFTER THAT GO TO YOUR COLD BED WHICH IS IN THE ATTIC.

Snow White walks OFFSTAGE dragging her mop dolefully. The Queen SHAKES HER HEAD.

Queen

HONESTLY, I DON'T KNOW WHAT ONE-IN-HELP IS COMIN' TO THESE DAYS. ESPE-CIALLY STEP-DAUGHTERS.

FADE OUT.

We have been involved mostly with writing so far. Now we are going on to other functions. However, even if you want only to write for a living, do go on and find out about the work of other people in the hierarchy of an animation staff. You will work better with them if you understand the part they play and the problems they face in production, especially if you try to draw and think about the various precepts I am teaching rather than just reading the text.

It doesn't matter if you have never drawn in your life. The result may be crude but at least you are starting to think like an animation writer. There is no way to become a successful writer in this field unless you can create and evaluate stories and gags from a graphic point of view.

So use stick figures or whatever mode of drawing you can manage, but draw a story sketch for everything you work on in this book.

# 6

## Character Design

In the average-sized studio, this job does not exist. Characters are designed by the layout person, or by one of the animators. However, in a large organization—the Disney studio, for example—a designer is a very important member of the crew. On a feature-length cartoon the main characters undergo extensive changes and improvements at the same time that the storyboard is being developed.

In a way, being a character designer is very similar to working as a casting director on a live-action film. A cast has to be created that will make a plausible combination of shapes and proportions that can house the personalities in the story. There has to be a feeling that there is a single point of view that has selected these particular components, a oneness that permeates each drawing.

For example, a cast that consisted of Herriman's Offissa Pup and Krazy Kat, Felix the Cat, and Disney's Pluto simply would be rejected by a motion-picture audience. The drawing styles are too disparate.

### Reference Material

Normally, an artist has favorite combinations of sizes, shapes, and proportions, which he or she will probably use all during working life,

**71**

Character designs for *The Opera Caper* by Gil Miret. Written by Shamus Culhane and Joseph Szabo. © 1967 by Famous Studio.

unconsciously or not. A character designer has no such comfortable career. He or she must deliberately and consciously seek variety in designing, ignoring natural feelings.

So it imperative that early on such a designer begins to gather a morgue and never stops collecting good material. From time to time, the morgue must be examined and outdated material weeded out. Newspapers, comic books, magazines, and coffee-table books contain such an enormous quantity of material for the character designer that it is important to begin collecting with a very high standard of acceptance. The morgue is not necessarily used for copying somebody else's ideas; rather, it is a springboard, a guide to combinations of proportions that are not native to this particular designer's mind.

## Stylized or Life-Quality?

Attention must be paid to the use of the characters. Are they going to be in a high-style unconventional film? If so, they are not going to be called upon to accomplish acting with life-quality as in a typical Disney film.

If the film is going to use very stylized animation, it is possible to design characters who are only drawn to look good in one view. Otherwise, be sure that the model sheet has all of the necessary views of the character. Don't stymie the animator with a three-quarter rear view that is not shown on the model sheet.

*The Yellow Submarine* is a good example of very high-style designing of characters who could not be used except in very limited camera angles. There is nothing wrong with this approach as long as all the people involved realize that there are limitations to the animation and do not attempt to draw life-quality movements with high-style figures.

*Nu Wa Patches the Sky,* by Quian Yun Da. Goddess Nu is a figure in ancient Chinese mythology believed to have created the first human beings.

*The Fire Boy,* by Wang Baiyong. A boy seizes back the source of life from a demon, but gives his life to his nation's happiness.

Sketches by Cliff Roberts of Red Riding Hood for *The Stuck-Up Wolf.* © 1967 by Famous Studio.

## What Is Good Design?

What good designing amounts to is the selection of unexpected and, therefore, humorous combinations of shapes. After looking at a series of cartoons featuring animals in the Disney style (which was imitated by almost all the other animation studios), it is refreshing to see Sullivant's approach. Like all great cartoonists, he has his own private brand of humor.

One of the paradoxes of drawing cartoons of animals is that in order to be able to omit, exaggerate, or diminish the proportions of an animal, it is vital that the artist know what the structure of the animal is in real

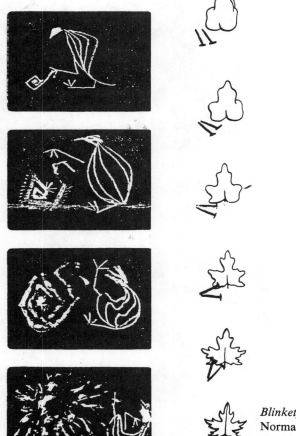

*Blinkety Blank,* animated by Norman McLaren in 1954. Courtesy of the National Film Board of Canada.

life. Therefore, the morgue should contain as many photographs and drawings of various animals as possible.

## The Model Sheet

A model sheet should first contain a number of views of a character in a neutral pose, and cover all aspects of the action in the storyboard. If time and the budget permit, it is useful to draw a number of poses depicting various emotions. But more valuable to the animator is the information about what the character looks like in a relaxed state. He or she can take it from there.

## Sensible Use of Color

Some designers have a carefree attitude about the number of colors they assign to their characters. Opaquing cels can be an expensive operation; the more different colors the painter has to use, the greater the possibility of making mistakes. A good strong statement with a few colors is a big help to the background painter because it is easier to control the color perspective of the set so that the characters do not merge with the backgrounds.

It is important to remember that the style of drawings used by the designer, to a large extent, will govern the appearance of the whole picture because the drawings of the layouts for the various scenes will have to reflect that style.

Some of the larger animation studios not only have character designers, they also have artists who specialize in creating props (such as the dwarf's organ in the entertainment sequence in *Snow White*), and other artists who paint atmosphere sketches. This work has no relation to the kind of drawings used in story sketches, which are inspirational rather than utilitarian.

## Will It Animate?

A character may have gone through many major changes during the course of its development, but the final judgment of the character's usefulness has to come from the animation department.

A scene from *36 Characters,* a film in which Chinese pictograph characters come to life. Conceived by A Da and produced at the Shanghai Animation Studio in 1984.

During the production of *Pinocchio,* Norman Ferguson and I animated about a hundred feet of the Fox before we realized that his nose was too long. Every time his head turned, his nose seemed to sweep across the screen. Ferguson redesigned him with a much shorter snout; we junked all the first attempts to animate him, and there were no more problems. Here the Fox had been under the scrutiny of Walt Disney, the directors, and many other artists, yet it wasn't until the Fox was actually animated that a serious flaw was discovered. After he was corrected, the Fox proved to be one of the most successful characters in the film. It doesn't matter how talented the designer is, or how attractive the character seems to be, there is only one acid test—will it animate?

# 7

## The Director I:
### Story, Casting, Music, and Sound

For an aspiring student of animation who has an image of a director as a heroic figure, such as the captain of a great ship, standing on the bridge issuing calm and measured commands to a scurrying crew, I reluctantly erase this noble dream.

The reality is that it is a hectic position. In a large studio, the image might be more akin to a stagecoach driver handling a six-horse team, with each animal trying to pull away from its neighbor. Writers, designers, layout artists, animators, and background renderers all jockey for the director's attention in order to gain the approval of some idea within their particular function in the filmmaking process. Camera operators have been known to call the director at three in the morning to ask for an opinion about some problem on a rush job.

The difficulty is that each personality must be handled with care, whether it involves the acceptance or rejection of an idea, because one of the most important aspects of directing is guiding the crew into making a good film while at the same time sustaining the morale.

Psychologically the director is a parental figure. Whether or not this role is accepted might easily be the difference between a well-run crew and a group split by personality problems. From the director all blessings flow, be it a compliment for a job well done, a recommendation

Doctor and Mrs. DeSoto pull the tooth of a rather testy patient. From *Doctor DeSoto,* a film by Michael Sporn, adapted from a book by William Steig.

for a raise, or a shift into a position with more responsibility.

Like children in a family, the crew rarely see the director as a person with strengths and weaknesses. So if you are suffering from the tensions of the director's job, don't expect sympathy from your crew. If you need to cry on somebody's shoulder, do it at home. Any attempt to pour out your complaints to a member of the crew will result in one of two things: That person, or any other member of the group who hears about it, will resent your attempt to shift some of your burden; or if he or she accepts the role of Father Confessor, you will find that you have usually created a kind of Cardinal Richelieu who will try to manipulate you from this advantageous position.

If all this sounds cynical, I can only say that it is an analysis based on observation and evaluation.

One of the nerve-racking aspects of directing is the fact that the relationship between director and crew is constantly being tested, and sometimes accidentally skewed.

An absentminded hello in the hall may easily be construed as a frosty greeting. A seemingly perfunctory acceptance of someone's finished work, instead of the expected compliment, might just mean that you were in a hurry to get to a story meeting, but to the person involved, it might look as if even his or her best efforts are regarded as pedestrian.

It is difficult to keep in mind that you are "onstage" at all times, but it is a psychological fact, and the cornerstone of your relationship to your crew. Don't dismiss these observations as my personal foibles. Accepting them as sound precepts may make the difference between enjoying the relationship with the crew or working with a sullen or indifferent group that barely meets your requirements.

Of course it is possible to work as a director in a very small studio, even a one-man operation, doing all the functions of filmmaking on your own; but for most of us, such a luxury is beyond our experience or expectations.

The director directing television commercials, half-hour specials, or feature pictures needs a nimble mind. One time, one of my best animators asked for a chance to direct. He was doing very well on his first assignment until I interrupted him. It was time to start conferring with the writers about the next picture. He found it confusing to be handing out work to his animators one moment and then suddenly having to adjust to thinking about the complexities of a new story plot.

I reminded him that normally he would not only be working with

In the last seventeen years, Frédéric Bàck has made seven short films of ten minutes or less. After trying a number of techniques, he has finally settled on using frosted cels and color pencils.

A rendering by Frédéric Bàck on a frosted cel for his spirited dance film *Crac!*

his animators and talking with his writers at the same time but he would also have a picture in the ink-and-paint department, and another being readied for a final recording. At that point, he just gave up and went back to animation. His mind wasn't equipped to handle such constant juggling.

Yet there are some of us who actually enjoy the tension, the need to make quick but accurate decisions; who are able to leap from a background problem to the intricacies of a multireel sound track and still give each situation its full measure of attention. These people are not intimidated or pressured by the fact that a myriad of similar problems are waiting to be solved.

What is exhilarating to one mind is an impossible burden to another; so if you need to work without interruption, don't look for a job as an animation director in a studio. Look for an abandoned lighthouse.

## What's So Funny About That?

As a director, you may find yourself with a writing staff whose humor is very different from your own. This can be a liability or an asset, depending on how you handle the situation. Obviously, there is little point in trying to wrench the crew around to your brand of humor. A style cannot be discarded like shucking off a jacket.

It will be useful to point out in a casual way that you have a rather different view of humor, which is no indictment of theirs. Indeed, you might suggest that it will be interesting to mesh them together and see what happens. While this might sound like blandishment, there is a possibility of truth in the statement.

I am reminded of my association with Bugs Hardaway and Milt

Schaffer at the Walt Lantz studio. A more unlikely amalgam of talents can scarcely be imagined. Bugs Hardaway was an expatriate Kansan with the earthy barnyard humor of his background. Schaffer came from the more sophisticated story department of the Walt Disney studio.

Milt tried manfully to present me with stories that made sense accordingly to the tenets of the Disney organization, an approach that Bugs rejected with a derisive stream of tobacco juice.

To him a gag was a gag. The fact that it was out of character, or did not advance the plot, he dismissed with impatience as too scientific and technical for an animated cartoon—this at a time when I was deep in the writings of Sergei Eisenstein! I was discreet enough not to advertise this fact.

I believe both Hardaway and Schaffer were at first rather appalled by my experiments in frenetic cutting à la Eisenstein. Hardaway remarked after looking at my pencil test of *The Barber of Seville,* "It looks like a Chinese goulash."

After we made a few pictures together, we managed a truce. I recognized that Bugs did have a raw kind of humor, and Milt could manage to eke out a story line most of the time; and both accepted the fact that my fast cutting was being enjoyed by the audience. We managed to put together several better-than-average cartoons.

Caroline Leaf, one of the outstanding filmmakers of the National Film Board of Canada, was the last person to be hired by the Board from the United States, more than a decade ago. Photo courtesy of the National Film Board of Canada.

*The Owl Who Married a Goose* is an Eskimo folktale. It was made by Caroline Leaf, and is a classic example of sand animation. Courtesy of the National Film Board of Canada.

In the preliminary thinking about a new story, do not be swept away by one very funny gag. Directors have to be thinking about the whole story. After the one great gag has been submitted, wait, but not too long, for the premise. What is the story? Do not accept the possibility of getting a story structure later. Insist on the development of a complete story that can be told in two short sentences, and it should wrap up. The idea of thinking up an ending later should set off gongs in your head. *Don't allow it, ever!*

It is important, too, that the writers understand that you are a creative person. The storyboard is not going to be put on the screen in its original shape. Gags are going to be added; dead material (at least dead in your estimation) is going to be cut; and the whole structure of the picture is going to stay malleable, subject to the ideas of every creative person who works on the film, right down to the final screening in sweatbox. A director is a receptacle for ideas, not some kind of ambulatory copy machine for the storyboard.

We've said there are two basic story structures—there's a third that is really a variation of the first. One type is just a series of gags, such as Chuck Jones's Road Runner pictures and the Kinney brothers' how-to-do-it cartoons featuring Goofy. Another is the kind of story

Ishu Patel is an animator known for his sensitive approach to music, which is always intimately bonded to the rhythm of his films. Photo courtesy of the National Film Board of Canada.

*Paradise,* designed and animated by Ishu Patel. It is a story about two birds, each envious of the other. This is his fifteenth film for the National Film Board of Canada.

that develops situation by situation from a beginning: *Three Little Pigs,* for example, or *Snow White and the Seven Dwarfs.* A third type was something that developed in the Disney studios, where their story department became really adept at milking a funny situation. They found that having four or five sequences built around comic situations made for a very satisfactory picture, and thus the variation was born.

*Hawaiian Holiday* is such a film. It opens with Minnie doing a hula while Mickey plays the guitar. Then Donald Duck essays a hula, which ends when his grass skirt catches fire. Then the action cuts to Pluto and a starfish. After a chase that ends in the surf, Goofy and a surfboard take up a sequence. The story then goes back to Pluto, who encounters a belligerent crab. Goofy and the surfboard follow, ending with Goofy buried in the sand, with his surfboard acting as a headstone. Mickey, Minnie, and Donald gather around the "grave," laughing as the film ends with an *Iris out.*

What is important to remember is that at no time in the entire picture were all the principals together. It was clearly just a string of funny sequences, just as Road Runner cartoons are a string of funny gags.

It is better to direct the story toward one type of story construction. Above all else, the picture must have a satisfactory ending. After a poor start, a story can be rescued with a funny ending; but conversely, there is no way to leave an audience with a good feeling if the ending is poor.

## The Story Session

At the first session for a new picture, have the ears of a lynx for the half-formed sentence, a murmured suggestion almost lost in the exchange of thoughts. That might very well be the springboard for a great cartoon. So don't pay attention to the loudest voices to the exclusion of more timid ideas.

Don't take over the meeting. Be more the observer. You will have ample time later to put forth your own thoughts. Give the writers free rein, and stay unobtrusive, unless there is a reason to reject an idea out of hand—a gag that is out of character, objectionable material, such as poking fun at ethnic groups or religions, or something too pornographic for this particular studio. If the group runs into a block and the meeting stalls, come to the rescue. It is expected of you. Revive the enthusiasm by prodding the group about the material they have put forth so far. What else could they have done with a given situation? Have they been thinking of a gag for the wrong character? Put them back on the rails with a series of ideas of your own.

## Disney Saves *Pinocchio*

Not every director is a good writer but most usually have a good sense of structure. Walt Disney had, among his other talents, a very keen nose for the solution to writer's block. When *Pinocchio* got off to a floundering start, it was apparent as the rushes started to come in that there was a great need for some unifying factor. The picture seemed fragmented.

The writers were not able to solve the problem within the framework of the plot they had created. It followed the original book fairly closely. Disney pressured them to go beyond the book and create a brand new character, the practical, conscientious Jiminy Cricket. Not only did he pull the plot together but Jiminy almost stole the picture from Pinocchio.

If there is a block in the writing, look beyond the plot structure that has led to the cul-de-sac and find a breakthrough as Disney did.

Don't accept a story as completed unless you are satisfied that there are no weak spots in the picture as far as you know at that point. If there are, don't accept the story; make the crew work until the plot is strengthened. Remember that the director is solely responsible for the finished film. After a screening of the picture, nobody wants to hear that the writers did a poor job. It is up to the director to wring a good story out of them in the first place.

## The Casting Session

When the storyboard is finished and the script typed, it is time for a casting session. There are formidable do's and don'ts in handling the actors. First, bear in mind that, contrary to Alfred Hithcock's dismissal of actors as "talking furniture," they are people looking for work. I think a casting session must be the most difficult part of an actor's life.

Naturally, there are going to be rejections for one reason or another, even when the actors are all seasoned veterans. When it is necessary to weed out, do it gently. A small compliment and your regrets will go a long way to keep an actor's spirits up.

Selecting voices for a picture is something like creating orchestration. Get into the habit of not looking at the people while they are working. They are not going to appear on the screen, so concentrate on the voice quality. Avoid like a plague any similarity among the voices you choose. I remember one horrendous piece of miscasting in a film starring Jimmy Stewart and Henry Fonda. For the entire film, each one tried to outstumble and outstutter the other. It was like watching a taffy pull.

At the start of a recording, do not sit in the control booth like Zeus, ready to hurl thunderbolts. Whether it is a television spot, a half-hour special, or a feature picture, before the actual recording starts, go down

Gene and Zdenka Deitch. In thirty years of filmmaking, Deitch has won one Oscar and has been nominated for an award five times. Zdenka is a talented production manager. They work together in their studio in Prague. Photo courtesy of Weston Woods Studios, Weston, Connecticut.

An illustration from *Where the Wild Things Are*. It took Gene Deitch five years of experimenting before he found a way to transfer Maurice Sendak's complex technique to the screen. Photo courtesy of Weston Woods Studios, Weston, Connecticut.

and mingle with the actors. I usually have some Xeroxed drawings of the various characters, which I show to the actors so they can get a better mental picture of their roles.

In the beginning, I warn everybody that during this first reading I am going to interrupt anytime I feel that I am not getting what I need. I stay on the floor, where I can talk directly to an actor and explain why the reading is not quite what I had in mind. This is the time to listen to suggestions and try out different approaches, so the reading will go along by fits and starts.

Be patient. The actors have only had a script to read for a few days, but you may have been brooding over the picture for a month or more. Let them get the feel of it. Don't stop correcting and changing until you are sure that everybody is confident and ready to make a serious attempt at a recording.

I have one eccentricity, that is, from this point on I am always recording. Tape is cheap, and you never know when some inspired performance will go a-glimmering if the tape isn't rolling, never to be achieved again. I have seen actors lose all their enthusiasm because they were rehearsed to the point of tedium before the director was willing to try for a recording.

Avoid dull recitation by having the scripts placed on stands to keep both hands free. Never allow an actor to hold the script in one hand and cup the other hand behind his ear. It may enable the actor to hear his own voice better but there is no way to use *body English* when the hands are not free. The results are bound to be as restrained as the hands.

To understand the importance of the body in acting, try this experiment: Turn off the sound on your television and watch something where the action and speech are exaggerated, a game show, for example. See how the whole body, especially the head and hands, is involved. Then you will realized how important it is not to restrain the hands during a recording. The lack of body English is bound to result in the lines being read aloud rather than the actor becoming emotionally involved.

Actors who are new to animation are usually inclined to be a little bit self-conscious and it may take them a while to loosen up and have some fun with the dialogue.

Never read a line for an actor who is not interpreting the role the way you see it even though it may be exasperating. Try making your needs known in a different way. Make it as clear as possible. That is why you are the director. Then try again. If you give a line reading, it is a confession that you weren't reaching the actor or that you need to do a better casting job. Don't necessarily blame the actor.

Never staple or bind scripts. The pages should be loose to enable the actor to turn them quietly. Stapled or bound scripts are almost sure to rustle as they are being handled, spoiling what may have been a good take.

During the recording, the assistant director or some one else able to take neat notes should be keeping track of good and bad takes. Each recording should have an oral identification and an evaluation by the director. Sometimes the sound operator will add ideas as well, and these should be noted. The director should never get involved in these mechanics. Your function is to listen to the track and weigh every word, every phrase.

At times, when a section of the recording has been going very well and suddenly there is a bobble of some kind, it is good for the director to call into the mike and instruct the actors to go back a few sentences and resume the dialogue. That way, the momentum, which made for a good track so far, is not lost.

When a given line doesn't sound right, make a recording of it anyway; then make a version that seems to be an improvement. That way, when the track is assembled, you have a choice. If your judgment was wrong, you can always go back to the original dialogue.

## Regional Speech

Unless you are using an accent in the track for a purpose, watch out for local interpretations of words. Middle westerners have several pronunciations that are native to the region. They say "mirrr" instead of "mirror," "Hairy" instead of "Harry," "watter" for "water," and "Mery" for "Mary." New Yorkers drop a "g" at the end of a word and have a habit of hooking a hard "g" to the word following, as in Long-Island.

Canadians can be distinguished by their saying "ruff" for "roof," "aboot," not "about." People all over the United States say "blesshoo" instead of "bless you," and there is a whole school of what I call Grunt English. They say "buh-hind," "tuh-day," and "buh-low."

There is a group that is conspiring to obliterate the letter "t." They say things such as, "I had an innerview with a denis." Weather forecasters use phrases such as, "There is a frunnel system . . ." Other people

*The Boy and the Snow Goose,* 1984 by Gayle Thomas. This award-winning artist has worked as assistant animator, background artist, and project coordinator as well as animator and director at the National Film Board of Canada.

carefully maim "luxury" into "luggzury." The list is endless. Cultivate a sharp ear for odd pronunciations. They may be quite acceptable on a local level but I think they have no place in a sound track that is going to be used nationally.

Again, during recording, retain the habit of not watching the actors. You are making a sound track, so your function is to listen, not to look. Usually I close my eyes, that way, I can really focus on listening.

Watch out for speech patterns such as the habit some actors have of dropping their volume near the end of a sentence. It can be corrected during the final recording but why have to contend with it? Make the actor aware of the problem by running an example from the tape; don't just tell him or her. Many people are completely unaware of this habit.

The reader will probably have become aware of one of my techniques: I try to break down every operation into separate steps. It is amazing how people can make things difficult for themselves by overlapping functions or trying to do several things at once. I notice that some workers will want to do this in spite of the fact that step-by-step is obviously more efficient. I am convinced that there is a type of person who likes to struggle and suffer—a vestige of our puritanical background.

## Collecting Actors

When the recording is finished, go down on the floor and take the time to say good-bye to each person. Plan to use the most outstanding actors again. Over the years, you should build up a stable of talent. There are some directors and producers who are always looking for new talent, ignoring actors they have used before. I think this is a misplaced feeling of power, or a case of the grass looking greener on the other side of the fence.

If you use the same actor many times, a fine relationship develops. You can both explore the possibilities of this particular talent in ways that would have been impossible during a casual relationship.

## Casting for Rotoscope

Since *Snow White,* a very different type of recording has developed at the Disney studios. Ever since that time, the company has leaned heavily on the use of rotoscope. In this procedure, the live actors go through the motion of the action and their images are traced as a guide for the animators. So in the search for specific characters during a casting session, there is an emphasis on the physical appearance of the actor, as well as the voice quality. He or she must conform in general to the design of the cartoon character because not only is the voice going to be recorded but the action is going to be photographed.

The action and voice for the particular sequence are then shot and reshot until it satisfies not only the director but the story people and even the animator. If it doesn't, the call goes out for another actor.

Although the sequence may very well be one side of a two-character conversation, the other character is often not even present; indeed, at this point, what is shot may only be a fragment of the role. Months may go by before additional dialogue and action are recorded and photographed.

The theory, as propounded by its adherents, is that the rotoscope tracings of the live action are a guide for the animators and help them make better cartoons. The detractors say that the idea of giving animators tracings of the actors' interpretations of the roles is similar in

Danish-born animator Kaj Pindal worked for many years at the National Film Board of Canada. Among his best known films are *What on Earth?* and *I Know an Old Lady Who Swallowed a Fly.*

*I Know an Old Lady Who Swallowed a Fly,* by Kaj Pindal and Derek Lamb; a National Film Board of Canada picture. Lamb and Pindal often worked together, and Lamb said that working with Pindal was like collaborating with a great pantomimist.

principle to giving the actor a line reading. They feel it hobbles the animator in much the same way.

I take this view. I think that after a certain amount of animation of *Snow White* was finished, Walt and his directors should have seen that it was quite possible to create very fine animation without the laborious photography of the actors and the subsequent tracing of their actions. According to Grim Natwick, he animated about a hundred scenes of *Snow White,* and most of them were done without the aid of the rotoscoped drawings. He merely used the first and last tracings to be sure that he hooked up to the scenes before and after the one on which he was working. He then flipped through the tracings a few times but he never referred to them while he was animating. It is doubtful that Walt Disney ever became aware that his safeguard against poor animation was being flouted this way.

As for recording piecemeal, those opposed to the method say that the whole system is similar to shooting out of context on a live-action film. Recording bits and pieces of a role, often months apart, has been the bane of any actor who has had enough experience in the theater to realize that there is a power and scope in acting on the stage that is rarely realized on film because of the loss of momentum when working out of context. However, this modus operandi has become standard procedure at the Disney studios.

## Recording Music

In addition to recording the dialogue, in certain types of pictures it is necessary to record sections of the music track before the annotation of the bar sheets can begin. And here is a place where a lot of care must be taken.

As a director, I have learned to hate songs that are often written into a script with scant regard for the fact that they interrupt both the pace of the film and the plot development. No audience wants to watch a sequence in which the characters stand around mouthing lyrics while the action grinds to a screeching halt.

Yet with proper awareness of this danger, the story can be so constructed that the singer or singers can perform and have interesting action as well, and then the plot moves forward. The action can include other characters who are acting out parts of the story as they listen. There is no better example of masterful handling of plot and song working together than in *Snow White and the Seven Dwarfs.* At no time during the entire film does one feel that the picture has stalled during a song.

One thing I insist on in the singing is good diction. What good are lyrics if the audience cannot understand them? One time I was directing a singing group and they were having difficulty with the word "doesn't." It kept sounding like "dozen." Finally, we hit on the device of having one girl lean into the mike at the appropriate time and instead of singing, just utter a distinct "t." It worked, too.

Often, it is necessary to prerecord bits of music before the score is written because the animation is going to follow the music note for note.

A good example of this approach is the opening sequence of Disney's *Hawaiian Holiday.* Minnie does a hula while Mickey plays the guitar. His fingers are in sync with every note in the music. Later, Pluto has an encounter with a crab and his chase of the Crab is a note-for-note interpretation of the score.

Darrell Calker, music composer at the Lantz studio, used this technique on all his scores for Lantz's Swing Symphonies. He would hire some virtuoso such as Nat King Cole, Bob Zurke, or Meade Lux Lewis to record a sequence of one or two minutes. The remainder of the score was written after the animation was finished.

It is fairly easy to detect prerecorded track; usually you can see the animation following the music note for note. The track reading must be very accurate since the musician is not wearing headphones to follow a *click track.* Because of that, the beat may vary one or two exposures in accordance with the performer's modulation. It is this subtle change of pace that is reflected in the animation and makes the coupling of the action and music so satisfying to the audience. This is unlike the use of a click track, which is bound to give the music a somewhat mechanical feeling.

## Fast Music; Fast Cutting

In the Lantz cartoon *The Barber of Seville,* we used a preproduction recording of Woody singing an aria, the "Largo al Factotum." The storymen, Hardaway and Schaffer, had ignored the possibilities in the fact that in the reprise the tempo of the aria doubled. To me, it was an opportunity to try out some of the principles of fast cutting that Sergei Eisenstein had expounded. Fortunately, it worked. This technique can

*Mindscape,* by Jacques Drouin, is one of a series of films he animated using the Alexander Alexieff pinscreen technique. This painstaking method involves a quarter of a million replaceable headless pins. They are inserted at various depths, producing an image on both sides of the screen. The illumination shapes the contours and allows for a full range of gray. The film is photographed in continuity from one frame to the next, and the animator is free to make his manipulation of the pins according to his creativity. Courtesy of the National Film Board of Canada.

be a source of great satisfaction to the audience because the listener has been taken on a kind of audio-visual steeplechase.

In spite of the advantages, the more timid directors, in fact whole studios, never tried fast cutting. There are no such sequences in the films of the Fleischers, Iwerks, or the early cartoons by Terrytoons, Famous, or Columbia.

As a pioneer in the field of animated television commercials, I introduced this technique in some of my earliest films. Now fast cutting is commonplace in both live-action and animated television spots. In fact, often there is such a bewildering succession of shots that the viewer is left wondering about the nature of the product being advertised.

## Sound Effects

One area of filmmaking that is often given short shrift is the art (and it is an art) of creating sound effects. In the early days of sound films, there was a tendency to use only natural sounds to embellish the action, even in animated cartoons.

It wasn't until Disney's *Tortoise and the Hare,* made in 1935, that a more creative approach to sound effects was devised. When the Hare dashed all over the court playing tennis with himself, there was a realistic ping as the racket struck the net, but when he slid to a stop in the opposite court, there was a loud automobile-brake screech. The audience reaction was so great that Disney set up a department specializing in sound effects. Directors should always be looking for creative sound effects. A good example happened when I was directing *The Night the Animals Talked,* a special being made at Gamma Film in Milan. The Italians were not very well versed in the technique of using sound effects, and I found their sound library to be very sparse.

In the film I had two pigs who lived in a mud wallow. They made some very acid remarks about the animals who lived in the barn. After each statement, they settled into the mud with a soggy splash. Gamma had nothing remotely like such an effect in the library. I was going to have to create it myself . . . but how?

I was still musing about it when we went to the commissary for lunch. This day, they happened to serve polenta, a kind of cornmeal mush. While I was stirring it up, I realized that the answer to my problem was literally under my nose.

After lunch, I went to the sound stage and ordered a bowl of polenta and a straw, to the mystification of the sound crew. When the food arrived, I placed the straw in the polenta and blew into it. A gurgling, sloppy burble emerged. I proceeded to make a series of short splashes, big blasts of mushy plops, and half a dozen sounds in between. We soon had enough of a library to take care of every pig movement the animators might conceive.

Keep your eyes open, even when you are not working on a specific problem. One night in a poker game, I realized that when a pack of cards was riffled briskly, it made a terrific snap, like the jaws of an animal. Years later I used the idea for the alligator in *Noah's Animals.* Again, here is the idea of the memory bank in action.

It is better for everything but the most common sounds to be prerecorded because usually there is a tendency to underestimate the time it takes for an unusual sound. There is nothing more frustrating than to find, when the editor is assembling sound effects, that one particularly good effect has to be discarded because of insufficient footage in the animation.

Realistic sounds such as dogs barking, hens clucking, cats meowing, loud crashes, different engine sounds, rain, birds, doors closing, and so

Børge Ring created Anna and Bella in its entirety; he even played the music for the sound track.

*Anna and Bella* by Børge Ring. Two aged sisters' memories are stirred by looking at an old photograph album. This film won an Academy Award in 1985, and other prizes.

on all can be bought from sound-effects libraries, either on tape or record albums.

In addition, be on the lookout for toys with odd sounds. There are musical toys such as slide whistles, kazoos, marimbas, drums, toy pianos, and pull-toys. Then there is the possibility of changing the character of sounds by slowing them up or speeding them. There are sound-effect libraries that have the machinery to do this kind of work.

There is no way to learn to create sound effects except by trial and error. It can be a fascinating area of filmmaking.

After all the recording is finished, the sound editor assembles the good takes. Often the beginning of one good take is spliced to the latter part of another. At this point, there is no need to try to cut the sound track into a finished form. The end result will be compiled from the director's bar sheets.

# 8

# The Director II:
## Preparing to Make Bar Sheets

While even live-action-film directors now use storyboards as a matter of course, the idea of preediting is what separates them from their animation counterparts. It is not unusual for a live-action film to be shot with a ratio of ten to one. In other words, ten minutes of film are shot in order to make one minute of finished film.

The director makes key shots, close-ups, medium shots, and other diverse camera efforts of a given sequence. The editor is given all these elements and has the responsibility of constructing picture from them.

In animation, the director makes the final decisions on every sequence. There is no multitude of shots from which to choose. There are only the single shots, which the director has created. The editor is reduced from a creative person to a splicer and librarian. The film has been preedited.

This is not sheer exhibitionism on the part of the animation director. It is a matter of a limited budget. So, in a five-minute cartoon, the director is expected to keep excess footage down to perhaps fifteen feet or less, as contrasted to the ten-to-one ratio of the live-action director.

Bar sheets are not used in live action. In animation, they are the director's blueprint of the entire picture. While at first glance they may seem to be formidable documents, taken one element at a time, they are soon quite understandable.

CHEST UP
THEN SLUMPS

Chuck Jones is a master of quick sketch. He studied the Nicolaides book *The Natural Way to Draw* for many years. These drawings show a sparkle and humor in just a few lines. They must be an inspiration for any animator. Warner Bros.

There are many ways for a director to work on a film. Much depends on a person's background, the skills he or she has in addition to directing. For example, I studied the violin for fifteen years, so I have a better than average knowledge of music. I also have worked as an animator and layout artist, painted backgrounds, and written scripts.

In my early years in the profession, I worked as a painter, inker, and checker. I even had a short and disastrous essay at animation photography. In other words, I have held all the creative jobs and most of the skilled positions at one time or another.

These days, talented artists are not wasted on the skilled jobs; they are put to work in areas that are more creative. Still, I am not sorry that I have this quite different background because I know the problems of inking, painting, and photography from personal experience. It has a lot to do with the way I approach directing.

## Sentence Measurement

While the editor is putting together the *good takes,* I prepare my personal script for sentence measurements. This is not to be confused with the word *analysis,* which the editor will do later. I need these measurements to compile my bar sheets.

Each sentence in the script is bracketed at the start and finish. Sometimes, certain key words within a sentence are also bracketed. These measurements are not accumulative. Each sentence is measured starting from one. I also need to know the number of blank exposures between each sentence. With this information, each sentence becomes an independent entity. I can place it on the bar sheets the way it was recorded, or I can put any number of feet between the end of the sentence and the beginning of the next. I always have perfect control because I know exactly the amount of footage with which I am dealing.

Of course, it is most important that the editor has been very careful to compute the dialogue footage to the exact exposure. Incorrect information would make for a number of technical difficulties, including a furious director.

## The Director's Rough Sketches

However, before the bar sheets can be worked on, I perform my most creative act as a director. As soon as I have the track measurements, I start making rough sketches of my conception of the action.

It would be very tidy to start working on sequence A, scene one, but believe me that is not going to give you control over the pace of the picture. You must establish parameters. Since the final sequence is the most important section of the film, it is best to start there. Because it

Director's roughs by Shamus Culhane for *The Last of the Red Hot Dragons,* Westfall Productions, Inc. Written by John Culhane, Charles Mortimer, and Shamus Culhane. Animated by Erredia 70.

is the culmination of the story, it should be the funniest, the most dramatic and compelling sequence in the picture. So I start sketching the action as I see it.

I use my drawing skills to enable me to visualize the action and stimulate my creativity. I draw at top speed, roughing out the poses with very little indication of a background, and no indication of the field size. No scene numbers or drawing numbers, either. All that material is sheer bookkeeping and has no place in my creative mood.

Very often, I do this work at night or on weekends because I want total focus on the problem of directing. If it is done during the workday, my assistant has strict orders that I am not to be interrupted for any reason. The right side of my brain must have an unimpeded session because in many ways the fate of the picture is being decided at this time.

This is the most exciting phase of the director's work. You must try to put yourself into that ruminative mood where you are at once the audience and the performer. The drawings that are being created are for your pleasure as the spectator. Draw whatever comes into your mind; keep it open to the most vagrant possibility. Discard it only when it so far from the story line that it is not feasible. Otherwise, explore every idea. After all, you are making drawings that at most take two minutes; throwing them away is no great hardship.

Do not stop for an instant until you have roughed out the key poses for the entire sequence. You will find that some scenes have required a single drawing to express your concept; others will have as many as ten or fifteen sketches. Put them in a folder and go to the next sequence.

## Pruning the Roughs

Choose the slowest one in terms of action; it, therefore, probably will be the slowest in terms of cutting.

Again, draw at top speed. Never stop to think. "Think" with your pencil. If you have arrived at some impasse, throw the drawings out and start at the point where the material was still good. Never correct a drawing. Throw it away instead the instant you see that it is unworkable. Erasing is using the left side of your brain, and you cannot be judgmental and creative at the same time.

This is the sequence that should undergo the most rigorous pruning. I have a rule of thumb; if I think that I would be bored by animating certain scenes, I try very hard to cut them out entirely. This is directly the obverse of my work on the last sequence, where, even if I know the picture's overall length is too great, I never skimp. I even add footage when I think of some action that was not on the storyboard.

When you have finished this pruning process, you now have established the parameters for the entire picture. No other sequence will be as slow as this section, or as fast-moving and dynamic as the previous one.

## Nuts and Bolts

At this point, it might be a good idea to go back to the finished work and indicate field sizes, camera moves, and scene numbers. Do each operation separately; don't do all three at once. If you are doing fields, for example, that is all you are thinking about.

Note that every sequence starts with scene one. I do that so I don't have to wait until the entire picture is on the bar sheets before I can begin to number each shot.

Take on the problem of the remaining sequences in order of their importance, paying strict attention to the tempo of cutting that has been set up by your two initial sequences. Now I know that there are many other ways of directing a film but I have never come across a method that can control the pace of a picture as well as this. However, directing is such a personal experience, that I am sure each of you will find some variation of my methods.

Realize that in making the rough sketches, I have not kept the layout artist from having a better camera angle than the one I have indicated. But it's then that person's job to convince me that the new camera angle *is* better. Often a discussion will result in still a third camera angle being chosen. The main point is that my sketches do not represent some ironclad concept. They will help the layout artist just as the storyboard drawings do. They provide a springboard for his or her ideas just as they did for mine.

The theory behind my choice of a camera angle is twofold. As soon as possible after establishing a long shot to set the locale, I want to move in and omit all extraneous detail. Next, I intend to give the audience a series of optical shocks. I want to make the eyes work to adjust to the procession of compositions from one shot to the next. I'll explain more about that in the following chapter.

There are a few basic approaches to scene cuts that are important. When setting up the cuts during dialogue, one can start the dialogue offscene or cut to a reaction shot before the end of a sentence. When you have two or more characters talking, overlapping the sentences and the scene cuts prevents a mechanical feeling in the editing.

Be careful about seeing to it that long stretches of dialogue are made interesting by some action germane to the plot. Once, during the production of a live-action film, I began to realize that a sequence between a boss and his salesman was going to be dull because of a lack of action. The salesman was getting orders to go out west but he was apprehensive because the last three salesmen before him had been shot dead.

The information was important to the plot but I didn't want to show two talking heads in an office. Suddenly, I got a brainstorm. We had not considered dressing the salesman while the men talked. Now we used it to embellish the dialogue.

The salesman, Orson Bean, really milked the dressing action. He was given a racoon cap and fringed buckskin jacket that had belonged to the last salesman. He did things such as poking a finger dubiously through a bullet hole in the jacket just as the boss was assuring him with false heartiness that it was a wonderful job opportunity for a young man. So the sequence, which might have been a pedestrian part of the picture, was one of the funniest.

The problem of providing enough interesting action often occurs in singing sequences. Study any Disney feature to see how the songs are always linked to the plot so that the story progresses even while the song goes on.

Do not always finish an action in the scene where it started. For example, in a scene of a character getting out of a chair, it is better to have the action start in that shot and finish in the following scene—making sure that the action matches, of course.

It isn't necessary to have connecting shots when going from one locale to another. For example, we see a person about to leave his house. Before we cut, somebody else's voice can be heard. In the next scene, we see another person who has been talking. *Truck* back and reveal our first character already seated in a chair, listening.

The more conventional approach would be to dissolve from the first shot to show a change of locale. A *fade out* would indicate the finish of a sequence. Sometimes for shock value, I fade out on a quiet scene, and instead of fading in on the succeeding shot, I cut. This is a good device if I want to jolt the audience with a very noisy sound track or a very vigorous action, contrasting it with the quiet scene preceding.

One psychological block to watch out for concerns the fact that storyboard paper usually has a printed field. These printed fields should not influence your choice of camera moves.

The camera plotting should be fluid, guided only by the need to keep the action framed in a good composition, which is why I rough out the action for myself without any attempt to circumscribe the movement of the characters with a previously determined field. Later, when I go back and add the field, I am giving this important function my full and undivided attention. For the most part, camera moves should be unobtrusive. Sometimes, a fairly subtle move can readjust a composition and save an action from being uncomfortably near the edge of the field.

As you do this work, preliminary to compiling the bar sheets, keep in mind that it is sharply divided between highly creative effort and bookkeeping. Never make the mistake of trying to do work in both categories simultaneously.

# 9

## The Director III:
### Bar Sheets and Track Analysis

First, you will note that the bar sheet is laid out in bars, similar to a sheet of music. This is because the music composer is going to write a score that will often closely interpret the action indicated in the bars.

### Following the Sample Bar Sheet

Aside from the job number, picture title, sequence letter, and page number, all of which are self-explanatory, there is a small box on the left labeled "beat." This fixes the tempo of this particular section of the film. It indicates that each bar is made up of two twelve-exposure beats.

I have chosen this tempo at random. It could have been a three-eight tempo, four-seven, or whatever tempo seems to best suit the action. The tempo is arrived at by a discussion with the composer if the score is going to be original. If the score is going to be library music, the choice is up to the director.

The scene numbers are circled for visibility. Next to them are short scene descriptions. The top two lines are marked "action." Because the action may be complicated, with several things happening at once, having two lines makes it easier to write the timing of the action more clearly.

The "x" you see at the beginning marks a beat. In this case, it indicates where Noah's foot hits the deck. Twelve exposures later, there is another step, and so on. We see that the fourth step is shorter, only eight exposures. Then Noah turns around, which takes sixteen exposures, going into a take that lasts another sixteen exposures.

There is a cut to scene fifteen. What has horrified Noah is a giant wave building up throughout this scene.

Cut to scene sixteen. On the nineteenth exposure, the wave crashes down on the ark.

Cut to scene seventeen. The ark comes into a shot of a whirlpool and starts spinning in the last twelve exposures of the shot.

Dissolve to scene eighteen, which is in the ship's interior. The elephant starts to spin with the momentum of the ark. On the twenty-fifth exposure, he hits a large group of animals and they all start to revolve. At this point, note that the music has gone into a waltz tempo, three-eight.

Cut to scene nineteen as the ark, still spinning, starts to approach the lip of a waterfall.

Cut to scene twenty as Noah grabs the wheel and starts to turn it at the rate of six exposures for each complete revolution.

## Indicating Dialogue

Returning to the beginning of the page, dialogue is indicated after six exposures of scene fourteen. The sentence is exactly thirty-three exposures long. I think you now understand why the track measurements have to be so accurate.

There is another sentence that starts eleven exposures after the beginning of scene fifteen, ending fourteen exposures into scene sixteen. A new sentence starts eight exposures before the end of the shot, continues through scene seventeen, and ends eighteen exposures into scene eighteen. There is a space of twenty-four exposures before a new sentence starts. This runs two exposures into scene nineteen.

## Camera Instructions

Going back to the beginning again, there are camera instructions. Scene fourteen has a truck back to a long shot, which starts on the twelfth exposure and ends thirty-seven exposures later.

JOB 86D

NOAH'S ARK
SEQ. M

SHEET #16

**BEAT** 2/12

14 NOAH LOOKS BACK

| | STEP 1 | STEP 2 | STEP 3 | STOP | TURN | TAKE HORRIFIED | 13 WAVE MOUNTING | WAVE FORMING | BUILDS UP |
|---|---|---|---|---|---|---|---|---|---|
| **ACTION** | | | | | | | | | |
| **DIALOGUE** | THE ARK IS OFF AT LAST > 9 | | TRUCK BACK TO LONG SHOT > | | | | | OH OH IT LOOKS | |
| **CAMERA** | | | | | | | | | |
| **SOUND** | FOOTSTEPS SOUND | | ← WIND EFFECT | | | | | ASCENDING | |
| **MUSIC** | AGGITATO | | | | | | | | |
| | 12 | 13 | 14 | 15 | 16 | 17 | 18 | 19 |

16 WAVE CRASHES

| | WAVE STARTS DOWN | CRASHES ON ARK | ARK ALMOST SUBMERGED | 17 ARK INTO WHIRLPOOL | ARK ENTERS SCENE | DRIFTING TOWARD WHIRLPOOL |
|---|---|---|---|---|---|---|
| **ACTION** | | | | | | |
| **DIALOGUE** | LIKE A SHORT TRIP > 4 | | ← NOAH WANTS EVERYBODY TO KEEP IN | | | |
| **CAMERA** | | | | | | |
| **SOUND** | WIND CONTINUES < BIG SPLASH | | ← WIND AND RAPIDS | | | |
| **MUSIC** | CONTINUE BUILDING UP ← LOUD CHORD | | DES CENDING | | | |
| | 50 | 51 | 52 | 53 | 54 | 55 | 56 | 57 |

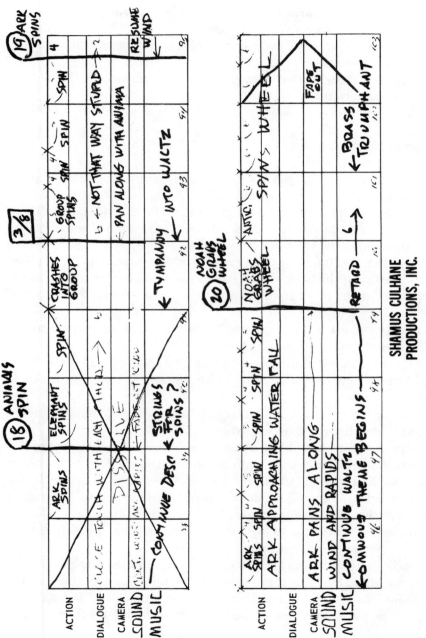

**SHAMUS CULHANE PRODUCTIONS, INC.**

Sample bar sheet, with all relevant information filled in.

There is a three-foot dissolve between scenes seventeen and eighteen, which is indicated by crossed lines. The scene number is always placed in the middle of the dissolve. A pan starts on the thirty-seventh exposure and is thirty-two exposures long.

Another pan starts at the beginning of scene nineteen and continues throughout the shot.

There is a fade-out twelve exposures long, indicated by the arrow's head in scene twenty.

## Sound Effects

Sound effects are next. Noah's footsteps are heard on the deck and a wind effect starts fourteen exposures before the end of scene fourteen.

The wind effect continues throughout scene fifteen and sixteen. There is a splash effect as the wave comes down on the ark, starting nineteen exposures after the start of scene sixteen.

Seventeen continues the wind but now adds the sound of rapids; then both fade out at the beginning of scene eighteen. There is a crash as the elephant hits the other animals twenty-five exposures after the start of the shot.

The wind effect is heard again at the beginning of scene nineteen and continues through scene twenty.

All the music notes are nonspecific but the effect called for is definite and certainly provides a composer with a sound structure on which to build the score.

For scene fourteen, I am suggesting a feeling of agitation, then a chord to emphasize Noah's horrified take.

Since the wave is building up in scene fifteen, I have a notation for an ascending phrase, which continues into sixteen, ending with a chord that coincides with the sound effect of the wave hitting the ark. In the final recording, I intend to mix the sound effect and music in such a way that the effect is dominant.

In scene seventeen, I suggest a descending theme opposing the ascending phrase in scene fifteen.

I indicate the possible use of strings to interpret the elephant's spins in scene eighteen; then a timpani beat to reinforce the effect as the elephant hits the group; and then resuming strings for the waltz.

In scene nineteen, the waltz continues but an ominous theme begins to overshadow it.

Scene twenty has the music retard, then a triumphant fanfare as Noah begins to control the ark.

You can see how a bar sheet is the blueprint for the whole picture, covering, as it does, all aspects of production. Taken one element at a time, it is not the formidable document it probably seemed to be before this explanation of each function.

Making the rough sketches and annotating the bar sheets would probably take three weeks to a month for a half-hour special, and as little as a day for a thirty-second television commercial.

## Why Use Bar Sheets?

There are directors who do not use bar sheets at all. Usually, they are directors who have risen from the ranks of the layout artists and designers without ever having done animation. So they write very general instructions in the action column of the exposure sheet, trusting that the animators will supply the detailed actions without further instruction. While it certainly is possible to produce and direct animation using this method, it has obvious disadvantages.

The musical structure is going to be by guess and by God, unlike the well-ordered suggestions indicated in the sample exposure sheet. During sweatbox sessions, a director who has been an animator can order the addition of three exposures here and five there with confidence in the resulting retake. Without the bar sheets, nobody can "read" the entire picture with a clear understanding of every department's contribution. It is doubtful whether a person who has not been an animator can ever develop and hone a sense of timing so keen that a twenty-fourth of a second is a distinct unit of measurement.

## Dialogue Track Analysis

While the director has been compiling the bar sheets, the editor has been analyzing the dialogue track. Each word is being broken down to its combination of vowels and consonants.

Editors unfamiliar with the proper analysis of a dialogue track, and who do not understand the way an animator goes about using this information, will often try to annotate the breakdown of the words by

brain and intuition about working with other creative people—are accompanied by a lack of interest in details of production, with a tendency to make mistakes on the bar sheets as a result.

## Correcting Bar Sheet Errors

It is up to the assistant to study the director and find out where there is a possibility of frequent error; for example, locating sentences on the bar sheets that are in the wrong place because the director has added up the number of exposures in the beats erroneously. This is a common mistake in the heat of creativity. When such an error occurs, the assistant calls it to the attention of the director. This can be corrected, assuming the assistant catches it. If it is just a question of one or two exposures short, the director can move the track at the beginning or end of the sentence to make up the deficit.

A longer mistake—perhaps ten exposures—is harder to correct, even when a sharp-eyed assistant finds it. The end of the sentence has an extra beat added and the bar sheet is marked accordingly. There is no way to add or cut out exposures that do not make a full beat if there is going to be an original score. One cannot omit or add eight exposures to a two-twelve beat, or five exposures to a three-eight waltz tempo. The correction would have to be an addition or deletion of twelve exposures in the former situation and eight in the latter.

It would be wrong to become smug about the fact that the director makes mistakes in details that have to be corrected. The kind of mind that has easy association with flights of fancy just usually does not have a tendency to be neat and orderly. Neither do sprinters make good weight lifters.

## Exposure Sheets

The assistant has the job of compiling the exposure sheets from the bar sheets and the editor's analysis of the dialogue. Of course, this transfer of information has to be correct to the last exposure. If the director has marked a sixteen-exposure-held pose on the bar sheets, he would not want to see it indicated as fourteen exposures on the exposure sheets.

The picture's title, animator, background number, sequence, scene, footage, and sheet numbers are self-explanatory, as is the start mark, field size, and position.

Sample exposure sheet.

In the action column, the beats are indicated—the first beat by an encircled cross; the second by a plain cross. Of course, the beats are numbered the same as the bar sheets.

The next column of numbers marked DIAL is solely for the use of the camera operator. Do not be confused by the fact that there is a line called DIALOGUE on the bar sheets and one called DIAL on the exposure sheets. The two have nothing to do with each other.

On the exposure sheets, dialogue is always written in the TRACK column. The *dial numbers* are always matched to the footage counter of the camera.

Very often during the course of the photography, the telephone must be answered or the errand boy brings in more new scenes. After the interruption, the camera operator returns to his work. There is a set of cels under the *platen*. The question is whether the work has been photographed before the interruption or not.

By checking the footage counter against the dial numbers on the exposure sheets, the camera operator can tell exactly what happened. Nobody else uses these numbers but they are important because they make it almost impossible to omit shooting a setup or inadvertently shooting it twice.

Dial numbers do not always start with #1. Sometimes, the cut occurs in the middle of a beat, so the starting number might be #7 or 8. It just depends on where the previous scene stopped. Wherever it is, the camera operator sets the footage counter accordingly before starting photography.

Another chore for the assistant director is the scheduling of meetings between the layout and background artists, animators, and the director. The assistant also sets up the pencil-test screening and the projection of the *dailies*.

## Revising the Bar Sheet

During discussion between the animators and the director about the pencil-test reel, the assistant is expected to make notes about the various changes, deletions, and additions that are going to be made. Later they are typed and each animator is sent a copy. During the next sweatbox session, the assistant refers to the notes to see to it that all changes have been made. All such notes are carefully stowed away and not thrown out until the answer print is approved.

It is a good idea to make the necessary changes on the bar sheets right after a sweatbox session while the material is still fresh in the mind of the assistant.

If a correction adds one beat, the assistant writes in the music line THREE BEAT MEASURE. If the change is two beats, a new bar is written marked "A" and the number of the previous bar. If the change is extensive and a number of bars are involved, it is best to extend the bars on the back of the previous page.

## Production Charts

Another important function is keeping the production chart up-to-date. When a given piece of work is started, the box is given a diagonal stroke, as indicated. This changes to a cross when the work is finished.

The assistant has to keep in daily touch with all department heads in order to keep the chart accurate. That way, the director can see at a glance whether the crew is on schedule. It is a good idea for the assistant to make daily rounds of the departments at the same time every day, either early in the morning or toward the late afternoon.

Never underestimate the value of the production chart, because in addition to showing the progress of the picture, it is a record of the reuse of cels and backgrounds in other than the original scenes.

One time I was directing a half-hour special in a studio that had never before done a film longer than a one-minute spot. To my annoyance and anxiety, the assistant director was taking a very slipshod approach to the production chart.

When all the work had been given out to the animators, I made the mistake of taking a two-week vacation. My assistant promptly abandoned the production chart as an irritating and useless bit of red tape.

By the time I returned, the studio was in a state of pandemonium. Backgrounds and cels that had to be reused in several future scenes had already been rephotographed and stored. But where? There were more than two hundred scenes already completed and stored in bins!

It took me and the crestfallen assistant more than a week of reorganization before we found the missing material and the production chart was once more up-to-date. In the interim, the studio was wasting precious hours looking through piles of scenes for cels and backgrounds that were holding up production. I would recommend that a production chart be made up for even a thirty-second spot.

## PALMOLIVE 60 SEC.

| | scene no. | feet | layout | bgrd | animator | assistant | pencil test | retake | re-use drgs | planning | Xerox ink | paint | check | color camera | retake camera |
|---|---|---|---|---|---|---|---|---|---|---|---|---|---|---|---|
| THREE SHOT | A1 | 3" | A1 | A1 | SAM | BILL | | | | MARY | | | JANE | | |
| C.U. FAT | A2 | 4" | A2 | A2 | SAM | BILL | | () | | MARY | | | | | |
| C.U. SKINNY | A3 | 2" | A1 | A1 | SAM | BILL | | O | A1 | MARY | | | | | |
| C.U. TINY | A4 | 3" | A4 | A4 | SAM | BILL | | O | | MARY | | | | | |
| FATTY SHAKES CAN | B1 | 3⁵ | B1 | B1 | TED | AL | | | | ALICE | | | JANE | | |
| SKINNY SCOURS | B2 | 4⁸ | B2 | B2 | TED | AL | | O | | ALICE | | | | | |
| TINY RINSES | C1 | 6⁵ | C1 | C1 | JOE | JOE | | O | | MARY | | | JANE | | |
| SPARKLES | C2 | 3⁷ | C2 | C2 | SAM | BILL | | | | MARY | | | | | |
| TINY SEES REFLECT. | C3 | 6⁵ | C1 | C1 | JOE | JOE | | | C1 | | | | JANE | | |
| SKINNY SKATES | C4 | 2° | A2 | A2 | TED | AL | | | A2 | | | | | | |
| FATTY AT CAN | D1 | 4³ | B1 | B1 | TED | AL | | | | ALICE | | | | | |
| SKINNY AND SON | D2 | 2⁹ | B2 | B2 | TED | AL | | | | | | | | | |
| TINY SMELLS GOOD | D3 | 3¹² | B1 | B1 | SAM | BILL | | O | B1 | JANE | | | | | |
| C.U. TITLE | E1 | 6⁹ | E1 | A2 | SAM | BILL | | O | D2 | | | | | | |

It can be seen from this production chart that all the layouts are completed, one background painted, all animation given out. Only D2 remains unfinished. The assistants have completed thirteen shots; eleven scenes have been approved in pencil test after three retakes had been completed. The planners have done eight scenes; five have been Xeroxed, four painted, three checked, two photographed and their retakes approved.

A chart like this should be brought up to date daily. It gives the director complete information about the flow of production in every department.

## Casting-Session Notes

During a casting session, the assistant should keep notes regarding the various comments made about the contenders, as well as the proper spelling of each name, and the address, telephone number, and Social Security number of the people selected for the picture. It is up to the assistant to find out whether the actors have any conflicts, such as work on a series that limits their available time. Then a schedule is set up for a recording, and, of course, each actor is notified.

Obviously, the major function of the assistant is to see to it that the director is spared all paperwork and any other details of the production that are not creative. A good assistant will study the work habits of the director (they are all different) to see where the director's job can be lightened.

# 11

## Field Guides, Peg Bars, and Pan Moves

When animated films were first produced, the equipment was very simple. The animator worked with a set of pegs screwed to a wooden drawing board. He had only one camera area in which to animate because the camera was immovable.

It was mounted on a camera stand made of strips of angle iron. The animation was placed on a table underneath the camera, and a rude framed glass, which was pressed down by hand, was the platen. The general effect of this rickety contrivance was as if somebody had been interrupted while building a rabbit hutch.

The first improvements on this jerry-built rig were made by John Oxberry, a very talented engineer and designer. Even his first camera stand was a big improvement because the camera could truck up and down. Oxberry kept improving his designs until he was building monster stands weighing thousands of pounds and operated by computers. Other designers followed suit and now camera stands are fully automated.

All these improvements did pose a problem for the studio staff because everybody from the director down had to be able to use all the facilities of the camera stand.

Temperamentally, creative people for the most part are not interested in machinery. Yet everyone concerned must become thoroughly familiar with the workings of a camera stand and the peg bars.

While the director has to be conversant with the process, he rarely has to do any of the mathematics because he deals in *thumbnail sketches* and rough drawings that have no indication of the camera area. Nobody else on the staff has such a luxury. Starting with the layouts, every drawing has to be assigned to an exact position in the camera field.

It would be almost a hopeless task to try to understand the following text by just reading it. It has to be a hands-on experience, using an animation board equipped with both still and traveling *peg bars,* 3-field paper, and both 12 and 16 fields. So, if you are just leafing through the book and do not have the equipment, skip this chapter.

Most of the time, animated films are produced using a 12 field, a camera area 9 × 12 inches. We use a grid called a 12 F guide. When the *field guide* is placed on the pegs, it makes it possible to compute an exact position for the animation camera within the periphery of the 12 field.

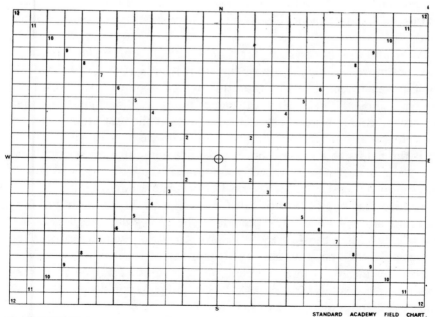

A 12-field chart.

Notice that all the field sizes have a common center. A simple command would be for the camera to come from a 12 F center to a 3 F center. The camera would be made to slide down the supporting columns. The nearer it got to the art work, the bigger the close-up. Finally, it would reach the 3 FC position and the photography would be resumed. The animator's command on the exposure sheet would be placed in the camera column and would read: Cut from 12 F to 3 FC

An arrow in the camera column would indicate the exposure where the cut would occur. The animator must include with the drawings in the scene a tracing of the #FC with the production name or number and the scene number. If there are a number of field sizes in a scene, they should be lettered "A," "B," "C," and so on. Make a rough drawing on a 12 F. Make a tracing of a 3 FC on it just to see how big a close-up you have made.

If, instead of a cut, we wanted to make a truck from a 12 F to a 3 FC, an arrow in the camera column would indicate the exact exposure for the start of the truck. The command would read: Start 48 exp. truck to 3 FC.

The animator does not decide on the length of the truck. That is the function of the director. The layout artist draws a field size. However, the animator may decide that it not quite accurate for the animation and needs an adjustment. This is often where sizes like 4½ and 3¼ are used.

When the instructions call for a field size off center, the procedure becomes more complex. Suppose the cut is from a 12 F to a 4 F 8 East. First make a tracing of a 4 FC, carefully indicating the center. Now take the tracing off the pegs, slide the center along the horizontal line that bisects the center of the 12 F until it arrives at the eastern edge of the 8 F. Now make another tracing of the 8 F in this new position. Write on it the field size and position, the picture name or number, and the scene number. If it was correctly computed, the east edge of the 4 F will be on the eastern edge of the 12 F on the guide.

Realize that one could not call for a 4 F 9 E. Try it. You will find that part of the 4 F would be outside of the 12 F guide. A quick check is made by adding the 4 and 9. Whenever the field size and any number for an off-center position add up to more than 12, it is incorrect.

Now for an even more complex move, from a 12 F to 6 F 3 West and 5 South, usually written as 6 F 3 W 5 So. Draw a 6 F at center. Slide the tracing along the center line as before to the west edge of 3 F. Now slide the tracing down south until the center is resting on the south edge of 5 F. Trace the field at that position and add the usual production number, and so on.

### *Exercise: Tracings of Various Field Positions*

Do the following exercises:
6 F 2 W 6 No to 9 F 3 So 3 E
3 F 7 W 6 No to 7 F 5 E 2 So
9 F 4 So to 4 F 3 No
10 F 2 W 1 No to 8 F 2 W 3 No

I hope you caught the erronious 9 F!

Normally no animation is photographed on an area smaller than a 3 F. Even on a 3 F, the inked or Xeroxed lines of the artwork should be rendered very thin; otherwise, the magnification of the lines will cause the drawing to appear too coarse.

In addition to the 12 F, there is a 16 F. The center of the 16 F is not the same as the center on the 12 F. Because the bottom edge of both fields are the same, the center of the 16 F is north of the center of the 12 F. When this field is used, the 12 F platen has to be removed and a 16 F platen installed. All camera moves must be computed from this new center. The method of arriving at field positions is exactly the same as it is on a 12 F.

Besides the mobility of the camera, there is still another movement in that the peg bars can slide east and west. They can be combined with trucks to make very complex action.

For example, we have a pan background on top pegs going to screen right at 1 inch per exposure. On the bottom pegs, we have a move to screen left at ¼ inch per exposure. If the pan on the top pegs were railroad tracks and the bottom pegs held a train, the effect would be that the train would be gaining on the camera.

While these two actions are going on, the camera could be trucking from a 16 F to a 3 F 13 W 7 So. Make these drawings and a tracing of the final field position, and, in effect, make a dry run as if the material was being shot.

The animator does not devise scenes of this complexity. The director and the layout artist would be responsible.

It is very important to be fully conversant with every aspect of the

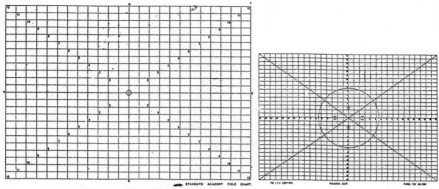

A comparison of a 12-field chart and a 16-field chart.

field guides and the peg movements. Make up your own exercises and practice until you are familiar with these tools.

A word of caution about still pegs. Both top and bottom pegs must have their centers lined up exactly with the center of the field guide you are using. Be sure never to allow a set of pegs to be inadvertently moved off center.

The start position of traveling pegs is always measured from the middle peg of the drawing to the middle of the field guide. For example, if the train in the exercise started offscreen and went through the scene and out of screen left, the animator would draw on 3-field paper. The first position of the paper would be with the extreme left set of peg holes at center. The drawing of the train would be made so that it was just outside of the field. The start mark is a vertical line that would be under the center peg hole. START would be added.

Now the drawing would be slid along the peg-bar groove until the train has cleared the field. Another vertical mark corresponding to the center of the field guide would be marked STOP.

In order to compute the speed of the peg move, the animator first checks on the screen time the director has indicated. Suppose it is 50 exposures. Now the length of the space between the start and stop marks is measured. Say this is 20 inches. Divide the 50 exposures into 20.00. The train will move to the left at .40 per exposure. Notice that we use the metric system, not inches. The 20 inches would be written as 20.00. The camera moves can be as slow as .01.

Three-field paper and cels are 10½ by 37½ inches. If you sketch this exercise and make the peg moves, you will see why the paper has to be 3 fields long. A shorter length would allow the edge of the paper or cel to show on the screen.

A layout sketch by Wayne Becker for *Noah's Animals.* Note the indication of a truck to a very small field. © 1975 by Westfall Productions, Inc.

Pan paper and cels can be bought in an animation-supply house, punched or unpunched. If you want to buy your own punch, be sure that it is capable of punching 3 or more field paper and cels. It is surprising that some expensive punches are only designed to punch for a 9 × 12 field.

One can tell at a glance whether or not a punch is going to be adequate. To the right of the right-hand die, there will be an auxiliary center peg very accurately placed, because after punching the first set of peg holes, the paper or cel is moved to the right and the middle hole placed on the auxiliary peg. When the punch is pressed down to make the next set of peg holes, the right-hand die must go smoothly into the hole that has already been punched. The die must not enlarge the hole by so much as a hair's breadth.

When the story calls for a violent impact caused by an earthquake or an explosion that seems to jar the camera, this effect is obtained by making a series of field sizes that jump from one position to the next, and may even tilt.

An example: We are on an 11 FC. The shake starts by calling for a 9 F 2 W 3 No. Then a 12 F, followed by 9 F, 2 No 3 So. Next a 12 F again, then 9 F 3 No 3 E, and so on. The shake can come to an abrupt halt, or it can gradually become a series of fields that are only one field size away from each other. The effect can be shot on ones or twos depending on the violence of the shake.

In making tilted fields, be sure that they still are confined to the field guide. This field position must be drawn, and if several are used, they must be identified by letters. For example, the camera column might read like this:

9 F 2 W 3 So
12 F
Tilt A

A *swish pan* coming to an abrupt halt can be accented by having the art go past the STOP mark, come back to a position before the STOP, go past it again, and so on. This would give an effect of a vibrating stop.

While most artists find all these measurements and grids a boring business, still, a sound knowledge of this aspect is as necessary as being able to draw well. The camera operator must have a set of readable and workable instructions. Exposure sheets have to be read and understood by every department in the production process. Take some pride in the fact that you are careful not to make 5 look like 8, or 7 resemble 1, and that your printed instructions are not like sandpiper tracks. Don't write instructions in longhand. Print everything. Over the years it has been established that the printed word is less likely to suffer from the kind of eccentricities that handwriting produces.

# 12

## Layouts I

Eugene Fedorenko, who worked with Derek Lamb on *Every Child,* the Academy Award winner in 1980, was one of his assistants on this title for *Mystery!* The other was Rose Newlove.

Before going into the problems of laying out advertising spots, half-hour specials, and feature films, there are two productions that do not fall into any of these categories: titles and animatics.

Before Saul Bass was called upon to design the titles for *Around the World in Eighty Days,* the credits for motion pictures were usually a fairly pedestrian chore. Bass solved Mike Todd's predicament about the pecking order of all the stars involved by making a series of caricatures.

The drawings delighted the audience; mollified the paranoic feelings of the actors and actresses; and a new field was opened to the animation profession.

Over the years, some very interesting combinations of live action, animation, rotoscope, and computer animation have been used for the creation of titles. Probably the most successful creations after *Around the World in Eighty Days* were the titles for the James Bond series.

Of course, there are many other films that are enhanced by titles that show a great deal of artistic talent. In fact, so many that it is not necessary to discuss them. It is probably more informative to bear down on the negative aspects of titles for films and channel signatures—aspects to be avoided.

## When the Title Art Overwhelms the Type

Many designers seem to have forgotten that the primary purpose of titles and signatures is to provide information to the audience. This information is in the form of lettering and is meant to be read without the reader having to run a gauntlet of artful devices that only make it difficult to absorb the text.

Currently, the television channels are given to what is possibly the worst use of computer animation. The artwork would not embellish the cover of a primary-school program celebrating Arbor Day. The cascade of sparks, waves of colored lights, soaring rectangles flying into the distance, and lettering—first offered upside down for some occult reason—are all devices designed to defeat the primary purpose of signatures, that is, readable printed information.

The audience is unable to get at this information until it has endured a number of optical insults.

The theatrical films do not fare much better. A conservative estimate would be that one out of four main and credit titles are illegible because the lettering is superimposed over a background that is not suitable. We have white lettering over cloud formations, and red text over lurid red sunsets. In many cases, the choice of type is poor. Either the lettering is too small or the choice is a spidery type with serifs, utterly unsuitable for viewing on television. (And what film does not end up on the tube?)

If you are given a title to produce, keep in mind that the basic reading speed of an audience is one foot a word. Any graphic embellishments should not stretch this reading time to the point of tedium. Try to talk your client out of a surfeit of artwork and design a neat, easy-to-read title instead. Maybe you can start a trend back to the real function of titles. The audience will be thankful.

## Animatics

The other diversion from the mainstream of production is the animatic, a brainchild of the ad agencies. It originated because of the blind faith agencies have in testing their handiwork before spending the entire sum allocated to a project. It is a film that is little more than photography of a storyboard, except that if there are pan backgrounds, they move; and trucks, fades, and dissolves are shot. The backgrounds are rendered and the characters are on cels in most cases. A dialogue track is made and sometimes music and sound effects are added.

An animatic can be so well done that one wonders why it cannot be used as is, instead of going on with additional work. One time, I made an animatic of a cereal that featured a zany rabbit. It had a number of pans, cuts, and zooms, which propelled the material along at a breakneck pace. When it was shown to the client, he announced that he was very well satisfied with the result. When could he start ordering prints? The panic-stricken account executive finally talked him into making a completely animated film, but it took some doing!

I equate the rather pathetic agency belief in the results of screening animatics for a selected audience with faith in the divine right of kings, and about as useful.

It is obvious that a selected audience is psychologically skewed, it is bound to be swayed in the direction of approving the production being shown. It has nothing in common with Joe Zilch, sitting with his shoes and shirt off, scratching his belly while swilling down a can of beer. He cannot possibly be looking at a finished television spot in the same mood as a member of a selected audience. This group is bound to be imbued with a sense of self-importance, and grateful to the agency for the privilege. Joe, on the other hand, is probably waiting with mounting impatience for the avalanche of ads to be over so that he can get back to his wrestling match or baseball game.

## Handling the Agency People

Don't try to talk the agency out of it. At least the animatic does provide a chance to establish the style of the finished film and to give some indication of the directorial approach. So it isn't totally a waste of money, although it is not the insurance of success the agency thinks it has achieved.

Unlike in the early days of television, the agencies now usually create their own storyboards long before they have selected a producer; thus, both the layout artist and the director are effectively tethered. Suggestions from either should be offered to the agency producer with infinite tact because somebody's toes are going to be stepped on, no matter how discreetly the change is suggested. So the director should weigh the value of a new idea very carefully, in terms of a cloud-free relationship with the agency crew, and consider whether this could provoke a vendetta with the art director, a writer perhaps, or God forbid, the account executive!

It is not necessarily the fault of the agency people. Perhaps they have had weeks of trial and rejection with a demanding passel of the client's personnel. A change might mean another nerve-racking conference in order to get approval of the new idea. In turn, who knows, the whole story structure might come under reexamination by a group absolutely ignorant of the most primary principles of picture making. With these factors to contend with, it is obvious that the average suggestion is going to get a short shrift from the agency. Tread carefully.

## A "Don't" for the Layout Artist

The first duty of a layout artist is to listen as the director presents ideas about the storyboard sketches, rough drawings of the action, and the cassette of the dialogue track. Unfortunately, many creative people have about as long an attention span as a kangaroo with its tail on fire.

I find nothing so exasperating as a layout artist who, immediately on hearing about the first few scenes slowly takes on a blank look, with eyes focused faraway. I finally fired such a person. He would happily interrupt me as I was talking about scene twenty with an enthusiastic idea that would change scene three. Had he waited until I was finished talking, he might have found that there was a reason in scene thirty for using the composition I had created for scene three.

## Control of the Audience

Theatrical set designers and directors have very little in common with animation layout people and cartoon directors, in that they have very

cut II RD /C--- NOAH LOOKS UP

SEQ (H) SC 19

ANIMALS: WHERE?... I DON'T SEE ANYTHING... OVER THERE... OVER THERE /... I CAN SEE HIM... ME too...

SEQ (H) SC 20

NOAH: NOW NOW CALM DOWN.

SEC TILTED?

IS OVERLAY K-10

NOAH SEQ I

Tilting the field back and forth gave the effect of the ship rocking. Drawings by Wayne Becker for *Noah's Animals*. Produced by Shamus Culhane Productions, Inc., for Westfall Productions, Inc.

tenuous control over the audience. They can attract the audience's attention to certain actors at various times, at least in theory. However, there is nothing to prevent some members of the audience from straying away from the designated action to turn a speculative eye toward the luscious figure of a secondary character.

This can't happen in motion pictures because the director gives the audience no choice but to look at the shot that has been preselected. In addition, the director decides on the amount of time that the audience will be allowed to look at a scene. So there is very tight control.

There are advantages and disadvantages to this situation. If the director stays too long on a camera angle, the audience will be bored. If the scene is cut too short, the audience will be irritated because the action was not comprehensible. In addition, it is up to the layout artist to design the sets so that their complexity, or the lack of it, is related to the screen time involved. This needs good judgment and an instinct for the amount of time the average person needs to absorb the details of a scene. Since there are no rules to govern these decisions, each new picture and every scene in it presents new problems, never ending.

However, if there is a good combination of screen time, interesting changes in composition, and just enough detail to embellish every scene, the director and layout artist will have proved to be a good team. One can understand how important it is that the layout artist pay attention to the production chart, not only to find out how much footage there is in every scene but also to make it possible to look ahead and see where animation and backgrounds are going to be reused, and to design the work accordingly.

# 13

## Layouts II:
### The Relationship of Scenes

A good way to start making layouts might be to draw thumbnail sketches covering a part of a sequence, such as all the shots in a certain interior or exterior on one piece of paper. That way, the chain of shots can be scanned to see to it that the camera angles conform to the principles of screen editing.

Often, a sequence starts with an explanatory long shot. To save money on background rendering, a director on a tight budget will go

In this layout drawing for *Noah's Animals*, Don Duga has carefully indicated the grain of the wood, instead of leaving it up to the background artist. A Shamus Culhane production for Westfall Productions, Inc.

on from there to a series of closer shots using the same background. While this is economical, it may not be the best camera angle for a given action. A better way might be to create several different angles, and to add some shots using the original long-shot background but with smaller field sizes.

## Screen Direction

These days, when there is a tendency to use many scenes in a sequence, these multiple cuts must be planned carefully to guard against an error in screen direction. There is a kind of unwritten set of rules that both the audience and the filmmakers follow. For example, if there is a shot of one character riding toward screen right and the following shot shows another horseman riding toward screen left, the audience will infer that the two will finally meet. Also if, as we alternate scenes of the two riders, we use closer and closer shots, the audience will see this as an indication that the meeting is imminent.

It would not do to start a character going screen right for a number of shots, then suddenly intersperse a scene where the character is going left. The inference there would be that the action has reversed itself. One rider has turned back.

An incidental tip on screen psychology is that if a character is doing something difficult, say a sequence of a man struggling through deep snowdrifts, it is better to show him going toward screen left because we in the Western world read from left to right. Thus, this action going screen left is against our natural mode of making our eyes travel and therefore it makes the action seem more difficult.

Head-on or tail-away shots are neutral in that they do not indicate a specific screen direction. Neutral, that is, as long as they show the character in the center of the screen. But if the character exits to screen left or right, that sets up a definite pattern of screen direction that must be followed.

When showing a menacing figure—a rhino attacking a group, for example—the action will not be dramatic enough if the charging rhino is only seen on a horizontal pan. A head-on shot would be much more effective because it puts the audience in the position of the hunters; whereas in the side view, the audience is in effect safely behind the camera.

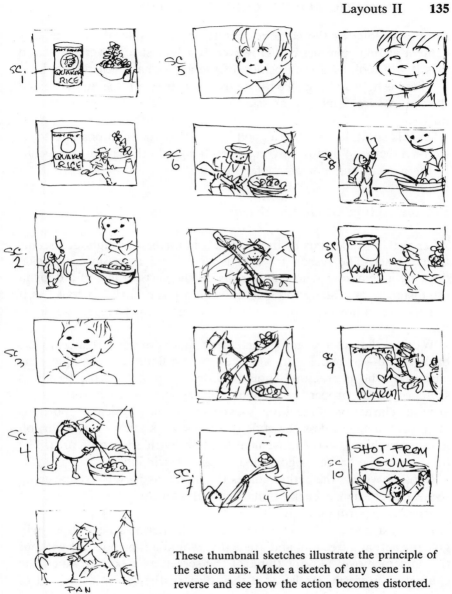

These thumbnail sketches illustrate the principle of the action axis. Make a sketch of any scene in reverse and see how the action becomes distorted.

## The Action Axis

In a sequence showing two or more actors, the *action axis* must be observed. This is an imaginary horizontal line that runs through the actors. As long as the camera operates on one side of the line, any camera angle is permissible. However, if a shot strays over the action axis it will look as if the position of the actors has been reversed.

There is no way to ignore these covenants between the audience and the filmmakers. Any transgression will be considered an unacceptable mistake.

At this point, it would be a good idea to take the thumbnail sketches to the director to discuss any possible changes in the layouts, revisions in the camera angle or character sketches.

## Let the Action Guide the Scene

After that, I would start by drawing the characters throughout a scene, then the set. The reason for that is to prevent a common mistake: drawing a character whose nose rests on the vertical line of a door in the distance; or placing the head in such a position that it looks as if it is wearing a flowerpot or some other object in the background on its head.

When a character is doing something that is directly related to the background—reaching into a basket on the floor, for example—the character who is reaching should be drawn first, then the basket is sketched in its proper position on the layout; never the other way around. The action of reaching is restricted by the physical proportions of the character (unless the style of the pictures allows for distortion in the stretching), so the movement has to be within a certain area. The position of the basket is governed by this restriction.

In other words, the action guides the layout artist into composing a scene rather than a background being drawn and the action of the characters superimposed on it.

Do not struggle to keep the camera still. Sometimes a slight pan will give the action a freedom and grace that would not be possible without the camera move. Do not think of the screen as a box in which the characters perform. Rather, see the edges of the screen as a kind of peephole through which one is looking at boundless space, north and south, as well as east and west.

## Television's Restricted Field

One nuisance is the fact that there is a cutoff area on television that pares down a twelve-field shot to a nine-field centered. In other words, anything outside of a nine-field shot will stand a good chance of not appearing on the television screen. So in composing layouts, there are really two working areas: the full field and the television field, which is always figured at three-fourths of the motion picture field. Whatever size the field is, the television cutoff must always be computed from the center of that field. There are no exceptions to this fact. All important action and all lettering must stay within the television field; otherwise, it will not appear on the tube.

## Using Overlays and Underlays

An *overlay* is a drawing of a portion of a background that is going to be rendered separately and pasted on a cel. It often is used over a character instead of having the inker match a complicated area so that the character seems to be behind it. A good example would be a person walking behind a picket fence. To have the fence a part of the background and to have to match each picket to the body so that this particular area is not painted would be a monumental job. It is so much easier to paint the whole body and place the picket fence on an overlay, saving the inker from a tedious matching job and the possibility of making a mistake.

Another use of overlays is to make them function as wild walls on a movie set. For a scene where the camera is going to have to pan into

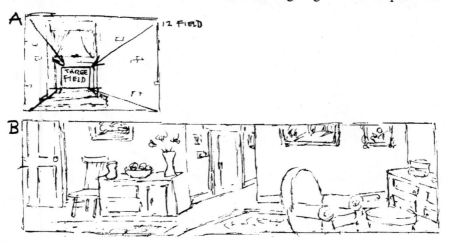

The camera trucks in past the window frame in A. This overlay is then removed, and the camera trucks back to a full 12 field as the artwork B pans to the left, revealing the other end of the room.

a window and along the interior of a room, the exterior wall and window are an overlay. When the camera has trucked down so far that it has gone past the window frame, the camera operator will remove the overlay wall, revealing the interior of the room, and pan along.

Another example would be a mountain road as seen by the driver of an automobile. It is rough and precipitous, with a big drop on the left and a steep vertical cliff rising next to the shoulder on the right. The camera trucks down as if the car was traveling along. When it reaches a point where the cliff edge is out of the field, the camera operator can remove the overlay, revealing another section of the road, perhaps a hairpin curve, which makes the camera truck back to a wide field.

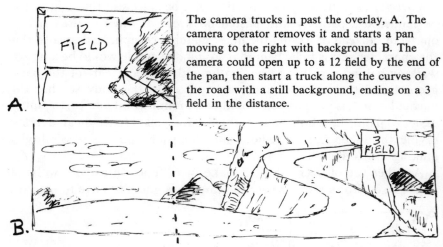

The camera trucks in past the overlay, A. The camera operator removes it and starts a pan moving to the right with background B. The camera could open up to a 12 field by the end of the pan, then start a truck along the curves of the road with a still background, ending on a 3 field in the distance.

An *underlay* also can be useful. On a horizontal pan, a section of the distant countryside and the sky are on an underlay, and the middle distance and foreground on an overlay. In between them is a train whose tracks are hidden by a depression in the ground. If the train enters at a speed that is faster than the overlay pan, and the underlay is going at a lesser speed, the result will be a three-dimensional effect.

Both layout paper and background paper come in a number of lengths, from one field to five or six fields. If, for some reason, long paper is not available, an overlay can be used to mask the join of the background paper. This seam is not necessarily a straight vertical line. It can be neatly curved to go behind any object as long as it is tall enough to hide every part of the seam: a tree, a well with a roof, a tall bush, or for the interior, a floor lamp, a chest of drawers, and so on.

Another type of pan is called a hook-up. As the name implies, both ends of the pan paper have exactly the same composition. When the camera operator comes to one end of the pan, he returns to the other. This cycled pan can go on indefinitely. The middle portion can be any length.

## Designing the Film

Usually the director has sketched out little more than a horizon line to go with the roughs of the action, leaving it up to the layout artist to style the picture. This is not a solo decision. It calls for a conference with the background artist and the director after a few exploratory layouts have been made. Now the layout artist is in a position to suggest the kind of medium that should be used.

Of course, the director has the final approval but very often follows the layout artist's advice. After all, that's the person who is going to design the film, and the choice of medium is going to influence the way the layouts are drawn. Art Heineman, one of the all-time great layout artists, liked to design his pictures for colored-paper backgrounds. This meant that all color areas were going to be flat surfaces with no gradations of value. As I recall, one of Heineman's best results was a brilliantly colored Walter Lantz cartoon, *The Greatest Man in Siam.*

In another musical film, *Boogie Woogie Man,* we even related the colors on the screen to the orchestration. The picture was designed with cold colors until the music reached a riff, then for that short time, we used backgrounds that were vivid orange, red, or yellow, then back to the cold blues, violets, and blacks, repeating the process on each riff.

The artists at UPA made no effort to give their films a feeling of realism. They did not attempt to hide the fact that their layouts, backgrounds, and characters were all very stylized drawings and paintings, the direct opposite of the Disney approach.

"Tom Terrific," a television series designed by Gene Deitch, had no backgrounds at all. The characters were inked or Xeroxed in a heavy black line and the action was played against colored paper, often without even a horizon line.

Whatever the medium that is going to be used to color the backgrounds, it should be decided upon before the layout drawings are very far along. The relationship between the layout artist and the background artist varies from team to team. There is no set rule about the division of work. Some layout artists will draw everything in meticulous detail; others will barely sketch in the salient features of the set. What is important is that each artist feel that his or her creative ability is not being curtailed or encroached upon. The director usually allows the two people to settle the peripheries of their work between them.

I would suggest that both the layout artist and the background artist study set design; so, for that matter, should the director. A good rule of thumb is that the composition of a shot should look unbalanced or empty until the characters are added. They are the hub of the composition, around which all the other components revolve. If a scene looks like a complete and finished entity without the characters, be wary. The composition may be so busy that the characters may not play easily in the space allotted to them.

Watch out for sequences of scenes that follow each other and have very similar compositions. The audience may find the film boring without knowing why. The human eye likes to work. It is a pleasure to have to keep making adjustments to variations of camera positions, different horizon placements, sudden moves from long shots to close-ups. All these visual exercises are a delight to the eye, completely separate from the plot or the acting ability of the players. Dull compositions can take the fine edge off a good story.

A montage with a good deal of fast cutting can be an exciting, thrilling visual experience. Sergei Eisenstein was an expert at creating them. In effect, he gave the audience an optical roller-coaster ride, and the people loved it. A study of his films reveals that the sequence of his compositions was always an important tool in his filmmaking.

I have nothing against unusual camera angles, providing they are doing a job, showing some important piece of business in the best possible composition. But I do not want an artful shot just as an extension of the layout artist's ego. My theory about the use of very unusual camera angles is that they are like condiments—to be used sparingly.

I have seen a crane shot used to show a group of children leaving school when a closer shot at eye-level would have been infinitely more interesting. Camera operators shooting films for television seem to like aerial shots; yet who needs to be watching from overhead while three detectives break down a door?

Sometimes I reject an odd point of view in a layout, to the artist's vexation. I explain that I try never to remind the audience that it is being manipulated, forced to look at the action from a point of view that we choose. So the gnat's-eye view in a shot is rejected in favor of a more normal and less obtrusive camera angle.

On the other hand, there are films such as Max Fleischer's *Mr. Bug Goes to Town* where the use of low-angle and aerial shots were an absolute necessity. The difference in size between the humans and the insects made for very tricky perspective shots, but they were germane to the story. They were necessary in order to establish and bring home forcefully to the audience how tiny and helpless the insects were and how precarious their existence was, living in such close proximity to human beings.

I hate to use a layout artist who draws characters badly. I don't want to have to tell an animator during a handout to ignore this or that drawing of the characters because it does not conform to the model sheet. Nothing is more dismaying to an animator than having to start working on a scene with a poor set of drawings that are a clumsy interpretation of the key poses. I think it often results in the animator not doing his or her best work.

Designing the sets may be the primary function of the layout artist, but character size, pose, and placement are important sources of information for the animator. Therefore, they should not be skimmed over. It is not a waste of time for the layout artist to practice drawing the characters in order to gain enough control over them to be able to draw a good key pose.

## Making Drawings for the Animator

Which drawings to make for the animator? The layout artist should be guided by a few simple rules. Obviously, it's necessary to draw the first and last pose of a scene in order to show the hookup between the connecting shots, if any.

Using my mode of directing, I come up with a pile of rough sketches I have made. If I have drawn them, it is because I feel that they are important factors in interpreting the action. They should be cleaned up against a very rough sketch of the set, which is going to be subject to many small changes as the various poses are finished. A very rough field size has been indicated on my sketches, but now is the time to zero in on the exact position and size of the field. Here is where one must not be restricted by the lines of the field. They are flexible parameters, not insurmountable barricades. A small, almost imperceptible camera move might provide a more comfortable feeling of space for the action. Remember your audience. You are dealing with the human eye, an exquisite instrument for gauging space and mass.

Throughout the picture, you are trying to manipulate the eye by swift changes in composition, providing adequate space for action, and giving satisfaction to the eye by the mix of long shots, close-ups, pans, and trucks that you and the director are using to interpret the story. The eye is quick to discern a shot where the action seems crowded by the set, hemmed in by the boundaries of the field. It is not a comfortable feeling.

## Layouts

The layout artist's job is very important because of the responsibility for the appearance, the graphic style of the film. Remember it is not your sole concern. A triad—the director, layout artist, and background artist—are all equally concerned. So be sure that right from the first handout of the picture there is a clear understanding of what the director wants as a final result, and that this feeling is shared by the background artist, as well.

During the first layouts, do not be hesitant about going to the director for approval of some aspect of the work that seems to be an improvement on the original concept but does deviate slightly. A good director will welcome the discussion; this kind of improvement keeps a film malleable, improving the original idea at every stage of production.

Above all, don't sulk if one of your ideas has been rejected. Remember that the director is responsible for every part of the picture. It's true he may have made a mistake in rejecting your suggestion, but like an umpire, he has to call them as he sees them. Be philosophical; if you still think it's a good idea, put it away in a file. Maybe it will be more applicable in another picture.

A whole spate of live-action pictures have been produced recently that feature wet streets at night. It took all this time for the live-action people to learn what a background artist such as Paul Julian was doing in Friz Freleng's Warner Brothers cartoons thirty years ago.

The streaks of varicolored lights from store windows and traffic lights reflected in the puddles make for most intriguing patterns, much more interesting than the same street when there has been no rain and the various lights are not reflecting in anything.

What it indicates is again a certain kind of thinking. Paul Julian was not painting a stereotype of a street. He was looking for a chance to depict one special street. The layout artist should have been doing the same thing. In Julian's case, he wasn't. But he did leave details for Julian to add, and embellish the backgrounds.

## The Morgue: A Visual Resource

This brings us to an important tool for the layout artist—the morgue. It is the difference between trying to fall back on one's memory all the time and leafing through dozens of ideas that might span ages of a particular culture.

I remember a story I wrote and directed about three kittens who lived in a house. I decided that the furniture should be Early American. We found some catalogues and magazines about antiques and proceeded to draw a series of tables, chairs, and other objects in this style. It made a very interesting-looking picture.

There is no background so prosaic that it offers nothing to to the layout artist's imagination—even so ordinary a subject as the front of a brick wall. Why not a wall that has been damaged and repaired with a different-sized brick? How about crowning the top with broken glass? What about a six-foot return at some point in that wall so that it is not just running parallel to the picture plane? Perhaps a cast-iron gate would enliven the shot.

In all cases, these embellishments should never impede or compete with the animation. When in doubt, leave it out.

Putting together a morgue should be fun. There is such a profusion of material that in no time one should have amassed a fairly large collection of information.

The trick is to have it properly catalogued. It has been said that a morgue is a collection of great material that happens to be of no use on the present assignment.

One of the chores is to have annual weeding-out projects so that the morgue is up-to-date and reflects your burgeoning knowledge of the layout business. Don't delegate this task to a subordinate. It is important that you do it and absorb information about the contents of your morgue. Then when you need a picture of an Eskimo snow knife, you pretty much know whether you have such a thing.

It is amazing how the memory can be honed to remember so much about the many pieces of information in a morgue. I remember once that I needed a shot of a pack of hounds. I immediately knew that I had such a shot. It was from the cover of a magazine and had one corner

# 14

## Animating

One of the most important factors in animating is a good work space. There should be a place to pin up model sheets so that they are always visible. You need a number of shelves for stacks of animation paper, rough sketches, and finished animation. Your desk should be broad enough to have room for a good pencil sharpener, a jar full of freshly sharpened pencils and colored crayon pencils, another jar for pencils with worn points, a small box full of erasers.

Your animation board should be large enough to contain the disk and your working set of exposure sheets. There should be a piece of beaverboard or similar compressed board. Your current section of the storyboard should be thumbtacked to it. It is to be hoped that you can leave all this set up so that it is instantly available at all times. Nothing is less conducive to enthusiastic work than having to drag the whole ensemble out of a closet and set it up before a drawing can be done.

The ideal components would include a tripod and a 16 mm camera rigged to shoot one exposure at a time. Of course, what's best to do, if you can afford it, is to run, do not walk, to your favorite photographer every time you have accumulated an hour's camera work, so that you can see your film as soon as possible, while the animation is still fresh in your mind. It would be a good idea to discuss your venture with the camera operator and find out how much footage can be shot in an hour. Estimates will differ.

Do not think that it would be time-saving to do the inbetweening and the animation simultaneously. Do it by steps. First the quick sketch, then the rough animation, numbering, spacing charts, and exposure sheets. Then the inbetweens. That is the way it will be done in the studio, so get used to the proper procedure.

This may seem to be an odd admonition but it is valid: Never forget your audience! The question might be put, "Which audience?" because American cartoons play all over the world.

Of course, there is no such thing as a typical audience. Even in the United States, we have vast ethnic differences. A canoe builder in Maine has very little in common with the lady owner of a dude ranch in Arizona, and even less with a fur cutter in New York City.

The audience of which you should be aware when you are animating is yourself.

You are being trained to make funny drawings, to caricature normal human situations and animal behavior so that you can appeal to the basic emotion shared by the whole of mankind—laughter.

This is why when you are animating, you must surrender to the tug of your emotions and draw from your feelings. You do not share your thinking processes with others, because you have a unique life experience. What you do share are feelings, sense of humor, a wry appreciation that we are an odd species, that working for a living and marriages have built-in problems that are universal, as do other relationships, such as children and parents.

So, as you animate, let yourself without reservation be both the entertainer and the entertained.

I am sure that by this time you have started to grumble about all this chatter about right side and left side of the brain. It is true that these theories are being proselytized by a drawing teacher who is not in the animation profession, but works in a California university, by an animator who is so old that he remembers when a hot dog cost a nickel, and also by a bevy of pointy-headed scientists who are as far removed from animated cartoons as they are from the Bushmen's circumcision rites.

Let us say that you are right. We just don't have the clout to convince you that the way we are trying to have you work and think is better than good old American common sense and a Pink Pearl eraser. Would you settle for Joan Miró, who said that "Creativity lies below the level of consciousness"? How about Gustave Moreau, Matisse's teacher:

"Art is the pursuit, by plastic means, of the expression of inner feelings"?

Matisse was aware of the need to divest himself of the restraints of painting and drawing with the left side of his brain. He just didn't know about the function of the left and right hemispheres, so he called them conscious and unconscious. But his words were true. He told his pupils that when they were drawing a tree, they should feel the growth, not get bogged down with the texture of the bark and the pattern of the limbs. It was more important to record the feelings that the tree aroused.

How about Samuel Johnson's version of my high-speed technique? I quote him loosely: "If I want to find out how good a sermon a churchman can write, I would have him write one as quickly as he can. Then go back and correct it." After he had designed one of the windows in the chapel at Vence and it had been installed, Matisse remembered that the motif was from a cloak that he had seen in a museum some thirty years before! Obviously, he had a memory bank.

Jean Charlot, the French artist and essayist, wrote in *An Artist on Art:* "We know by the letters of Van Gogh, that the great master of his type works with his mind at such a pitch that would be exhausting to sustain. Such exaltation is made fruitful only through long years of emotional experience and study. To such a master, the moment of work is what to the saint is the moment of ecstacy . . . to attempt a slowing down of his painting technique would result for the artist in a distinct loss, a muddling and an obscuring of the unmarred mental image that he envisions as a start."

It has been suggested that the reason our approach to creativity has been rejected so firmly is that people are frightened by the experience. The senses are heightened, very much as they are during a sexual encounter, and this seems almost sacrilegious during work hours. One is, according to our puritan ethos, suppose to suffer during the creative process, not have the equivalent of an orgasm.

The more I read about the process of creativity among famous artists in any medium, the more I am sure that their happy acceptance of this trancelike state is the reason for their greatness.

The human being can be very selective. During a day in the country, after the first few moments of awareness, the drone of the locusts can be edited out of the consciousness. I have heard that workers in garbage dumps soon learn to stop reacting to the stench.

People can also edit out other people.

It is surprising how many people go through life looking but not seeing. They have no interest in the activities around them, operating in a kind of limited consciousness. For an artist, and especially an animator, this self-imposed stupor is not acceptable.

Are you in a bus? How do old people sit down? How do the pelvis and shoulders work in a creaky body? What angles do they take in an effort to shift from a sitting to a standing position? What kind of expressions do the passengers have? Happy, dour, saturnine, vulpine, morbid, weary, hostile?

See the world around you. Even the most common activities are amazingly interesting. Here is a crowded market. See the tentative squeezing of fruit, the suspicious expression. The judgmental smelling of a melon. Is it fresh? The thoughtful rejection or the satisfied acceptance as it is placed carefully in the shopping cart.

Did you ever think how often humans can act like chickens? Watch people at a counter where clothing is on sale. The hands dart out and pluck at the material, give it a little shake, drop it and peck at some other piece, just like chickens scratching around a barnyard.

Eating is such an atavistic pursuit that a restaurant is a happy hunting ground for the observing artist. Here one can see gluttony, naked and unadorned. Repulsion to food, being acted out by the anorexic. The poor girl eating with her boyfriend, trying to ape the manners of a duchess, with her little finger cocked away from the handle of her coffee cup. The slob, head bent almost into his plate, grease trickling down his stubbled chin, shoveling food down his maw without stopping to taste it. Who can tell when one of these characters will be recalled from your memory bank twenty years from now to become a superb piece of animation?

## Learning to See

Observing the world around you with the keen eye of an animator should become second nature to you. But it will not happen overnight. For some time you will have to practice *seeing* instead of *looking* on a conscious level, asking yourself what is unique about the actions of some particular person, as if you were about to animate them. Later, the whole process will go on day after day and it will take an effort to realize consciously just what you are doing. Then one day, after you have just roughed out a sequence using the high-speed technique, you

Exercise: a drawing by Honoré Daumier. The slight tilt to the woman's head gives
the feeling that she is leaning over to look at her husband, while the husband's
uptilted nose makes one feel he is snoring. How else could this situation be
composed? How about a reversal of the roles? Do gesture drawings of these
situations.

will suddenly realize that you have incorporated into the animation an
incident you observed many years before.

Honoré Daumier, had he lived in modern times, would have been a
great animator because he was a great observer of the human condition.
He understood that for every mood there is a gesture, a pose that is the
essence of the feeling translated into kinetics. Looking at his drawings,
the nature of Daumier is revealed. He was a man who hated corruption
in high places, loved the poor, but enjoyed depicting their frailities with
a mixture of sympathy and irony. His drawings are worth intensive
study.

If you are just starting to learn animation, pay attention to your point
of view about the pictures you are working on. Norman Ferguson once
made the observation that fat animators like to draw fat people, and
thin animators animated thin characters very well. That may very well
be. One thing that is even more obvious is that animators who like to
draw pantomime are not usually as interested in fast comic action, such
as slapstick. See if you have a tendency in one direction or the other.

Not that you should try to specialize very early in your career. Still, why not not concentrate to a degree on that with which you feel most comfortable?

## Draftsmanship

There is no other factor as important to an animator as good draftsmanship. What good is it to have exciting ideas about your animation but find you are not able to put them on paper because of poor drawing

Exercise: Nobody ever drew corrupt authority with more venom than Daumier. This composition is almost like something we'd find on opening a photo album. Make several compositions of the same scene, but from different camera angles.

ability? Improving your drawing is going to be a lifelong chore, without limit. There is no way one can make a projection and say, "Five years from now, I will be able to draw as well as Tytla, Babbitt, or Børge Ring." One improves by plateaus, not by some steady ascension to perfection, as being on a ski lift. Some artists are late bloomers, others reach the apogee of their talent early in life.

## Starting Animation

When the animator is called into the director's office to pick up a sequence, it is understandably an exciting moment. Then you are a performer being called upon to interpret the ideas of several other people. The responsibility is yours alone, not to be shared with anybody else.

This feeling may make you impatient to start drawing as soon as possible. Instead, it is vitally important to listen very carefully as the director goes through the storyboard, layout drawings, and exposure sheets. There are dozens of details to absorb, so it is important to be sure that you understand them all. Better to ask questions now than to have to reanimate later.

Especially check the directions for specific actions as annotated on the exposure sheets. Does there seem to be enough screen time for a particular action? Perhaps the director's explanation has been too perfunctory. Question it.

It is not a bad idea for the animator to repeat the whole sequence back to the director, so that they will both be satisfied that everything is well understood.

If there are strange characters in the material, time must be taken to learn to draw them very well so that there is no need to keep checking with the model sheets. Not that the sheets should be filed out of sight; they should be plainly in sight at all times.

Learning to draw the characters may take anywhere from a few hours to several weeks. I spent a week just drawing the Fox's hands for my animation in *Pinocchio*. Unless the construction of the characters is well understood, there is the danger that the proportions will go astray during the heat of drawing the rough animation and all the animation will have to be redrawn. Why risk it?

When the character-drawing period is over and it is time to start animation, it is better not to rush into it. There should be a time of rumination, a leisurely examination of the story line, the layouts, and exposure sheets.

Benny Washam used to tell this story about me: When I went to Warner Brothers, Benny was curious about the way an ex-Disney animator would approach his work. We were supposed to animate twenty-five feet a week but to Washam's amazement, for three days I sat at my drawing board immobile, looking as if I was taking a catnap. Suddenly, in the last two days, I roughed out twenty-five feet. He decided to ask me why I did nothing for three days. I answered, "First I had to think about it."

In truth, I wasn't just thinking about the twenty-five feet. Chuck Jones had given me one half of a picture to animate, so I was thinking about the entire project. In no way would I consider those three days a waste of time.

The only drawing I had done during that time were some little doodles of various key poses, about one and a half inches high. These I had roughed out without looking at the layout artist's drawings of the same action. When it came time to actually start animating, I discarded the sketches. They were all well fixed in my mind, and since I intended to animate straight ahead, I didn't need them.

## Symmetrical Is Dull

There is a common fallacy in drawing animation that I call the Gemini Syndrome . . . the twins. Some artists, under the mistaken supposition that it looks neater, will draw a character standing with its weight evenly distributed on both feet, both hands in the same position, shoulders exactly horizontal, feet together, head and neck perfectly perpendicular.

What's wrong with this concept is that besides being the epitome of dullness, it doesn't exist in real life. The rare exception might be a West Pointer standing at attention in what they call a "brace."

Normally, a body has a number of points of imbalance, or what looks like imbalance. In truth, it is a system of easing tension by leveraging the balances along the spine and pelvis. A dropped shoulder on one side is answered by a drop in the pelvis on the opposite side; or, in an even more extreme way, which Michelangelo favored, balance is achieved by dropping both the shoulder and the pelvis on the same side.

Either position sets up a torsion in the body that makes it look alive,

A. The weight distributed evenly on both feet makes a static pose.
B. Both shoulder and pelvis dropped on the same side makes it look as if he is going to move forward with his right side.
C. The most dynamic action occurs when the angle of the shoulders and pelvis oppose each other.

whereas the Gemini Syndrome makes the figure look like a tailor's dummy, with no life-quality whatsoever.

This principle of asymmetry should be carried into details such as the placing of the eyes, the curve of the mouth, the angle of the cuffs, and alignment of the feet. In fact, one can say that the more the various elements in a drawing are asymmetrical, the more lifelike it will appear.

The principle of asymmetry even extends to actions. In the drawings of Fatty one can see that the hands in the first illustration are twins and therefore look stiff. In the second illustration, one sees that every effort has been made to avoid twin actions, and the result is infinitely more interesting.

## Torque

A feeling of tension can be created by torque—the twisting of parts of the body in contrast to each other; For example, making the head almost a profile, the chest less so, the pelvis a front view, the feet pigeon-toed.

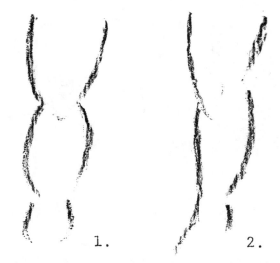

(Fig. 1) Twin curves are static and do not indicate masses or line of action.
(Fig. 2) This drawing has a definite line of action, and the variation of the curves and straight lines indicate form and movement.

Study the works of Michelangelo, Rodin, and Rubens. See how they twist forearms in opposition to biceps, and do the same with the muscles of the legs, and even to the torque of one finger against the next. Torque builds tension and tension means life-quality.

Torque is a form of distortion in that the artist has created a drawing that cannot be matched in real life without running the risk of dislocating a joint. There is, however, a limit to the amount of torque that can be achieved by the artist without going beyond the boundaries of believability. Don't make a drawing that has so much torque it looks like a victim of Torquemada's kindly ministrations.

Notice how twin curves of the leg have no motion, nothing for the eye to traverse; then see how curves not exactly juxtaposed allow the eye to move from one area to the next. Let me say again, in art, twins are a negation of life.

## Basic Procedures

In order to keep perfect control of the composition of a shot, the layout sketch of the background should be the bottom drawing on the pegs at all times, with the television area clearly marked in colored pencil. All important action should be confined to this area. Unfortunately, when the animation is being done to television specifications, you lose that taut feeling in the relationship between the action and the edges of the screen.

The Gemini Syndrome can take all the interest out of an action, as seen in the upper row of figures, whereas using variation can result in more lifelike action.

The layout artist, when drawing the key poses, can only give a rough estimate of the field positions and sizes. It is really up to the animator to make the final decision, so the layout artist's fields should always be open to close scrutiny. Is this the best field size, or should it be a little larger—or smaller? Would a little off center be better? These questions should be asked after the animation is all finished.

When drawing the rough animation, always work on the bottom pegs. If the drawings are on top pegs, one has to use both hands to flip two drawings; whereas on bottom pegs, the drawings can be tucked between each finger, making it possible, using a rolling motion, to see how five drawings animate.

Of course, when the animation is being cleaned up, the assistant will put all held cels on top pegs, making it easy for the camera operator to strip off in one swift motion from the bottom pegs the cels that have been photographed.

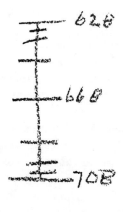

In the lower right-hand corner of every drawing is the drawing number, and when necessary, a spacing chart. This information is always written outside the field.

## Testing the Action

When I first went to work with Erredia 70, the best animation group in Milan, I picked up a stack of animated drawings and flipped them. The animators gasped in astonishment and implored me to show them how to do it.

Then I found out that these animators were all self-taught. They had learned the principles of animation by renting Disney short subjects and running the scenes over and over on a Moviola, so they had never learned about flipping drawings.

It is really quite simple. Stack the papers with the lowest numbers on the bottom. Remember to slide them so that there is an angle of forty-five degrees to the edge of the stack. Then the thumb slowly travels across the bevel, flipping the drawings. With practice, one can flip a scene containing several hundred drawings and view the action quite clearly.

When doing high-speed roughs, it is not a good idea to stop working to flip the drawings. Do it at lunchtime or at the end of the day. Remember that one cannot be creative and critical at the same time.

## The Two Approaches

There are two main approaches to doing animation. One is called "pose-to-pose." Progress through a scene, drawing the key poses until they are all completed. Then go back to add incidental drawings, and spacing charts for the inbetweens.

The second method is called "animating straight ahead." As the name implies, the animator starts on the first drawing and keeps on going, not stopping to make key drawings. Instead, the main poses come about because the previous action leads into them. They are not predetermined.

Straight-ahead animation has advantages. There is spontaneity, and the method will probably lead to more complex and lifelike action. However, this method may not achieve the solid poses that are possible in pose-to-pose animation.

Many animators work with a combination of both methods in one scene, drawing key poses where they are uncertain of the action, and plunging straight ahead where the overall movement is more important than single poses would be. It is hard to believe that any real spontaneity can be possible by this kind of mishmash.

There is another compromise, introduced by Norm Ferguson. He would initially sketch a number of key poses in rough drawings about an inch and a half high. Then he would start to animate straight ahead,

Michelangelo's "Adam" in the Sistine Chapel. Note the torque in the outstretched arm and the extended leg. The line of action is clearly apparent.

having solved in his mind the basic geometry of each important pose. Thus, he had the advantage of exploring his key poses first, then arriving at some variation on them when he was animating straight ahead. This seems to me to be the best of the two worlds.

Of course there are some scenes that by their very nature must be animated pose-to-pose. A good example are the shots of the dwarfs returning home, singing "Heigh-Ho."

The main problem here was that each dwarf had his own characteristic manner of walking. Yet no dwarf could be allowed to lose ground and leave a gap in the line or speed up and start treading on the heels of the dwarf in front of him.

It often took a whole day or more to map out the positioning of all fourteen feet in a given scene, so there was no possibility of working straight ahead.

Another example of pose-to-pose animation was my stint in *Pinocchio,* where the Fox, Cat, and Coachman are plotting in the Red Lobster Inn. Here I needed to gauge the amount of restraint I would have to use in the secondary action of the Cat so that he would not interfere with the main action between the Fox and the Coachman. Therefore, I chose, and I think rightly, to abandon my usual high-speed technique, and to draw slowly and carefully.

Several good examples of the use of high-speed straight-ahead animation are my Pluto and the Crab sequence in *Hawaiian Holiday;* the first half of *Inki and the Mynah Bird* (Warners); and the soldiers in Faith and John Hubley's *The Hat.*

Normally, I am reluctant to abandon straight-ahead animation because then there is no possibility of creating those happy accidents that come about when the right side of the brain is functioning without interference.

If I have decided that I am going to animate straight ahead, I get ready for the onslaught by seeing to it that there is a large supply of sharpened soft pencils and a huge stack of paper. The eraser is conspicuous by its absence. My assistant is warned not to talk and not to allow any kind of interruption. Classical music, not too bombastic, is usually the way in which I arrive at that dreamy state of mind that signals that the left side of my brain has been lured into a state of somnolence.

While the exposure sheet is kept just a quick glance away, I have no intention of stopping to write on it. I am not even going to stop drawing to number the drawings.

Many animators make the mistake of starting a pose by drawing the head. A Renaissance artist put it very succinctly when he said that the

Quick sketch by Shamus Culhane. In these swans, the line-of-action principle is obvious.

only time you start with the head when drawing a figure is when the person has been hanged!

## The Line of Action

Every drawing should have a very clear line of action. The principle of torque is only going to work if it is following a definite line of action right down to the fingertips, the tilt of a hat, the curve of a tail. The eye derives enormous satisfaction in following this line. When there is no planned line of action, the drawing will probably look disjointed, as if the parts do not fit together.

For many years at the beginning of animation, one can see that this principle was not understood. Even in the early Mickey Mouse cartoons, he and the other characters were obviously made up of separate parts. Ub Iwerks, creator of Mickey, was considered at the beginning of sound films to be the best animator in the business, yet his drawings in *Steamboat Willie* show no hint that he understood the line-of-action principle.

Often in the silent days, the characters were drawn using a nickel for tracing a circle for the head, and a half-dollar for the body. The real adjustment toward more sophisticated body construction was led by Fred Moore. He redesigned Mickey, giving him a pear-shaped body instead of one made of two separate parts.

The impetus for the direction of the line of action can come only from feeling what happens to a body when it is expressing a particular emotion. It is really the idea behind a gesture drawing. Every human being while growing up begins to become an expert at reading the quality of other people's emotions from overall posture, as well as facial expressions. We animators have to become superexperts.

Unlike in real life, we can carry the line-of-action principle one step further. We can invest the clothing of a character with the capacity to reflect the character's mood. This idea was also unknown in the early days of animation, even at the Disney studio. It probably developed with experiments in carrying the line of action to its ultimate. Once arrived at, however, it has become a valuable tool. Always remember that clothing can "act," too.


## Perspective

There is a way of drawing that will inevitably result in an uninteresting pose. That is when perspective is avoided. Very often, it happens because the animator started to draw an arm or a leg from the torso outward. A hand can express emotion; an elbow or forearm cannot. So why place these parts in a prominent place in the drawing?

The best way to avoid these boring parts is to start by first drawing the hand where you want it in the pose, then attaching the arm to it. Very often, it will be in such acute perspective that it is not noticeable.

One time, while I was working on a drawing of the Fox in *Pinocchio,* the pose was giving me trouble. The character's head just didn't seem to be resting in his palm. Norman Ferguson came along and redrew it. He first drew the head at the angle that was needed. Then he sketched the hand cradling the head. Then he made an arm and finally the body. In other words, all the elements that made up that drawing were done in the order of their importance. That was one of the most important things I learned at Disney's.

Are you going to draw two characters glaring at each other eyeball to eyeball? With Fergie's lesson in mind, I would begin by drawing the eyes, not by laying in the two bodies and finally getting down to the details such as eyes. In this case, the eyes are the most important element in the drawing. If they are not in exactly the right position, the rest of the drawing is meaningless. Now I think you can see why automatically starting a drawing with the head shows a lack of feeling for the pose. Begin with the most important element no matter what it is or where it is going to be in the gesture.

This method of drawing will almost force perspective into the drawing, making it much more interesting.


## Stretch and Squash

The early animators had not thought of another principle, which also came from the Disney animators: stretch and squash. If they had, they certainly would not have used coins to construct their characters. There were distortions in the animation in the early cartoons. Very often, there was an increase in the volume of the figure.

There is no way that life-quality can be animated when there is a change in the volume of the character. The principle of stretch and squash is like pressing down on a balloon, or pulling and stretching it. The shape will be different but the volume of the balloon will remain the same. Such distortions will be accepted by the audience as being in the realm of possibility, but an increase or decrease in volume will not.

It is astonishing how much stretch and squash there is in nature. We have all seen photos of fighters being punched in the jaw. The amount of dislocation and distortion in the face is incredible. Often the amateur photographer will take a shot of somebody talking. The picture is rejected because it doesn't resemble the subject. Maybe it was taken just at the instant that the subject made a sound such as "oo" or "ch." Normally, the various distortions used to make human speech are unnoticed because they are so common, so such a picture is rejected. Yet the distortion of the mouth in talking is an essential movement.

A long study of Muybridge's books on human and animal motion will reveal just how important squash and stretch is in every kind of action.

## Anticipation

Another important principle overlooked by the early animators was anticipation. Nobody thought that an action meant a shift in the center of gravity, which had to be started by a countershift. The most obvious example would be the windup of a baseball pitcher before he throws the ball.

Nobody could throw a ball very hard if the throw started with the pitcher in a standing position, both feet on the ground, with his arms dangling at his sides. It is a principle that the more violent the action is going to be, the more violent the anticipation. This is why a pitcher goes through all those contortions in order to throw a baseball ninety miles an hour.

Even the most subtle action needs anticipation. For example, a slow, lazy person is going to start a shambling walk from a standing position in which his weight is equally distributed on both feet. There is no way that this character can animate with life-quality without dropping the whole weight of his body on one leg so that the other leg can clear the ground and start a step. Besides this shift, the body may lean back slightly at the same time, then thrust forward into the beginning of the first step.

A study of anticipation leads naturally into the principle of overlapping action. In nature, there is no such thing as all the elements of a body arriving at the apex of an action at the same time. Even in a simple action such as coming to a stop, certain parts of the body will slow to a stop; others will go past the final point and settle back into the pose.

### Exercise: Anticipation and Overlapping Action

For an example, do a scene of Skinny doing a standing broad jump. First try it yourself to find out how it feels. You will find that the arms are doing actions much different from the rest of the body. First the body rises as the arms are coming up to an overhead position. Then the arms arc back behind the body after the body squats. Next the arms fly out and the body follows their momentum, arriving at a high point. The legs follow, then lead the descent. The arms remain high, but after the legs impact, the body follows. After that, the arms descend. This is a classic example of the various parts of the body acting independently of each other, yet all obeying the laws of anticipating and overlapping action.

Now make Fatty and Tiny broad jump, too, keeping in mind that Fatty is going to make a ponderous effort and not cover much ground; Skinny is going to jump the farthest because of his long legs and agility; Tiny will be able to leap like a little animal because he is so close to the ground. Remember the principle of overlapping action; no part of a body is going to work in concert with any other area. Feel the difference in the efforts of each character, using very fast sketches. Let the drawings happen and see just what comes about as a result.

Now go back and this time use the pose-to-pose technique. Remember to avoid the Gemini Syndrome; use torque where possible; and maintain the line of action, which should be easy to analyze in this type of action. Don't avoid using perspective. Make these particular jumps from a front view.

Now that you are familiar with successful broad jumps, try three unsuccessful attempts. Fatty falls on his rump; Skinny ends on his face; and Tiny lands on his stomach. All in high-speed technique. Now do the same action in pose-to-pose style, but this time have Fatty fall on his stomach, Tiny land on his rump, and Skinny end up with his rear in the air and his face on the ground. Do not look at your previous drawings for inspiration, and certainly do not copy them. Try to draw from your feelings. If you were in a movie house watching these three characters animate, what would make you laugh?

If you started making them jump from left to right, reverse them when switching from the straight-ahead to the pose-to-pose technique. That way, you will not tend to copy the former action. Remember that these are comics—make the action funny! Don't forget the secondary action of the clothing and be sure that it fits the movement of the characters, violent when the action is violent, and restrained where it isn't. Look for the clothing to react to the movement rather than animating with the action. It always happens later. Clothing doesn't instigate action; it is a victim of it.

## Eye Movements

Sometimes it is necessary to animate such a small action that it seems impossible to have the audience notice it. This is where the principle of anticipation comes to the rescue. If we made Fatty wink without anticipation, there would be very little movement between an open eye and a closed one.

However, using a big anticipation involving the whole face, the dropped jaw and raised eyebrows signal to the audience that an action is about to occur. Thus, what might have been an undetected movement is seen because it is done with a broad scope.

Do your own version of Fatty winking, then draw Skinny and Tiny doing the same. Realize that both Skinny and Tiny have much less meat on their faces than Fatty. Animate the winks accordingly. Can you find a way to bring their caps into the action?

Always think of eyes and eyebrows as one unit. The eyebrow is not something pasted on the forehead, independent of the eye. Feel how the eyebrow going into a frown is pressing down on the eye and changing its shape. When the eyebrows go up in surprise, the shape of the eyes should change accordingly.

Make frowns and raised eyebrows using all three characters in a three-quarter front view.

While we are on the subject of eyes, never have a scene go by without blinks. A dark-colored character like Pluto could blink very quickly. One drawing of the lid almost closed, a closed eye, and a lid halfway back up will do the job very well because the white of the eyeball is so conspicuous.

When a character has normal skin tones, the contrast between the white of the eyeball and the skin is not enough to do a satisfactory blink with the speed of Pluto's eyes; it will take more drawings. However long you take to make a blink, be sure that it happens. A character that does not blink suddenly becomes a lifeless dummy, all the life-quality gone.

Sometimes when there is a radical change of gaze, I use a blink to make it memorable. For example, Pluto is looking straight ahead, thinking. He blinks and when his eye reopens, he is now looking up at the ceiling.

It is amazing how the spacing of the pupils and the angle of the axis will change an expression. Draw a head-on view of Fatty. On a separate paper draw eyes and pupils. See what happens when you sketch a series of eyes whose pupils range from walleyed to cross-eyed.

Now keep one pupil looking straight ahead and start changing the axis of the other pupil in a series of drawings. Then draw eyes that are different shapes. Remember when the audience looks at a character, the first place they look is the eyes, then the rest of the face. Skillful placement of the pupils and the shape of the eyes will give a wide range of possibilities in making your characters act.

Even the size of the pupils can be important. Draw a front view of

Exercise: To see how the placement of the pupils and eyelids dominate the expression, trace these drawings with blank eyes. Over a lightboard, on a separate sheet of paper, draw various eyes and eylids.

Skinny with an expression of horror. Draw the pupils on a separate paper at their normal size. Now make another sketch of them almost as pinpoints and slightly crossed. See how the look of horror has been intensified?

## Reaction Is Important

One common error in animating secondary action is to stop the reaction too soon. For example, if a long-eared dog comes to a stop after a fast run, his ears will continue to travel at the same speed that he was going because they are only fastened to his head on one end. Therefore, the ears are like a pendulum. When they reach the end of the arc, they swing back. If the dog isn't moving, the ears will continue to swing back and forth, each time with a lesser arc. Finally, if the dog stays still long enough, they will come to a stop, but it will take a long time. Probably they will still be swinging when the dog elects to start moving again. Make a dog turn his head from side to front view. Now it is better to err on the side of continuing the swinging, because as long as it is happening, the audience will pay no attention to their action. The real

Very often the body's action tells more about the emotions involved than the face. Drawings by Shamus Culhane.

mistake is to make the ears stop swinging too soon. That will certainly make the audience examine the ears to see why they defied the laws of momentum. After a two-foot hold, the dog turns back to a side view.

The same principle holds for all kinds of attachments, such as skirts, tails, long coats, and so on. The tendency is to make them stop reacting too soon.

## Action: Shape and Pace

In analyzing action, if you have been really animating from your feelings, you will find that all the actions you have drawn describe arcs, some shallow, some deep. There are rarely actions that move in straight lines—it is no accident. There are no straight lines in the natural movements of any living creature—man, animal, bird, or fish. They all move by arcs, whether it is the action of a fishtail, the sweep of a bird's wing, the lope of a wolf, or a man and woman doing a tango.

In addition, there is another precept: Most actions tend to start

Exposure sheet for an action showing Tiny stealing a coin from Fatty.

slowly, accelerate in the middle, and slow down to a stop. This is the main reason that spacing charts were developed. Do make a practice of indicating the position of inbetweens by using spacing charts, even if you are doing all your own drawings.

While on the subject of inbetweens, it is a good idea to indicate the curve of an arc on one of your key drawings so that the inbetweener does not decide that the shortest line between two points makes the best inbetween, thus giving you a series of septagons or octagons.

Again, it is a good idea to go back to Muybridge to see how this important principle is carried out in live action.

It would be impossible to animate with life-quality if the action consisted of straight lines and movement that maintained a constant speed.

## Timing

When drawing pantomime, the timing of an action is probably the main problem for the animator. Timing, that is the passage from one pose to the other, is the way in which the mental and emotional attitudes of the actor are revealed. Pantomime is choreographed as strictly as a ballet. While the poses tell the story, it is the timing that intrigues the audience. In a way, it is more important than the poses because it gives us such specific information about the personality of the actor. If one were to give the same set of key drawings to two animators and ask them to create spacing charts, I am sure that they would end up with two entirely different interpretations because of the fact that each animator would sense the character's emotional structure differently and would indicate the timing accordingly.

The eye delights in sudden changes from slow movement, or no animation at all, to frenzied action. This unexpected change of pace captivates audiences the world over because it is part of the universal language of mankind.

Every great animator is a master of change of pace. The characters they drew became stars because of it. Norman Ferguson's Pluto, Art Babbitt's Goofy, Fred Moore's Mickey, Bill Tytla's Dumbo, and Dick Lundy's Donald Duck are all classic examples of incredibly talented pacing.

All their films should be studied. In addition, I recommend films by the greatest live pantomimist ever—Charlie Chaplin—as well as those of Buster Keaton, Laurel and Hardy, Harpo Marx, Harold Lloyd, and the modern master, Marcel Marceau. Animators and live pantomimists have a problem in common: They all have to edit the timing of their movements, so they are all valuable to the student of animation.

## Staging

Another lesson that can be learned from a study of these stars, both graphic and live, is staging. Of all the people I have mentioned, again Charlie Chaplin is the master. Remember that in most cases the audience is seeing the material for the first time. Thus, it is necessary that it be presented and displayed in such a manner that the action can be easily "read."

Chaplin usually prefaced a gag by presenting a preliminary stage. If he opened a door with a key, he first flourished it briefly as he took it out of his pocket, instead of shoving it right into the keyhole without any audience preparation.

Disney animators and directors learned this principle very well. After 1934, it was one of the tools that was used regularly in making their films.

### Exercise: Action in Silhouette

One way to find out whether your key drawing is really working is to make a silhouette out of it. The action should be understood in spite of the fact that there is no detail. Now try this exercise: In a waist-high shot, Fatty puts his hand in his pocket (remember about the anticipation), fumbles around, and comes up with a single coin, which he shows to Tiny very proudly. Remember to have Tiny react to all of Fatty's movements in a restrained manner.

Suddenly, Tiny snatches the coin and runs out. Fatty stands still for a moment with his fingers still together, as if he was still holding the coin. Suddenly, he realizes that it is gone. He opens his hand and looks at the palm, then goes into a frenzied attempt to run, but spins in place for a second until he gets traction. Then he runs out.

This action has been right to left. Now reverse the action and do the same action pose to pose, not copying any of the poses you arrived at in animating straight ahead. Make Fatty take the coin from a different pocket.

Draw these two exercises before going on to read the following text. You made a choice of the hand that Fatty used for his action.

Brush drawing by Shamus Culhane showing the importance of the silhouette in depicting various stances of an animal.

Looking back, was it the correct one? Did the hand and coin clear the mass of Fatty's body to make a clean silhouette, easy to read?

There are two extreme methods of reacting to a situation. Suppose we have an elephant walking along with that grandly ponderous stride indicative of the fact that this elephant knows he is lord of all he surveys. Suddenly, a mouse confronts him. Now we all know that the elephant is going to be running away, but how will this particular animal do it?

One, he could let out a bellow and run back where he came from, so fast that his exit is just a blur and some small clouds of dust. Two, he could be paralyzed with fright, unable to move, just standing there trembling. Then slowly, never losing sight of the mouse, he could start to sneak off, then suddenly run off.

Here we have two different kinds of timing. Both, in effect, doing the same action yet different in interpretation. Look for these possible extremes from slow to fast or vice versa in all pantomime situations. Remember that a funny situation and good poses are only part of filmmaking; timing is the other essential ingredient.

## Fast Action: Blurring

Using fast action reminds me that we have not explained the use of blurred action, usually called speed lines.

If very fast action is photographed and the shutter speed is not fast enough to stop the action in focus, there will be a blur on the trailing edge, where details of several images will be seen. This indicates that the object traveled some distance across the camera field before the shutter closed.

We have copied that principle in animating very fast action. Our multiple images, as the live-action ones, are distinguished by having a hard outline on the leading edge of the last image. In fact, except for some blur on the trailing edge, the last image is almost in focus.

The animator has to keep these principles in mind when he animates. He must not only draw the outlines of details such as the eyes, nose, mouth, hat, and so on but has to show the painter how the color is going to trail off. The blur effect is more than just a scribble of lines. The principles must be followed.

A good way to animate a vibration that starts vigorously and dies down is to make a set of drawings for the left side of the action and a group for the right. The vibration is caused by the way the action is notated on the exposure sheet. Make an action of Skinny with his finger in a light socket, vibrating. Remember to draw a leading and a trailing edge, more blur at the start and almost none at the finish.

Staggered drawings show tension. In this case, make a series of drawings with regular inbetweens. The staggered effect is made by the way the drawings are notated on the exposure sheet.

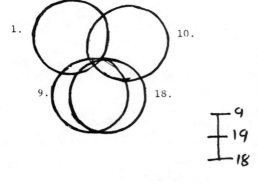

This is a diagram of a potential head vibration as an example of the juxtapositioning of the two sides of the action. The inbetweens, 2 to 8 and 11 to 17, can be slowed in and out or evenly spaced. The blurring is going to be more extensive on the early numbers, and practically nonexistent as the heads come close.

| PICTURE | ANIMATOR | DRAWINGS USED FROM | BACK GROUND |
|---|---|---|---|
| | | | |

**SHAMUS CULHANE PROD. INC.**

## VIBRATION

| DIAL | ACTION | DIAL | TRACK | 1 | 2 | 3 | 4 | 5 |
|---|---|---|---|---|---|---|---|---|
| 1 | | 1 | | 1 | | | | |
| 2 | | 2 | | | | | | |
| 3 | VIBRATION | 3 | | 10 | | | | |
| 4 | | 4 | | | | | | |
| 5 | STARTS | 5 | | 2 | | | | |
| 6 | | 6 | | | | | | |
| 7 | WIFE | 7 | | 11 | | | | |
| 8 | | 8 | | | | | | |
| 9 | | 9 | | 3 | | | | |
| 0 | | 0 | | | | | | |
| 1 | | 1 | | 12 | | | | |
| 2 | | 2 | | | | | | |
| 3 | | 3 | | 4 | | | | |
| 4 | | 4 | | | | | | |
| 5 | | 5 | | 13 | | | | |
| 6 | | 6 | | | | | | |
| 7 | | 7 | | 5 | | | | |
| 8 | | 8 | | | | | | |
| 9 | | 9 | | 14 | | | | |
| 0 | | 0 | | | | | | |
| 1 | | 1 | | 6 | | | | |
| 2 | GRADUALLY | 2 | | | | | | |
| 3 | DIMINISHES | 3 | | 15 | | | | |
| 4 | | 4 | | | | | | |
| 5 | | 5 | | 7 | | | | |
| 6 | | 6 | | | | | | |
| 7 | | 7 | | 16 | | | | |
| 8 | | 8 | | | | | | |
| 9 | | 9 | | 8 | | | | |
| 0 | | 0 | | | | | | |
| 1 | | 1 | | 17 | | | | |
| 2 | | 2 | | | | | | |
| 3 | | 3 | | 9 | | | | |
| 4 | | 4 | | | | | | |
| 5 | | 5 | | 18 | | | | |
| 6 | | 6 | | | | | | |
| 7 | | 7 | | 9 | | | | |
| 8 | | 8 | | | | | | |
| 9 | | 9 | | 18 | | | | |
| 0 | | 0 | | | | | | |
| 1 | | 1 | | 9 | | | | |
| 2 | | 2 | | | | | | |
| 3 | | 3 | | 18 | | | | |
| 4 | | 4 | | | | | | |
| 5 | STOPS | 5 | | 19 | | | | |
| 6 | | 6 | | | | | | |
| 7 | | 7 | | | | | | |
| 8 | | 8 | | | | | | |

Exposure sheet of a vibration.

Staggered drawings are the best way to show extreme tension. Note the two examples of spacing charts. The one on the right as it is exposed will show a sharp pull ending with great effort. The chart on the left will start with tension already established. The pulling action could be repeated by exposing the drawings in reverse, going back to drawing #1 and repeating the action.

## Double Takes

As you probably know, in acting parlance a "take" is a start of surprise. A double take is a bit more complicated. The character looks at or hears something and has no reaction. Then the full import of what the character has seen will penetrate and there will be a reaction. The interval between the two—no reaction and realization—may be long or short depending on the mentality of the character. A quite long interval gives the audience a chance to savor the fact that the character has not understood what has been seen or heard.

I have purposely made that passage pedantic because I want to explain the very basic underlying mechanics before we get into the technique of double takes. The numerous variations are something else again.

The double take was first brought to perfection by such masters as Charlie Chaplin, Buster Keaton, Harry Langdon, and W. C. Fields. Fields, a master juggler, used this skill in depicting a frightened or surprised take. When he reacted, his hands flew up to his hat as if to keep it from flying off. His fumbling fingers in fact did make the hat rise well into the air, and he would end the take by stopping the fumbling and cramming the hat solidly on his head.

# TWO EXAMPLES OF STAGGERED EXPOSING

| DIAL | ACTION | DIAL | TRACK | 1 | 2 | 3 | 4 | 5 | |
|---|---|---|---|---|---|---|---|---|---|
| 1 | | 1 | | | | 1 | | | |
| 2 | | 2 | | | | | | | |
| 3 | | 3 | | 2 | | 2 | | | |
| 4 | | 4 | | | | | | | |
| 5 | | 5 | | 1 | | 3 | | | |
| 6 | | 6 | | | | | | | |
| 7 | | 7 | | 2 | | 4 | | | |
| 8 | | 8 | | | | | | | |
| 9 | | 9 | | 3 | | 3 | | | |
| 0 | | 10 | | | | | | | |
| 1 | | 1 | | 2 | | U | | | |
| 2 | | 2 | | | | | | | |
| 3 | | 3 | | 3 | | 5 | | | |
| 4 | | 4 | | | | | | | |
| 5 | | 5 | | 4 | | u | | | |
| 6 | | 6 | | | | | | | |
| 7 | | 7 | | 3 | | 5 | | | |
| 8 | | 8 | | | | | | | |
| 9 | | 9 | | 4 | | 6 | | | |
| 0 | | 20 | | | | | | | |
| 1 | | 1 | | 5 | | 5 | | | |
| 2 | | 2 | | | | | | | |
| 3 | | 3 | | 4 | | 6 | | | |
| 4 | | 4 | | | | | | | |
| 5 | | 5 | | 6 | | 7 | | | |
| 6 | | 6 | | | | | | | |
| 7 | | 7 | | 6 | | 6 | | | |
| 8 | | 8 | | | | | | | |
| 9 | | 9 | | 5 | | 7 | | | |
| 0 | | 30 | | | | | | | |
| 1 | | 1 | | 6 | | 8 | | | |
| 2 | | 2 | | | | | | | |
| 3 | | 3 | | 7 | | 7 | | | |
| 4 | | 4 | | | | | | | |
| 5 | | 5 | | 6 | | 5 | | | |
| 6 | | 6 | | | | | | | |
| 7 | | 7 | | 7 | | 9 | | | |
| 8 | | 8 | | | | | | | |
| 9 | | 9 | | 8 | | 8 | | | |
| 0 | | 40 | | | | | | | |
| 1 | | 1 | | 7 | | 9 | | | |
| 2 | | 2 | | | | | | | |
| 3 | | 3 | | 8 | | 8 | | | |
| 4 | | 4 | | | | | | | |
| 5 | RIGHT COLUMN RELAX PULL | 5 | | 9 | | 9 | | | |
| 6 | | 6 | | | | | | | |
| 7 | | 7 | | 8 | | 8 | | | |
| 8 | | 8 | | | | | | | |
| 9 | | 9 | | 9 | | 7 | | | |
| 0 | | 50 | | | | | | | |
| 1 | | 1 | | 8 | | 6 | | | |
| 2 | | 2 | | | | | | | |
| 3 | | 3 | | 9 | | 5 | | | |
| 4 | | 4 | | | | | | | |
| 5 | | 5 | | 8 | | 4 | | | |
| 6 | LEFT COLUMN RELAX PULL — RIGHT COLUMN RESUME PULL | 6 | | | | | | | |
| 7 | | 7 | | 9 | | 3 | | | |
| 8 | | 8 | | | | | | | |
| 9 | | 9 | | 8 | | 4 | | | |
| 0 | | 60 | | | | | | | |
| 1 | | 1 | | 7 | | 5 | | | |
| 2 | | 2 | | | | | | | |
| 3 | | 3 | | 6 | | 6 | | | |
| 4 | | 4 | | | | | | | |
| 5 | | 5 | | 5 | | 7 | | | |
| 6 | | 6 | | | | | | | |
| 7 | | 7 | | 4 | | 6 | | | |
| 8 | | 8 | | | | | | | |
| 9 | | 9 | | 3 | | 7 | | | |
| 0 | | 70 | | | | | | | |
| 1 | | 1 | | 2 | | 8 | | | |
| 2 | | 2 | | | | | | | |
| 3 | | 3 | | 1 | | 7 | | | |
| 4 | | 4 | | | | | | | |
| 5 | LEFT COLUMN REPEAT STAGGER → | 5 | | | | 8 | | | |
| 6 | | 6 | | | | | | | |
| 7 | | 7 | | 2 | | 9 | | | |
| 8 | | 8 | | | | | | | |
| 9 | | 9 | | 1 | | 8 | | | |
| 0 | | 80 | | 2 | | | | | |

Exposure sheet showing two examples of staggered exposing.

In making a vibration, it is not necessary to have the correct number of eyes versus noses or caps. The vibration might extend to more multiple images than I have indicated, and they need not follow numerically. A random selection of images will give a feeling of confusion. The order of numbering on the sheets can even include the first drawing at times, even though it has no multiple images.

Flesh tints, the whites of the eyes, and other light values will be more conspicuous in a blurred image than darker values like the cap, shoes, or clothes. Therefore, it is very important that the light values follow through.

The Disney animators, when they turned away from slapstick to more complex acting, were quick to realize the comic possibilities of the double take—particularly W. C. Fields's version.

Dimetradon, a computer-generated 3-D model by Dick Lundin. © Computer Graphics Laboratories, Inc.

Creature, a self-portrait by computer artist Lee Manovitch. He used a number of computer techniques.

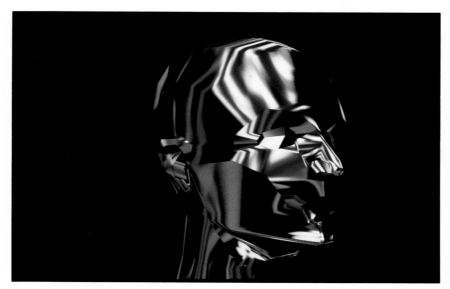

A twenty-two second logo for Robbins Research Institute, produced by Jim Lindner's company, the Fantastic Animation Machine. The head was first modeled in clay by art director Eileen O'Neill, then, using a three-dimensional digitizer, the information from the model was input into the computer. The head was rendered as highly reflective chrome surfaces, using a technique called environment mapping.

Six computer-generated paintings by Paul Xander, Sr., showing some of the possible techniques and textures.

*Exercise: Double Take I*

Do an exercise in which Fatty is sitting in a beach chair, sprawled out reading a newspaper. A lion enters the scene behind him and stands there looking menacing. Fatty turns a page and goes on to reading. After tilting his straw hat, he turns his head and looks the lion in the eye for fourteen exposures, then turns back to read. (This is a waist-high close-up.)

Suddenly, his eyes widen. Fatty holds this expression for sixteen exposures, then slowly, in fright, turns around into a pose exactly where he had been looking at the lion before, except that this time he is scared stiff. Then he goes into a Fields's hat routine with his own hat.

Next he makes a big anticipation and whisks off the screen in two drawings, leaving a puff of smoke to mark his exit. The lion's reaction is one of surprise at the take and then puzzlement after Fatty has run out. He might look at the audience blinking. Do the whole scene two exposures per drawing.

*Exercise: Double Take II*

In this next exercise, Skinny is climbing a cliff. In a niche in the rock is a nest. In the nest is a large eagle. Skinny is climbing hand over hand. Seeking a hold, without thinking he puts one hand on the top of the eagle's head and pushes himself up. Suddenly, he realizes that his hand is on something soft. His pose is such that he has one hand still on the rock, the other pressing the eagle down. He has a horrified expression. Slowly, he takes away the restraining hand and looks into the nest. The eagle slams into a nose-to-nose pose.

Skinny anticipates and pushes himself away from the cliff in a big take. He thrashes wildly for fourteen exposures, then plummets out of sight. The eagle stretches his neck to look down after him with a big smile.

## Animating Thought

For a long time, the only character who seemed to do any thinking on the screen was Felix the Cat. It was pretty crude stuff. Felix would stop in a pose and a light bulb would appear over his head. This indicated to the audience that he had an idea. Norman Ferguson, the Pluto

Two exposure sheets, showing different actions.

SKINNY
PATS EAGLE

| DIAL | ACTION | DIAL | TRACK | 1 | DIAL | ACTION | DIAL | TRACK | 1 |
|---|---|---|---|---|---|---|---|---|---|
| 1 | EAGLE | 1 | | | 1 | | 1 | | |
| 2 | SITTING | 2 | | | 2 | | 2 | | |
| 3 | | 3 | | | 3 | | 3 | | |
| 4 | ON | 4 | | | 4 | | 4 | | |
| 5 | NEST | 5 | | | 5 | PAT X | 5 | | |
| 6 | SKINNY'S | 6 | | | 6 | | 6 | | |
| 7 | HAND ON | 7 | | | 7 | PAT | 7 | | |
| 8 | | 8 | | | 8 | | 8 | | |
| 9 | FIELD ON | 9 | | | 9 | | 9 | | |
| 0 | PITCH X | 0 | | | 0 | | 0 | | |
| 1 | | 1 | | | 1 | | 1 | | |
| 2 | | 2 | | | 2 | | 2 | | |
| 3 | SKINNY | 3 | | | 3 | PAT X | 3 | | |
| 4 | PULLS HIS | 4 | | | 4 | | 4 | | |
| 5 | BODY UP | 5 | | | 5 | | 5 | | |
| 6 | | 6 | | | 6 | PAT X | 6 | | |
| 7 | | 7 | | | 7 | | 7 | | |
| 8 | | 8 | | | 8 | PAT X | 8 | | |
| 9 | | 9 | | | 9 | | 9 | | |
| 0 | | 0 | | | 0 | PAT X | 0 | | |
| 1 | | 1 | | | 1 | | 1 | | |
| 2 | | 2 | | | 2 | | 2 | | |
| 3 | HAND | 3 | | | 3 | ANTIC | 3 | | |
| 4 | GOES | 4 | | | 4 | | 4 | | |
| 5 | HIGH | 5 | | | 5 | SKINNY | 5 | | |
| 6 | | 6 | | | 6 | LOOKS | 6 | | |
| 7 | | 7 | | | 7 | INTO | 7 | | |
| 8 | | 8 | | | 8 | NEST - | 8 | | |
| 9 | | 9 | | | 9 | WITHDRAWING | 9 | | |
| 0 | GRABS | 0 | | | 0 | HAND | 0 | | |
| 1 | PITCH X | 1 | | | 1 | | 1 | | |
| 2 | | 2 | | | 2 | | 2 | | |
| 3 | | 3 | | | 3 | | 3 | | |
| 4 | | 4 | | | 4 | | 4 | | |
| 5 | PULLS | 5 | | | 5 | EAGLE | 5 | | |
| 6 | UP | 6 | | | 6 | ANTIC | 6 | | |
| 7 | | 7 | | | 7 | SLAMS X | 7 | | |
| 8 | | 8 | | | 8 | | 8 | | |
| 9 | | 9 | | | 9 | INTO | 9 | | |
| 0 | | 0 | | | 0 | NOSE TO | 0 | | |
| 1 | | 1 | | | 1 | | 1 | | |
| 2 | | 2 | | | 2 | NOSE | 2 | | |
| 3 | HAND | 3 | | | 3 | POSE | 3 | | |
| 4 | GOES | 4 | | | 4 | | 4 | | |
| 5 | HIGH | 5 | | | 5 | | 5 | | |
| 6 | | 6 | | | 6 | | 6 | | |
| 7 | | 7 | | | 7 | | 7 | | |
| 8 | | 8 | | | 8 | | 8 | | |
| 9 | | 9 | | | 9 | | 9 | | |
| 0 | | 0 | | | 0 | | 0 | | |
| 1 | HAND CENTER | 1 | | | 1 | | 1 | | |
| 2 | PRESSES | 2 | | | 2 | | 2 | | |
| 3 | DOWN | 3 | | | 3 | | 3 | | |
| 4 | | 4 | | | 4 | | 4 | | |
| 5 | | 5 | | | 5 | SKWAM | 5 | | |
| 6 | | 6 | | | 6 | INTO | 6 | | |
| 7 | | 7 | | | 7 | ANTIC | 7 | | |
| 8 | SKINNY | 8 | | | 8 | | 8 | | |
| 9 | INTO PERPLEXED | 9 | | | 9 | | 9 | | |
| 0 | EXPRESSION | 0 | | | 0 | EAGLE | 0 | | |
| 1 | | 1 | | | 1 | | 1 | | |
| 2 | | 2 | | | 2 | SMILES | 2 | | |
| 3 | | 3 | | | 3 | | 3 | | |
| 4 | | 4 | | | 4 | THRASHES | 4 | | |
| 5 | | 5 | | | 5 | AS HE | 5 | | |
| 6 | HOLD | 6 | | | 6 | | 6 | | |
| 7 | BLINKING | 7 | | | 7 | PUSHES FROM | 7 | | |
| 8 | | 8 | | | 8 | | 8 | | |
| 9 | | 9 | | | 9 | AWAY FROM | 9 | | |
| 0 | | 0 | | | 0 | | 0 | | |
| 1 | | 1 | | | 1 | EAGLE | 1 | | |
| 2 | | 2 | | | 2 | IN MID-AIR | 2 | | |
| 3 | | 3 | | | 3 | | 3 | | |
| 4 | | 4 | | | 4 | | 4 | | |
| 5 | | 5 | | | 5 | | 5 | | |
| 6 | | 6 | | | 6 | | 6 | | |
| 7 | | 7 | | | 7 | | 7 | | |
| 8 | HAND | 8 | | | 8 | HITS TO LEFT | 8 | | |
| 9 | UP | 9 | | | 9 | | 9 | | |
| 0 | | 0 | | | 0 | | 0 | | |

Look for every part of the body as well as the clothes for an opportunity to express an emotion. In this case, the ears prove to be useful.

expert, was the Disney animator who began to extrapolate humor from thought processes. To make this subtle form of acting enjoyable, the movement has to be kept to a minimum. For example, if Pluto was walking along and his paw suddenly became stuck on flypaper, he would come to a complete stop. Then his eyebrows would go into a frown. He would go from that to a slow blink. When his eyelids came back up, the audience would see that Pluto was now looking skyward—thinking.

The only movement on the screen would have been Pluto's eyes and eyebrows. There is not much chance of putting over acting such as that while the character is moving around. An exception is when Snow White kisses Grumpy good-bye. He turns brusquely and starts walking toward the door. His steps get slower and slower because he cannot maintain his pretense of being such a curmudgeon, and his heart melts. While Tytla did change the dwarf's expression as he walked, Grumpy's change of pace really did most of the acting.

But, as a general rule, since the thinking process is usually only reflected in the face, the elements there—the eyes and mouth—are too small to compete with large parts of the body, if those are in motion, as well.

## Hands

It is vitally important to learn how to draw hands very well so that animating them becomes second nature and there is no struggle to attain a pose of the hands that would impede high-speed drawing. Keep in mind that the line of action of a hand runs into the forearm; it does not stop at the wrist. Of course, the same thing holds for the feet. As the hands, they are not separate attachments. The line of action flows into the legs.

In order to "read" the emotions of a character, the audience first looks at the face, then the hands, after that, the body, starting with the upper torso.

Hands are very important in revealing attitudes. I remember making dozens and dozens of the Fox's hands before I started animating my first scene in *Pinocchio*. I wanted his hands to appear elegant but to overact. When he was posturing around with his cigar, I wanted the audience to realize that this nimble manipulation of the cigar was his idea of how a gentleman would handle it; but, in keeping with his con man flamboyance, it was overdone.

When I first started to direct live-action television spots, I decided to go to an acting class to see whether there was any difference between directing animators and live actors. I found that there wasn't but did learn that both animators and actors had the same difficulty in dealing with hands.

Dave Pressman, the director, had to struggle with the student actors to make them use their hands. The youngsters usually would keep them hanging stiffly, put them behind their backs, or in their pockets. If they did manage to use them in accenting speech, they often kept their fingers together in what I began to call "mittens." It was all remarkably similar to the efforts of a novice or untalented animator.

I cannot stress enough the importance of being able to draw hands with ease, because they are such an important factor in staging. When animating a scene in which one hand is going to be directly engaged in some activity, make sure that you pick the correct hand to do the job. There is always one best choice, whether it is because of the staging or because there is going to be a complication in the following action if the wrong hand is used.

## Relation Between Characters

A common error by novice animators when handling a scene with two characters is to animate one figure right through the scene, then go back and do the other. Nothing could be less advantageous to the composition of the shot, and also to the feeling that the two characters make

Exercise: Make gesture drawings of the three characters in tight compositions like this. See how important it is to gauge the proper distance between the forms.

Exercise: Make a tracing of each character on separate pieces of paper. Over the lightboard, take them off the pegs and shift them back and forth to understand how delicate the balance is between the forms, how easy it is to make too much space between them, or to give a crowded feeling.

one entity. There is the danger that at some point the space between the characters will be too great, or conversely, too small.

### Exercise: Relation Between Characters

Do the following experiment: Make a drawing of Tiny in an attitude of terror. On another sheet of paper, draw Fatty in a menacing pose.

Now start by placing the two characters at opposite sides of the screen. Gradually push the two elves nearer and nearer. Finally, you will reach a point where there is an optimum amount of space between them. A little more and you start to find that they are uncomfortably close. A movement of an eighth of an inch this way or that makes a decided difference. This is very true in drawing groups. *Snow White* contains many scenes that are superb examples of controlling composition in crowd shots.

Another source of study are the reactions of the other dwarfs when one of them speaks. These reactions are very subtle and in no instance steal the scene, yet the emotional tension between the speaker and the group never slackens or stops.

In response to the import of the dialogue, the characters blink, their jaws drop, they look at one another in dismay, draw back in consternation. Each dwarf reacts according to his character. The one thing they don't do is just stand there. This is why *Snow White* should be seen many times. The secondary action is so well done, it is worthwhile to ignore the main actors and concentrate on the reactions of the group. This is also true of the animals and birds.

## Animals

The superb animation of the birds and animals in *Snow White* is far superior to the standards of any other studio existing at that time. The reason for it was that Walt Disney believed in the value of observation. Instead of stereotyped action, he wanted a version of movement that was based on the real thing.

That was the reason he had hired Don Graham to run art classes for the study of the movement of humans, and also to take groups to the Los Angeles zoo for three-hour sessions. The artists were urged not only to draw but to make notes about behavior, as well. If they felt like it, the entire session was devoted to observation and note taking, instead of sketching.

For *Bambi,* Disney hired Rico LeBrun, an internationally famous animal draftsman, to teach his artists the finer points of animal anatomy. The result was that *Bambi* reached new heights in animal animation, even surpassing the fine animation in *Snow White.*

There is no doubt that animal animation is a specialty that has to be studied quite separately from other types of animation. There were only

Sullivant had the kind of draftsmanship one associates with preliminary sketches made for sculpture. His forms were solid, rounded shapes.

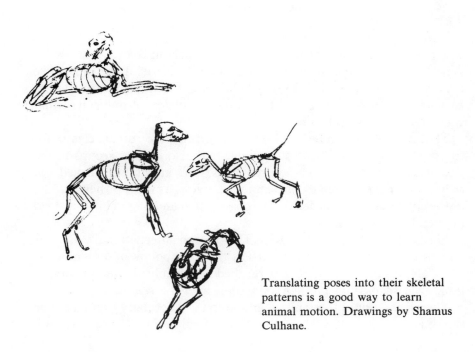

Translating poses into their skeletal patterns is a good way to learn animal motion. Drawings by Shamus Culhane.

about four animators at Disney's who were acknowledged to be Pluto specialists, and the figure never increased. Eric Larson led a small group that handled all the animals and birds in *Snow White;* and later a very small group of animals specialists did the main animation in *Bambi.*

It is necessary to know the skeletal structure and the construction of the muscles in order to caricature an animal's movements. This takes long hours of observation and sketching. I became very interested in cats, so I collected a group of twenty-four of them, ranging from small kittens to rheumatic old tabbys. None of them were allowed in my house, I hasten to add, but when I went out into the yard with a sketch pad, there were always a number of cats around.

Don Graham had some interesting comments about animals. One was that predator's eyes are in the front of the skull. The eyes of animals such as lions, tigers, or wolves were good for stalking. Their prey, herbivorous animals such as deer, antelope, cows, and bulls, all had their eyes on the sides of the head, enabling them to keep an efficient watch for predators.

Graham likened the spine of a four-legged animal to a bridge, with the legs serving as abutments. I found this concept very useful in my animal drawing. (It also gave me a greater appreciation of the miracle

T.S. Sullivant's animals are never made up of graceful curves like animation characters. While this style would not be difficult to animate, oddly enough Sullivant never influenced Disney's, or any other studio.

that let human beings upend the bridge and walk upright on two of the abutments.)

One of the big differences between humans and animals is that one can see very subtle emotions in the human face. Emotions in animals are not so easily recognized. A bear has no expression at all. There is no way to tell from his "face" whether he is going to walk away amiably or rear up and crush your rib cage.

Other animals signal their emotions by reactions and movements that involve the whole body in ways that humans cannot match. Hair bristles into a ruff, claws are unsheathed, tails fluff out, whiskers fan back. An enraged elephant can bring its ears forward so that they look like sails. Each species has its own way to express emotion with parts of the body.

There is only one way to learn this body language—observation and drawing. One of the dead ends in animation came about after Disney's success with his animals in feature films; just about every studio in the

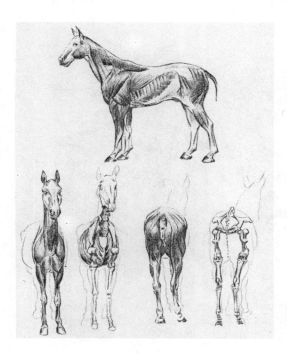

A study by Shamus Culhane. It is only by thoroughly understanding the skeleton and musculature of an animal that one can caricature it.

A quick sketch by Shamus Culhane. Note that this drawing accentuates the planes of the dog.

business decided to copy his style of animal drawings. So for forty years we have had a surfeit of cute squirrels, cuddly bunnies, and dear little baby birds, ad nauseam.

Yet, Garfield the Cat, the animals of Sullivant, Krazy Kat (the comic strip Kat, not the animated abomination), and a few other characters show that we need not be bogged down in a style that seems just too saccharine for the Atomic Age.

Drawing from *I Know an Old Lady Who Swallowed a Fly.* Kaj Pindal has a very personal approach to drawing animals, far removed from the conventional style used in many studios at the time this cartoon was made. A National Film Board of Canada production, 1963.

Arthur Babbitt, one of the all-time great animators, drew these various walks and runs as a guide for the puppeteers who worked on Lou Bunin's *Alice in Wonderland*.

### Researching Animals

A really serious student of animal animation, besides spending a lot of time at the zoo, will also study at places like the American Museum of Natural History in New York City. It is difficult to draw an animal in the zoo because, more often than not, halfway through your drawing the animal will change its pose.

So I suggest that before tackling the drawing of a particular live animal, it would be best to concentrate on a study of the skeleton and to try making simple drawings of it. Before you work on the large, most important muscles, make sure that you are so familiar with the skeleton that you can make high-speed sketches easily. Remember one large difference between the primates, including humans, and other mammals—the shoulder blades lie across the back in the former and are upright along the sides of the rib cage in four-footed beasts.

When a man or monkey crouches on all fours, the shoulder blades slide along the back. In four-footed animals, the shoulder blades, being upright, jut out from the silhouette. Armed with information about the bones and muscles, one can go to the zoo and quickly sketch in the main muscles and planes before the animal starts to move into another pose. Pencil is the best medium for this work, although litho crayon can also be used.

It is only when you are equipped with a sound knowledge of the construction of an animal and its characteristic movements that you can start to caricature it in a personal way and not just ape the traditional Disney approach.

### Walking and Running

Heretofore, I have made no mention of the mechanics of walking and running. The reason is that I consider them too difficult for the average student to handle. One must be aware of the principles of anticipation, overlapping action, the line of action, slowing in and out, and squash and stretch before learning the principles of locomotion.

First, let it be understood that just standing still is a tremendous feat of balancing. Watching a baby try to stand is a way to appreciate just how difficult it is. Yet, as we grow up, we learn to balance unconsciously, even though at all times the muscles along the spine are having a tug-of-war to maintain the balance around the center of gravity.

Both walking and running are in effect stopping one's self from falling face forward by interposing a leg. We call it taking a step. Make a drawing of Skinny with only one leg, standing at attention. Now make him lean forward as if he was starting to walk. As his body tips, the center of gravity changes. If the action continues, it is obvious that he will fall flat. It is only when one's off leg is brought into play that a fall is prevented. It is important to get the feel of that movement so that the principle of the walk can be well understood. The only difference in the run is that the runner is taking a series of leaps, which if not stopped by the off leg, would end with the runner face forward on the ground.

Overlapping occurs in the action of the arms and hands. They do not reach their extreme positions at the same time as the legs. The slower the walk, the more time elapses between the foot striking the ground and the drawing of the extreme of action of the arms and hands. In a fast run, the overlap between the leg and arm/hand action may be only one exposure.

Animation in which there is no overlapping action will look mechanical. You can see it in early cartoons. Because the principle of overlapping was unknown, none of the characters walked or ran in a lifelike way. The animators drew the extreme position of the arm/hand action on the same drawing as the extreme foot/leg movement, and the characters moved like windup toys.

In discussing early animation, it must be understood that we always have to make one exception: Winsor McCay. He never fell into these traps. Intuitively, he used every one of the principles I have been teaching. That is almost as amazing as the fact that he had no disciples. Nobody tried to learn to animate by studying McCay's pictures. Thirty years went by before the Disney animators started to grope towards life-quality animation, and they didn't learn from McCay. His work had been almost forgotten.

## Styles of Walking

It is astounding how mankind, with everybody equipped with the same system of skeleton and musculature, manages to create so many diverse types and styles of walking. A slight twist of the ankles and we have a splayfooted duck walk; a twist in the other direction and we have a pigeon-toed walk. With a maladjusted tibia, a shambling knock-kneed trudge is created.

There are people who walk leaning backward at such an acute angle that they look as if they are climbing invisible stairs; others walk head bent as if they are searching for lost dimes. Some walkers swing their arms sideways instead of back and forth, giving the effect of marching to inaudible music. All these variations are a visual feast for the observing animator. One should never go down the street without automatically checking the pedestrians for an unusual walk. When you find one, take the time to study the mechanics so that you go off with a complete understanding of the reason why this particular walk *is* unusual.

## Styles of Running

Now that jogging has become such an integral part of the street scene, it affords the animator a golden opportunity to store different types of runs in the memory bank. The ideal movement is a kind of pumping action, with the hands going well ahead of the chest, then going back to slightly past the middle of the chest. The hands should be clenched in a semifist, but loosely. What we see on the street is often a parody of this action. Some joggers scarcely pump at all; others move their arms across their chests; others allow the hands to dangle off the wrists, flopping like limp rags with every step.

The legs should be covering a normal distance, carrying the feet well out in front of the body, and as much as two feet behind the body at the end of a stride. In a very fast run, the feet are lifted high off the ground; in a jog, they barely skim along.

What we often see is a kind of baby toddle, with such a short stride that the runner scarcely appears to be moving, or the legs are carried so far apart that the jogger seems to be playing a constricted type of hopscotch.

A fat person will have overlapping action in the breasts and stomach, the mass coming down after the foot strikes the ground, then dragging as the torso lifts into the next stride. Thin people usually have more bounce when running or walking than fat people.

Old people with stiff joints, or others who have severe physical handicaps, should be studied to see how they manage to maintain a precarious balance.

In order to make a smooth walk or run, both legs have to measure the same stride; right and left legs must use the same number of drawings and follow the same pattern of spacing charts. Failure to follow these rules will result in an uneven run or walk. It is a good practice to draw one full step of a leg, then go back and draw the other, matching all the positions of the first leg and, of course, allowing for perspective in the far leg. This will give you a perfectly smooth walk or run.

## Using Drawings in Cycles

In the very early days of animation, Bill Nolan, a brilliant animator, conceived the idea of making walks and runs with the body animating in one place and the feet moving as if on a treadmill. Not only that, he thought of the use of drawings in cycles so that they could be repeated indefinitely. In other words, if a walk is twelve exposures to a step, then drawing number twenty-three is followed by drawing number one.

Measurements are now computed in hundredths of an inch. Animators used to use fractions; imagine trying to find the total length of a pan by adding one-sixteenth, one-quarter, five-eighths, nine-sixteenths, and so on. Numbers such as .10, .15, .25, .45, .60, .75, 1.00 are much easier.

## Background Speeds

One important feature of a pan walk or run is the fact that once the foot is on the ground, it must follow a steady progression. It must go back in exactly the same amount of travel as the background or the character will appear to be sliding.

The speed of the background is determined by the amount of travel the foot makes on the ground. This can be arrived at before the inbetweens are made by measuring the distance between the feet of the two extreme drawings of the step that is on the ground, then dividing the distance by the number of exposures per step.

It is rarely a good idea to animate pan walks or runs on two exposures a drawing because the action will appear to be jerky, unless the pan speed is around .10 per exposure.

### Exercises: Walking and Running

Do the following exercises:

Fatty is exhausted, walking twenty-four exposures to the step. In other words, a cycle in which drawing one follows drawing forty-seven.

Explore the pose in a gesture drawing, where you feel the drag of gravitation. Feel the emotion of tiredness in the little fat guy. Is his head down, never rising with the movement of the torso, or does it come up and flop down shortly after the foot hits the ground? Do his arms barely swing? Has his back become bowed so that his hands hang listlessly in front of him? Do his eyes close and half-open as he trudges along? Is the mouth open in breathlessness, or is it grimly closed with the corners down? Are his feet barely skimming the ground, or is he in a kind of stumble where his feet come up high and slam down? Does the toe of the back foot drag along the ground for a few exposures before Fatty can lift it? Are his clothes expressing his exhaustion? Make this action a side view going left to right. Be sure to photograph about five feet of the animation so that it can be a loop on the editing machine. Because this will be a very slow walk, use two exposures per drawing.

Tiny is very happy, bouncing along in a walk, sixteen exposures to the step. Is his hat cocked and are his other clothes expressing his state of mind? What are his hands doing to look cocky? Are they stuck in his belt? Are his thumbs tucked into his armpits? Are his arms describing big arcs as he bounds along?

Skinny is part of a parade, marching along to a twelve beat. Is he stiff-legged as the English at the changing of the guard, or is he ramrod straight, strutting like a West Pointer? What can you incorporate about his attitude into his clothing? Make this scene a head-on shot.

Tiny is very tired, walking along at twenty exposures to the step. What have you learned from Fatty's walk that will help the audience to read the emotion in this scene, even if it is a rear view? Use two exposures per drawing.

Fatty is jogging left to right at eight exposures per step. Show him running with one of the faulty techniques I have described. Remember that his belly is going to overlap his main body action, not only when he is coming down on one foot but as he lifts off again.

Tiny is running left to right, four exposures to the step. He is looking back in horror. Remember that during a fast run, there is scarcely any bounce in the body because he is skimming along the ground. Do you need speed lines? If so, do you remember the principle of the leading edge being less blurred than the trailing edge?

Skinny in a front view is loping along at seven exposures to the step. He is running with great confidence, and it is justified because he is using his arms and hands properly.

You will see how the difference in height and weight affect both the walk and the run. Keep in mind that all clothes are subject to overlapping. Since you are drawing cycles of each character, be sure that the animation of the clothing hooks up smoothly and that the clothing is being motivated by the momentum of the body. Study the problem carefully and don't just fake the movement, because it is a part of the exercise.

If any walk or run is uneven in that one leg is working differently from the other, you have not matched the leg action properly. Remember that the spacing of the action and the pattern of the spacing charts have to be exactly the same for both legs. Do not read further until these exercises are mastered.

Fatty has a huge bandage on his leg, as if he had the gout. Make him hobble along, fourteen exposures to the step. The bandaged foot is going to drag along, barely lifting off the ground, and there is going to have to be much more side sway than in a normal walk. His expression should be one of great pain.

Make a front view of Skinny. He is walking Indian style in that his leading foot lands right in front of the one behind. This makes the arc of his foot curve outward in the middle of a stride as it goes past the other leg. It is like a Charlie Chaplin walk, with his feet splayed out.

Tiny skips along on twelve exposures each skip. He is very bouncy and happy. Make sure that the action of his cap and clothing reflect the jerk as he leaps up, and the squash as he lands. Be sure that the movements are caused by the momentum and direction of the body's action.

Animate Skinny in a sneak. Try out the action yourself and you will find that as the leading foot goes forward, the body rears back to keep in balance. After the foot is planted, there is a fast move forward, which ends in a semicrouch as the weight is transferred to that foot. This is a good opportunity to study the shifting of weight, which is basic to a walk or run, but never so obvious as in a sneak.

## Animal Movement

I think you will agree that walking and running demand all your drafting skill and a sound knowledge of the principles of movement. Animal walking and running are more complex.

Sullivant, especially, has a very strong approach to animal drawing. His style is more of a caricature, a reverse of the normal proportions

Sullivant's choices of shapes in caricaturing an animal always made for a very solid construction.

Unlike the cuddly rabbits in theatrical animation, T. S. Sullivant's animals are more straightforward in being caricatures, rather than abstractions.

T. S. Sullivant was not just an animal cartoonist. He was a superb caricaturist, whose figures had a very personal brand of humor, very different from the conventionalized interpretation that was dutifully followed by all the studios making theatrical animation.

Instead of drawing the lion's mane in one solid piece, Sullivant divides it and gives his lion a crewcut.

of the heads and bodies. The huge heads that he gives his animals would, in fact, be ideal for animation. Instead of being cute, I would classify his characters as droll.

### Exercise: Animals

Using Sullivant's point of view, do the following exercises:

Draw a model sheet of a pig with a very large head, little pushed-in snout, and a small body.

Draw a model sheet of a moose with a huge head and antlers, and a small body with fairly large feet.

Draw a model sheet of an alligator with a very large head, a long snout with big teeth, and a very small body and tail.

Draw an elephant with a large head and a very small body. It has a short but thick trunk.

Draw a cobra with its hood extended, and a big split tongue. The body is very small.

Now reverse all the proportions and make all these animals with very small heads and huge bodies, but with very short legs and large feet.

When doing quick sketches, look for the opportunity to draw views in sharp perspective. Good animation requires the ability to draw action from any angle. Drawings by Shamus Culhane.

Be sure that each model sheet has a set of positions giving enough information to enable an animator to draw any pose from any point of view—front, profile, or back.

Draw a model sheet of each animal, just the heads, depicting the following emotions: small smile; looking coy; a big laugh; astonishment; perplexity; peevishness; furious anger; fright. Pick any view that will best illustrate the emotion, but draw all the heads the same size.

Draw a model sheet of each animal acting out the above set of emotions, but this time draw the entire body. Do not use the same expression and view of the animals that you made for the previous model sheet.

Remember that a basic model sheet shows the character in a normal pose with a placid expression. Save the violent gestures and expressions for the other types of model sheets.

Remember how important the eyes are, and the fact that the mouth is next in importance. When the audience is "reading" a pose the eyes are examined first, then the mouth, the attitude of the head, the shoulders, the hands, and finally the entire body, in that order.

Remember that the size of the pupils and their position are most important, and the eyeballs should not be drawn like twins. Nor does the axis of both eyes have to be the same. In a smile, the mouth may very well curve up more on one side than the other. Teeth are not always neatly proportioned; they may be widely spaced or even missing. The poses should include some showing the character lying down, standing on its hind legs, or on all fours.

Push your proportions in a series of very rough sketches until you have exaggerated as far as you think possible. Then do your cleanups. After that, animate a cycle walk and a run of each character, walking on twelve exposures and running on five exposures.

This is an enormous amount of work. Do not expect to do it in a few days or even weeks.


## The Importance of Content

I am not deprecating the Disney achievements in the animating of animals, or any other type of animation for that matter. The studio has set a very high standard in every branch of filmmaking and is responsible for discovering practically every principle we use in full animation.

It seems to me that the fault in animation at the present time is in

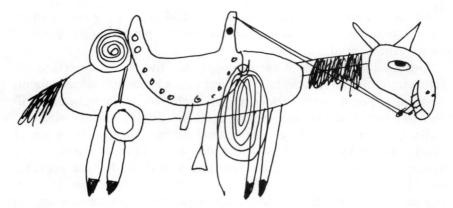

A simulated child's drawing for *The Stubborn Cowboy.* Drawn by Gil Miret.
© 1967 by Famous Studio.

the choice of subject matter. Writers such as Teddy Sears, Mike Maltese, Tedd Pierce, Tex Avery, Cliff Roberts, and Frank Tashlin turned
out films that showed by their content that the creators knew their
contemporary public. They created films that to this day remain mile-
stones of the art form. This in spite of the fact that they were working
in commercial studios.

Except for Ralph Bakshi, the choice of subject matter in commercial
film production is pedestrian and unimaginative. It remains for artists
such as Derek Lamb, Norman McLaren, Frédéric Bàck, Børge Ring,
and Caroline Leaf, who are not connected to commercial studios, to
produce films that by their content, style, and overall approach are
directed to the current film audience. It is dismal to see just how far
behind the commercial film studios have fallen.

## Animating Humans

You may wonder to what this diatribe is leading up. The subject is the
human figure.

There was a time in the 1920s when it was considered that Bridgeman's books on anatomy were the immutable answer to learning to
animate humans. Bridgeman approached the musculature as if the body
were made up of a series of cigar boxes.

I believe that Bridgeman's methodology is very valuable if you are
thinking of going into the cigar business. Otherwise, it is a ponderous

simplification of the complex shapes that make up the human figure. Happily, the method is rarely taught now, just as animators have stopped using nickels and half-dollars to draw animation.

Way back in 1938, the Disney animators, Grim Natwick especially, left no doubt that the human figure could be animated. After *Snow White,* the door was open. The problem was that very few studios took advantage of it, with the exception of Ralph Bakshi.

One of my frustrations is that while I was producer at Famous studios, I wanted to make a Sholem Aleichem story, in somewhat the style of Chagall, and I wasn't allowed to do it on the grounds that the Board of Directors at Paramount (most members of which were Jewish) might take offense. That was more than twenty years ago but I still fret when I think about it because this is the general direction in which animation should be going. There is so much world literature that is just waiting to be interpreted by animation—the most modern, most innovative graphic art.

Instead, animation of the human figure in the commercial studios is being used in Saturday-morning children's television programs and in

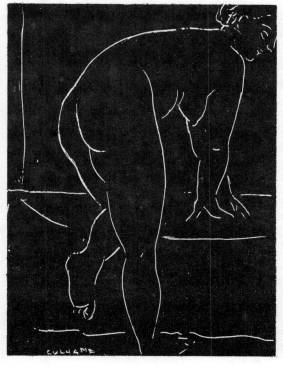

An animator or layout artist should get used to visualizing in line, rather than seeing the figure in light and shade. A scratch-board drawing by Shamus Culhane.

feature films that are based on fantasy so banal that it churns the stomach. The drawing style is obviously spawned by comic-book illustration.

I would say that it is important for the animator to learn how to draw the human figure in line. Forget painting and shading. The obvious commercial approach would be to copy the artwork in comic books until you have developed a style that is similar. Not all of the drawing in those magazines is poor, but most of it is a bag of tricks—masses of muscles and vacuous faces. But I am urging the student to learn how to animate the human figure. Someday a producer might come along with a really worthwhile script about people, real people. You would not want to be caught without experience and lose your chance at a film with literary quality.

You can be sure that all the principles I have been expounding are a necessary part of learning how to animate the human figure.

## Adapting Human Movement for Animation

The big problem that one has to face is the fact that everybody in the audience is going to be an expert on how humans move. This makes it pointless to attempt to use rotoscope or any other device in order to imitate human action. I believe the answer lies somewhere in working out a mode of movement that is edited action, just the way that the animals in *Bambi* and the dwarfs in *Snow White* were. An audience will accept any convention, any point of view, as long as it is carried out consistently. I think there is less chance of rejection by this approach than by that of stupidly trying to draw animation with all the complexity of live action. In the first place, it can't be done; and in the second place, why try to recreate the approach of the Hudson River School of painting? It fizzled out like a soggy firecracker. After the viewers marveled at a match head that looked as if it could be picked off the canvas or a torn envelope that uncannily simulated real life, they got bored with it.

Imitation of real life is not art, and art is what we are involved with, despite mutters to the contrary from Madison Avenue and the networks. At present, except for television spots, almost all of the commercial animation being produced is aimed at kids, but I doubt that this situation will last very long. It just happens that many of the production markets are controlled by toy manufacturers, but patience! This too shall pass. We have to look to the independent filmmakers to lead us out of this graphic and literary wilderness.

### Exercise: Cleanup Drawings

For an exercise, reach into a stack of your quick-sketch exercises and select a drawing at random. I stipulate random because I don't want you to pick out an easy one. Whatever the subject matter—your hand, dear old mother, or the house cat—make a cleanup of the drawing, being sure that you are using the contours to delineate form.

Draw steadily not quickly so that the final result isn't sketchy. Every closed area should be just that . . . closed, just as one would clean up a bit of rough animation so that the color areas were contained. Don't draw slowly, either, because your lines will lose their crispness. If you don't like a particular line, rub it out. This may sound like heresy in view of my earlier insistence on not correcting your roughs. But now you are working with the left side of your brain, using the drawing skills you have acquired in the past, so it is proper to be critical and wholly intellectual.

You are, of course, doing this on your animation board with the underneath light on. Now discard the rough after you have compared both drawings to see whether you have maintained the vigor that you have in the rough. If you have not, perhaps it would be better to do the cleanup again from scratch. If it meets with your approval, take a fresh sheet of paper and this time work with your cleaned-up drawing underneath.

Make a new drawing, not a tracing. The object is to make this drawing somewhat stylized. Think of it as a drawing that is going to be animated. When you have completed this exercise, choose another rough of the same subject at random. Clean this up on one drawing and stylize it on another.

Using the stylized drawings as extremes, animate seven inbetweens that start with a slow out and slow in to a stop. If you need it, rough out the main inbetweens with a light-blue pencil before you draw the cleanup.

Take another gesture drawing of a different subject and see whether you can possibly make a stylized drawing without doing the preliminary cleanup. Do a second drawing of another gesture, then seven inbetweens. Do one set of drawings every day. In these exercises did you remember not to make the movement in a straight line? Did some parts go beyond the stopping point and settle back into the final position? Did you think of torque, the line of action?

While you must never consciously think of these rules while you are making gesture drawings, use them as a checklist for cleanups.

# 15

## Animating Dialogue

The advent of sound films threw the entire profession of animation into utter confusion. In the first place, the film speed per second went from sixteen exposures to twenty-four, ruining the animator's sense of timing. It had to be learned all over again.

But that was nothing compared to the perplexities of making the characters speak. There were various theories, some absolutely absurd now that we can look back. One, a Fleischer idea, was that the mouth closed after every word! Imagine the mess that made of the dialogue!

Another, more prevalent theory was that when there was a loud voice, the character's mouth should be opened so wide it looked as if the jaw was dislocated. Some of the early Betty Boops not only had huge open mouths for loud vowels but a kind of Ubangi-like protrusion for "oo" sounds.

### Body Movement in Speech

Despite attempts to get along with these misconceptions, there was no satisfactory interpretation of dialogue until it was discovered at Disney's that there was a definite need for body English. The louder the volume, the more violent the effort of the body to produce it. The size of the mouth was a very minor contribution to the end result.

Long after this principle was understood at the Disney studio, the rest of the business was still trying to interpret loud sounds by making wide-open mouths with no particular body movement. It wasn't until some animators left Disney and worked in other studios that the principles of dialogue were diffused throughout the industry.

As late as 1939, the Fleischer animators had not gotten the message. Ex-Disney animator Al Eugster roughed out a scene for *Gulliver's Travels* and, following the Disney technique, omitted the mouths. They would be added later if the body movements were in sync. Dave Fleischer, the producer, commented on the accuracy of the mouth action during a sweatbox session. When he was told that there were no mouths, he couldn't believe it. The sync was perfect. He was mystified when the scene was projected again and he saw that indeed there were no mouths.

Before we go into the mechanics of dialogue, I want you to look at a game show and watch it with the sound off. Look at the bobbing and weaving heads, the waving hands and body movements. Don't observe newscasters. They are reading copy, not talking naturally. However, you might note that some of them have developed mannerisms, consciously doing a little bobbing and weaving to avoid looking like a static talking head.

A great deal of negative information can be learned by studying television spots where the announcer is a company officer, not a trained actor. Most of them are frightened by the camera, so they have to be coached to make natural body movements as they speak. Often they overdo it and end up looking like somebody trying to flag down a steamboat.

I have been very amused, now that Madison Avenue has entered politics, at the attempts to liven up the images of various politicians—both famous and infamous—on television, using what I call "artificial gesticulation."

I found ex-President Nixon especially hilarious on television. He must have been an assiduous student of his Madison Avenue mentors, because it was obvious that he had learned, by diligent rehearsal, to make a series of gestures to fit each speech, right down to the diffident wave to the audience at the finish. The only problem was that he was always out of sync. His key words were emphasized by very strong hand gestures. But they were made without conviction; every move was the result of long practice. Thus, these physical accents occurred at precisely the same time as the accents in his speech.

Unfortunately for Nixon, nobody talks that way. Accented gestures always *precede* emphasized words or phrases by anywhere from three or four exposures to fifteen or twenty. They are never in exact sync with the words.

So watch for ex-presidents of companies or ex-presidents of the United States who try to reach the public via television. It's your chance to see some very bad animation in live action.

What is probably the very best piece of dialogue animation was done by Bill Tytla in *Pinocchio.* Stromboli's struggle to pronounce English words when he is talking to Pinocchio in his caravan is a fabulous interpretation. Tytla had to have observed many foreigners to be able to create the body English, the futile hand gestures, and the frustrated head shakes as Stromboli tortures his mouth into unfamiliar shapes to pronounce those strange sounds that are English.

Watch for old Jimmy Cagney movies to see a very odd style, a very personal quirk in mouth action. Often when Cagney was about to speak, he would purse his mouth up into the position long before the sound emerged. If he was about to start a sentence with "You . . ." his mouth would assume the "oo" position as much as ten or twenty exposures in advance. I wouldn't recommend this as a normal speech pattern, but it is good to recognize all the possibilities.

All the Disney feature films have superlative dialogue animation in that the acting that goes along with the speech is always the result of much analysis, a searching examination of the motivation, the speaker's character, and the story situation. Disney animation of life-quality dialogue is unrivaled.

## Mouth Action

At UPA and subsequently at the Hubley studio, we find that meticulous mouth action is ignored completely. The characters may start a sentence in sync but the resulting conglomeration of mouth drawings bear only a vague resemblance to the sounds that are being interpreted. Luckily, they usually end in sync, too. This approach is in line with the informal approach to animation, which emphasized the fact that the audience was watching drawings, not little live animals or people. Esthetically, it would be pointless to animate the bodies in this fashion but have the mouths in perfect sync. The movement of both the bodies and mouths in these stylized films accurately reflect a specific point of view.

Bill Melendez's Charlie Brown half-hour specials have a style of mouth action that falls somewhere in the cusp. His animators pay slightly more attention to major vowel sounds than the UPA animators did, but they still use a very stylized approach compared to the intricate Disney interpretation of dialogue.

## Synchronizing Speech

In the Disney technique, all the body action is animated first and the accents in the gestures are hit right on the exposure throughout the scene. Then with the help of the editor, the film is run through an editing machine and the action is first shown the way it was photographed. Then the action reel is put back exposure by exposure, one accent at a time, until the relationship between the accent in the gesture and the accent in the dialogue look correct.

Unfortunately, there is no rule that governs the number of exposures by which the action should precede the dialogue. Usually, I put back the action reel three or four exposures, and that ordinarily will do the job. However, sometimes it will go to five or six.

To a large extent, it depends on the style of the speaker. A drawl will usually look best with the body's accent happening quite a bit before the speech accent. A very staccato delivery will need less time.

If the delivery style is consistent, very often one readjustment of the animation reel will put the whole scene in sync, but I wouldn't rely on it. Try each major gesture to see whether the sync can be improved by readjusting it still more. It is surprising how even a move of one exposure can improve the sync.

## Animating Speech

How does one go about animating a character talking without having it end up with a piece of acting that makes it look like a semaphore?

The way I go about it is to start running my cassette over and over until the fact that it is English seems to fade away and be replaced by the knowledge that the track is also a series of sounds with a cadence.

Also, some of the sounds are more outstanding than others because of an increase in the volume. I am no longer listening to English; the track has become an abstraction.

When I can hear it in my head and understand the pattern of the sound, as a musical composition, I start to make some very small sketches of the salient poses—a very few. Then I discard them and begin to animate high-speed roughs, not stopping until I have completed the scene.

This is not always my technique. When there is a need to animate very small, subtle movements, I switch to pose-to-pose animation. My sequence in *Pinocchio* where the Fox, Cat, and Coachman plot in the Red Lobster Inn is a good example. Even so, I still play my cassette until the dialogue has become an abstraction. I can still think in terms of cadence, as well as the literal meaning of the speech, so that the movement can be made into a form of choreography in which the body is moving to the cadence as well as the meaning. I find that this approach effectively blocks the possibility of making gestures that are too profuse and do not fit the dialogue.

Having made notes in the *cutting room* about the various shifts in the animation, I usually have my assistant rewrite the exposure sheets with the corrections, and sometimes even animate these adjustments. This is a good way to start to expand your assistant's skills. I usually go on from there to allowing him or her to make small corrections in other areas; finally branching out to animating small scenes and eventually to becoming a full-fledged animator. This is much the best way to learn not only the fundamentals but a particular animator's point of view.

## Keeping Your Standards High

I worked as a kind of assistant to Bill Roberts at Disney's, doing nothing but reanimating his sweatbox changes for almost six months. When I think of Roberts, I think of Van Gogh. They both drew painfully; theirs was no God-given facility, but it was scrupulously honest. I equate some of Van Gogh's drawings of the potato eaters with Bill Roberts's animation. Awkward, searching for truth, they suffered in the cause of honesty.

Working so intimately with Roberts, I changed from an artist who lacked a real dedication to the craft to the zealot I have become. I recently was reading about one of my favorite characters in history,

Samuel Johnson. I have often marveled at his struggle to exist as a writer. Often he was forced to accept the most banal and commercialized forms of writing in order to make a bare living. Yet, no matter if it was a job as a ghostwriter for a member of Parliament or one of research for his famous dictionary, Sam Johnson gave each project his best efforts.

Here is a lesson for all of you. In the course of your career in this profession, you will no doubt have to work on material that is commercial trash. Ignore the lack of artistic value and work on it according to your own standards, and I hope you keep them high. If it is limited animation, concentrate on the line of action you can create for a pose. Or, as I did, learn to become a layout artist while working on very cheap bits of animation.

I realize that it is a constant struggle against commercialism. I never heard of a businessman who implored the artists he hired to do better work. Therefore, you will have to maintain your own integrity. Sometimes it will cost you money, but you can always make money. What you cannot very easily repair is the loss of the honesty that makes you do your best possible work at all times. Many people still in the animation business who worked in what we call The Golden Age of Animation could not rise to the pain of meeting those standards again. They have succumbed to the quasi-bookkeeping techniques of limited animation, which have robbed them of their artistic moral fiber. Guard your integrity! I see that I have wandered far afield, but in a good cause.

## How Sounds Are Made

To get back to the problem of mouth action . . . it is not a good idea to pick up a pencil and start drawing mouths throughout a scene, starting with drawing one. A much better control can be attained with a little more analytical approach, but first one must learn all the positions that the mouth takes to make English sounds. We will go through them starting with the sounds one makes with the lips closed. They will be either "m," "b," or "p." The lips may be their normal width, or they may be pursed closed. That width is going to be determined by the sounds directly before and after the word.

I would suggest that a good-sized mirror is going to be a big help until you understand the principle of mouth sizes. Try to say "boob" with the same "b" sizes at the beginning and end. You will find that if the preceding sound is the "oo" for "you," the two "b"'s in "boob" will

1 is the position for the sounds of *M, B,* or *P.* This position works when the preceding sound is made with a wide mouth. When the preceding mouth was an *OH* or *OO* sound, the closed mouth is more pursed, as in 2.

3 or 4 will make the sounds for *C* as in *center, D, J, R, S, Z,* and *X.* However, if an *OH* or *OO* sound precedes it, again the mouth will be pursed.

5 is used to make *F* or *V* if the dialogue is fairly slow, otherwise position 3 will do the job.

6 is used for the *TH* sound if the dialogue is slow. Otherwise use a mouth like 4.

7 is used for *N* and *L* when the speech is rapid; if it is deliberate, 8 is called for.

9 makes sounds like *E, K,* hard *C* as in *cat,* and *U* as in *hug.*

10 is used for the wide-open vowels like *AH, AY.*

11 is the *OH* sound or the start of *OO.*

12 makes the end of the *OH* or *OO* sound. It need not be very distorted, especially if the speech is fast.

be pursed up. If the preceding word was "the," the first "b" will be wide and the second one pursed.

When studying mouth action in a mirror, don't start exaggerating the mouth positions. Talk normally at regular speed. Do it over and over if you have to, just don't slow down and start looking like somebody whose bubble gum got caught in a filling.

The next position to study is the case of the exposed clenched teeth as in "c," "d," "g," "j," "r," "s," "t," "z," and "x." This is not so simple, either. All these sounds can also be made with the teeth slightly apart, particularly in fast talking. Usually the top and bottom rows of teeth are visible, but it depends on the size of the teeth. A character with buckteeth might not show the bottom row at all. It's a matter of the animator's interpretation.

For "f" and "v," in the early days of sound, the animators carefully tucked the lower lip under the top teeth, but I believe this is a convention that would only be useful in saying a heavily emphasized word such as an emphatic *"very!"* The tip of the tongue showing between the teeth makes "th."

Partially opened teeth, wide enough to see that the tip of the tongue is behind the upper front teeth, is the basic position for "n," and "l." In rapid speech, this tongue position can be ignored, but the teeth still have to be partially opened.

The same degree of slightly parted teeth, this time with the tongue lying flat, will take care of "e," "k," and "u" when it is pronounced "uh" as in "luxury."

The widest open mouths are used for vowel sounds such as "ah," "ay," "aw," "eye," and "h," when it is used as an aspirate, as in the word *hurry.*

The sound "oh" is really two mouth positions, a wide, rounded, open mouth, then a pursed mouth in the "oo" position for the finish of the sound. The letter "w" uses the same position as "oo"; so does "q."

Keep talking in the mirror, or have other people talk and watch them. There are fascinating variations in speech habits. Some people make a crooked mouth when they start to speak. Mae West's jaw made a semicircle when she said, "Come up and see me some time." People with bulldog jaws look very different from those with an overbite.

## Select Key Sounds

When animating mouth action, be careful not to overdo it. It is not necessary to make a drawing for every consonant. People slur over consonants. When they don't, the effect is very irritating to watch. So, when in doubt, underplay the action and you probably will be right.

## The Sequence of Drawing

If you start with drawing one and go forward, I doubt that the animation will be correct, because there is no control. The approach I have devised is almost foolproof. The first thing that I do is to draw all the

**SHAKE HANDS**

| DIAL | ACTION | DIAL | TRACK | 1 |
|---|---|---|---|---|
| 1 | | 1 | | |
| 2 | | 2 | | |
| 3 | | 3 | | |
| 4 | | 4 | | |
| 5 | | 5 | H | |
| 6 | | 6 | | |
| 7 | | 7 | O | |
| 8 | | 8 | | |
| 9 | F   X | 9 | | |
| 10 | /0 | 10 | | |
| 1 | | 1 | | |
| 2 | | 2 | W | |
| 3 | | 3 | | |
| 4 | | 4 | D | |
| 5 | | 5 | | |
| 6 | | 6 | | |
| 7 | | 7 | | |
| 8 | | 8 | O | |
| 9 | | 9 | | |
| 20 | | 20 | | |
| 1 | | 1 | | |
| 2 | T | 2 | | |
| 3 | | 3 | Y | |
| 4 | | 4 | OU | |
| 5 | | 5 | | |
| 6 | | 6 | | |
| 7 | | 7 | | |
| 8 | | 8 | | |
| 9 | | 9 | D | |
| 30 | | 30 | | |
| 1 | | 1 | | |
| 2 | | 2 | O | |
| 3 | | 3 | | |
| 4 | | 4 | | |
| 5 | | 5 | | |
| 6 | | 6 | | |
| 7 | | 7 | | |
| 8 | | 8 | | |
| 9 | | 40 | | |
| 40 | | 1 | | |
| 1 | | 2 | | |
| 2 | | 3 | | |
| 3 | | 4 | | |
| 4 | | 5 | T | |
| 5 | | 6 | | |
| 6 | | 7 | | |
| 7 | | 8 | | |
| 8 | | 9 | M | |
| 9 | | 50 | | |
| 50 | | 1 | Y | |
| 1 | | 2 | E | |
| 2 | | 3 | | |
| 3 | | 4 | R | |
| 4 | | 5 | | |
| 5 | | 6 | | |
| 6 | | 7 | | |
| 7 | | 8 | | |
| 8 | | 9 | | |
| 9 | | 60 | W | |
| 60 | | 1 | E | |
| 1 | | 2 | | |
| 2 | | 3 | | |
| 3 | | 4 | | |
| 4 | | 5 | | |
| 5 | | 6 | LL | |
| 6 | | 7 | | |
| 7 | | 8 | | |
| 8 | | 9 | | |
| 9 | | 70 | | |
| 70 | | 1 | | |
| 1 | | 2 | CUT ↑ | |
| 2 | | 3 | | |
| 3 | | 4 | | |
| 4 | | 5 | | |
| 5 | | 6 | | |
| 6 | | 7 | | |
| 7 | | 8 | | |
| 8 | | 9 | | |
| 9 | | 80 | | |
| 80 | | 0 | | |

**THE BRITISH ARE COMING!**

| DIAL | ACTION | DIAL | TRACK | 1 |
|---|---|---|---|---|
| 1 | | 1 | | |
| 2 | | 2 | | |
| 3 | | 3 | | |
| 4 | IT'S | 4 | | |
| 5 | GETTING | 5 | | |
| 6 | | 6 | | |
| 7 | | 7 | TH | |
| 8 | | 8 | | |
| 9 | | 9 | | |
| 10 | | 10 | | |
| 1 | | 1 | EE | |
| 2 | | 2 | | |
| 3 | | 3 | | |
| 4 | | 4 | | |
| 5 | | 5 | | |
| 6 | | 6 | | |
| 7 | | 7 | BR | |
| 8 | | 8 | | |
| 9 | | 9 | | |
| 20 | | 20 | I | |
| 1 | | 1 | | |
| 2 | | 2 | | |
| 3 | | 3 | T | |
| 4 | | 4 | | |
| 5 | | 5 | | |
| 6 | | 6 | | |
| 7 | | 7 | | |
| 8 | | 8 | SH | |
| 9 | | 9 | | |
| 30 | | 30 | | |
| 1 | | 1 | A | |
| 2 | | 2 | | |
| 3 | | 3 | | |
| 4 | | 4 | | |
| 5 | | 5 | RE | |
| 6 | | 6 | | |
| 7 | | 7 | C | |
| 8 | | 8 | | |
| 9 | | 9 | O | |
| 40 | | 40 | | |
| 1 | | 1 | | |
| 2 | | 2 | | |
| 3 | | 3 | M | |
| 4 | | 4 | | |
| 5 | | 5 | I | |
| 6 | | 6 | | |
| 7 | | 7 | | |
| 8 | | 8 | NG | |
| 9 | | 9 | | |
| 50 | | 50 | | |
| 1 | | 1 | BR | |
| 2 | | 2 | I | |
| 3 | | 3 | | |
| 4 | | 4 | T | |
| 5 | | 5 | | |
| 6 | | 6 | | |
| 7 | | 7 | SH | |
| 8 | | 8 | | |
| 9 | | 9 | A | |
| 60 | | 60 | | |
| 1 | | 1 | RE | |
| 2 | | 2 | | |
| 3 | | 3 | | |
| 4 | | 4 | | |
| 5 | | 5 | | |
| 6 | | 6 | C | |
| 7 | | 7 | O | |
| 8 | | 8 | | |
| 9 | | 9 | | |
| 70 | | 70 | | |
| 1 | | 1 | M | |
| 2 | | 2 | | |
| 3 | | 3 | I | |
| 4 | | 4 | | |
| 5 | | 5 | | |
| 6 | | 6 | | |
| 7 | | 7 | | |
| 8 | | 8 | NG | |
| 9 | | 9 | | |
| 80 | | 80 | | |
| 0 | | 0 | | |

**PLAYING CARDS**

| DIAL | ACTION | DIAL | TRACK | 1 |
|---|---|---|---|---|
| 1 | | 1 | | |
| 2 | | 2 | | |
| 3 | | 3 | | |
| 4 | THE | 4 | | |
| 5 | LESS | 5 | | |
| 6 | | 6 | | |
| 7 | HAPPY | 7 | | |
| 8 | | 8 | | |
| 9 | | 9 | | |
| 10 | | 10 | | |
| 1 | | 1 | | |
| 2 | | 2 | | |
| 3 | | 3 | | |
| 4 | | 4 | | |
| 5 | | 5 | | |
| 6 | | 6 | | |
| 7 | TINY | 7 | | |
| 8 | SPEAKS | 8 | | |
| 9 | | 9 | | |
| 20 | | 20 | | |
| 1 | | 1 | | |
| 2 | | 2 | P | |
| 3 | | 3 | | |
| 4 | | 4 | | |
| 5 | | 5 | | |
| 6 | | 6 | | |
| 7 | | 7 | | |
| 8 | | 8 | | |
| 9 | | 9 | | |
| 30 | | 30 | | |
| 1 | | 1 | | |
| 2 | | 2 | | |
| 3 | | 3 | | |
| 4 | | 4 | | |
| 5 | TINY | 5 | N | |
| 6 | ANSWERS | 6 | | |
| 7 | | 7 | | |
| 8 | | 8 | O | |
| 9 | | 9 | | |
| 40 | | 40 | | |
| 1 | | 1 | I | |
| 2 | | 2 | | |
| 3 | | 3 | M | |
| 4 | | 4 | | |
| 5 | GRABS | 5 | E | |
| 6 | FOR | 6 | | |
| 7 | MONEY | 7 | | |
| 8 | | 8 | | |
| 9 | | 9 | | |
| 50 | | 50 | | |
| 1 | | 1 | | |
| 2 | | 2 | | |
| 3 | | 3 | | |
| 4 | | 4 | | |
| 5 | | 5 | | |
| 6 | THROWS | 6 | | |
| 7 | IT | 7 | | |
| 8 | ON | 8 | | |
| 9 | TABLE | 9 | | |
| 60 | | 60 | O | |
| 1 | | 1 | | |
| 2 | | 2 | | |
| 3 | | 3 | NE | |
| 4 | | 4 | | |
| 5 | | 5 | P | |
| 6 | | 6 | | |
| 7 | | 7 | | |
| 8 | | 8 | | |
| 9 | | 9 | | |
| 70 | | 70 | CK | |
| 1 | | 1 | | |
| 2 | | 2 | | |
| 3 | | 3 | | |
| 4 | | 4 | | |
| 5 | | 5 | | |
| 6 | | 6 | | |
| 7 | | 7 | CUT ↑ | |
| 8 | | 8 | | |
| 9 | | 9 | | |
| 80 | | 80 | | |
| 0 | | 0 | | |

Exposure sheet showing dialogue.

closed mouths, paying attention to the sound before and after this particular position, to be sure that I am drawing a proper width for the mouth in each case.

Next, I do all the mouths with closed teeth showing. After that, I listen to my cassette very carefully and pick out the loudest vowel in the sentence. Having drawn that, I do the next-loudest vowel, and on through the sentence, until they are all drawn. Of course, the loudest vowel is going to have the widest open mouth, and the mouths are less wide as the volume diminishes.

After that, you can see that the remaining animation is a simple matter of inbetweens. With this system, there is no way that a secondary vowel will have a bigger mouth than the louder vowels.

Of course, this careful approach only pertains to animation with life-quality. For more abstract animation à la UPA, forget the whole system and just follow your instincts. In any event, you won't be able to animate exact mouth actions because the editor will not supply you with a detailed analysis of the track.

In these next exercises, you will note that I have not written exact directions for the various movements because they are so dependent on the manner in which the animator handles the relationship between the dialogue and the action.

If you have the facilities, by all means do a recording and get a track analysis word by word. Then animate the action, have it photographed; then after making whatever adjustments are necessary to obtain good sync, animate the mouths.

If you have no way of getting a recording, I suggest that you still do the animation in two stages, action first and then the mouths after all the inbetweens are done.

### Exercise: Dialogue

First is a waist-high shot with Skinny already in position, but Fatty has to take one step as he extends his hand.

Rough out the animation. "How do you do?" from Fatty. Skinny's rejoinder, "I'm very well." Fatty is hearty and vigorous in contrast to Skinny's more reserved manner. They are both smiling and friendly. Do the cleanups, then the mouths.

In exercise 2, we have a mystified Skinny watching Tiny as he runs in with excitement. After he skids in, Tiny never stands still, but there is a pattern of steps in the cadence and meaning of the words that should give you a clue as to when he bobs up and down. Have Skinny react to the words but be very restrained so that he does not take the audience's attention away from Tiny.

In exercise 3, we have a medium shot of the three elves playing cards. Be sure that the elves react to each other's dialogue. Have their eyes follow the action precisely. When the scene opens, Fatty and Tiny are looking at their hands and reacting. Fatty becomes mournful while Tiny gets happier. Keep these actions well under control because the main action is Skinny's. When he says, "I pass," he addresses Tiny, but as soon as he finishes "pass," he looks to Fatty for confirmation.

As Fatty talks, Tiny goes into a wondering look, then a big happy grin as he shouts, "Not me!" Be sure everybody keeps reacting to the dialogue. I don't mean that they have to move around a lot; this is mostly a facial reaction. Don't make too many changes of expression, just let it come the way it feels. Do draw all three characters at the same time, not one and then the other. Keep in mind the need for tension between one body and the other, and an overall composition. For that reason, I suggest that you draw a very small table so that the elves are almost cramped. That way, the composition will be somewhat easier to work out.

Remember to draw the most important parts first. In this case, I would draw the position of the cards for all three before I did anything else, then the heads. Keep in mind the exercise of Fatty menacing Tiny, and the way he changed his tension as you moved the drawings back and forth. Those heads should set up a tension. Put Skinny in the middle, with a rather hopeless expression as he reaches for the card— Fatty to the left, Tiny to the right. It will not be necessary to show the denomination of Tiny's cards, although in the normal course of events, the next shot would be a close-up of his hand.

This chapter on mouth action is difficult, but if you take it in stages, you will find it easier. I would say that at first it will be hard to create good poses without overacting. On the other hand, each pose should be a well-worked-out drawing, using perspective where it applies, a strong line of action, and so clear a presentation that it would make a good silhouette.

What I have mentioned about the sequence of drawing the parts of a drawing is one of the most important aspects of building a rough. At first, you may have to be vaguely conscious of the rule as you draw. Later, it will be second nature because you will feel the pose, and that feeling will urge you to start where the emotion is strongest.

Would it surprise you to know that the very last thing I would draw, if I were animating this card-playing shot, would be the table? When you think about it, everything else is more important. The table should be the result of the positioning of the bodies, not the other way around. Yet I believe that most artists, even professionals, would start by drawing the table.

It is this attention to principles that made the Disney animators the best in the business year after year. No other group was ever so analytical; and it paid off. I hope as a result of reading this book, and doing the exercises honestly, you will become a thoughtful artist.

## Beware Overgesticulation

Keep in mind the pitfall of overgesticulating along with the dialogue. You can always add a gesture if you find that the figure seems not to be properly interpreting the dialogue. It is more difficult to excise a gesture, because the remaining material may not hook up very well. If you run the silent animation on a projector, usually it will look jerky. If it doesn't, you probably have not accented the gestures enough. You can always modify a too-violent accent, but it is difficult to invigorate a movement without changing the whole concept.

## The Secondary Players

Pay attention to the reactions of secondary players in a scene. They always should be reacting to the situation. This may be entirely a facial reaction, but what with blinks, eyes widening in astonishment, jaws dropping, or closing mouths, there are plenty of subtle ways to keep the tension between the secondary and major characters.

The audience will probably pay no attention to the secondary characters, but, if by chance they do, there should be some interesting acting going on to reinforce the scene, not just a figure staring into space in the general direction of the major action. Nothing will kill a scene faster.

### Further Exercises

Obviously doing three exercises of mouth action is not going to make you an expert. Devise your own exercises. Just to make it less easy, ask someone else to give you a sentence to animate. Even if they answer, "Gee, I wouldn't be able to think of any," use that as a line to animate. Accept it as an assignment, whatever it is. The basic trouble with working by yourself is that you are not really being commanded to do a certain exercise. It is very easy to dream up an assignment and then drop it if it doesn't come easily. Avoid that by asking somebody else for an idea for a scene, then do it as if it were an assignment in a studio.

# 16

## Production Tips

Now that there are Xerox machines that can enlarge or reduce drawings, use them and avoid having to animate very small figures. Instead, animate them at a comfortable size and have them reduced. Remember, too, that one can take the reduced copies and run them through again, making them even smaller. We once made figures one-fourth as large as the original drawings. Imagine the problems in trying to animate characters five-eighths of an inch high!

Another good idea is the use of models. In Disney's *Beach Picnic,* I had to animate a rubber inflatable horse that was working with Pluto. To my astonishment, I couldn't do it. No matter how I animated it, the subtle inaccuracies in the perspective made the toy look alive. We solved that problem by making a mock-up of a rubber horse exactly like the drawing on the model sheet. Then it was photographed from all the angles I needed for my animation. I was given prints of all these shots and it was a simple matter to trace them very carefully and draw the inbetweens meticulously. The end result was a perfectly lifeless rubber horse bobbing around in the water.

Another time, I was directing a television spot at Erredia in Milan. In lieu of a proper model sheet, the agency sent us just one drawing of a very complex dragon, and a side view at that. We began to make front and three-quarter views but we soon realized that it was going to be a difficult job. However, one of the animators was a skillful sculptor. He took the drawing home and came back two days later with a large clay model of the beast. We made photographs of various views of it and gave each animator a set. What would have been a horrendous struggle to animate became no problem at all.

Like making out time cards, writing up exposure sheets can be a profound bore, but think of the camera operator and don't scribble the numbers so that they look like a Linear B granary list.

When the scene is using cels from another shot, it is a good idea to write those numbers in red pencil. If the scene uses a second group of cels from still another shot, use a blue pencil. Avoid light blue because it will be difficult to read under the camera lights. You can see from these admonishments that, contrary to popular belief, I think of camera operators as human beings.

I like to letter the drawings in addition to numbering them, because I believe it cuts down the number of errors the painters make. The most common error is to use a set of colors designated for another cel level. This will cause a flash on the screen because the character will suddenly become lighter or darker. It is a difficult mistake to catch in the checking department. Even the expert checkers at Disney's have allowed color flashes to appear in many of the studio's short subjects.

By affixing a letter after the drawing number, one can tell without looking at the exposure sheet which level this drawing is using. I use A for the lowest level, B for the next, and so on. Nobody uses more than five levels because, although the cels seem to be transparent, they are not. They are a definite shade of light gray. This is why we have this complicated system of painting with Cartoon Colors, which compensates for the gray tint of the cel whenever we move a character to a different level.

It sometimes happens that a group of cels are going to be reused in another scene. However, for technical reasons, they are going to be on a different level. If they are going to work with other cels in the shot, you have three choices.

1. Use them with the wrong color on them and risk a color jump.
2. ReXerox and paint new cels with the adjusted color. In this case, half the possible profit is lost in the extra wages, taxes, and union fees.
3. If it is possible when the reused cels are being shot, cut to a different

field. When they have all been photographed, cut back to the original field. The color jump is now contained in a separate scene, which can be corrected in the lab. What cannot be corrected is a scene were the old cels are used with the new.

If you are trying to establish a reputation as a great animator, you are going to be living under two standards of quality, yours, and the studios. Yours should be much higher. Above all, do not send a scene into the pencil-test reel if it is not your best effort. If it is rejected by the director, you have accomplished two negative things. First, you can animate shots with poor quality. More important, you do not seem to have the judgment to differentiate between good and bad work.

A few scenes like that and you are pegged as an animator whose work is uneven, when your real goal is to be known in your unit as an artist who never deviates from top-quality work. A good reputation makes you eligible for all the vital sequences, no matter how difficult. With a reputation for instability, you are going to be passed over for many interesting segments of your unit's films.

When the storyboards are moved into the director's room, I see nothing wrong in viewing the material and asking for a particular sequence that appeals to you. The director may not give it to you, but at least you have indicated the type of animation that excites your creativity.

If the director is an ex-animator, the exposure sheets probably will be planned to the last exposure. If this is so, then it follows that you animate the various actions as they are indicated. Occasionally, you may not be able to animate an action in the amount of screen time the director has specified. It is not a good idea to steal a few exposures from the following action. You may be throwing the action and music slightly out of sync. Why do it? Go to the director and explain your problem. It may be that you had not understood his approach to the action. If it is his mistake, he will accept it and add exposures to your scene to take care of the complete action. The change will be recorded in the bar sheets and no harm done.

There are two high points in an animator's life. One is standing in front of an editing machine right before your newest animation is going to be run, fresh from the lab. The other is seeing the same material now spliced into a pencil reel, knowing it is going to have to run the gauntlet of story people, the director and even your fellow animators.

Now, most directors are able to ask for changes, additions, or deletions with no particular impatience. However, there are exceptions. Ben Sharpsteen at Disney's would instruct the hapless animator about his changes with obvious irritation. This would be compounded by the fact that, as the reel was run back and the same material screened again, Sharpsteen would grow more petulant, as if the poor animator should somehow have fixed the offending animation and transported it by magic to the pencil-test reel before Sharpsteen had to look at the incorrect action again.

But for the most part, good directors do not have such psychological hang-ups. If your work is being criticized, it is normal to defend your point of view. However, having stated your case, do not become argumentative to the point where there is a wrangle. After all, the director has this huge advantage: He knows what the pace, the form, and the flowering of the humor should be, and the animator only knows about his own percentage of the picture. So don't become a forecastle lawyer and engage in long polemics.

What you are doing then, unwittingly perhaps, is wrestling the director for a piece of his authority, his empery.

## Handling Retakes

There are usually two kinds of retakes: One is adding to the shot, a process that may involve a few exposures or a few feet. The other is where a section of the film is excised altogether. For the latter, simply draw a large X over the section involved on the exposure sheet. For additions, cut the exposure sheet where the new action starts and paste on enough footage to take care of the retake. Be sure that your assistant changes all the dial numbers right to the end of the scene. The result is that you will end up with at least one exposure sheet that is longer than the others. What of it? It certainly is better than wasting time rewriting old exposure sheets to take care of the new material. Be sure your assistant shows the assistant director where you have added or cut footage so that the bar sheets can be kept up-to-date.

If the animation to be changed was initially done in pose-to-pose technique, make your changes in that mode. If the work was drawn at high-speed, make your changes the same way, even if the retake is only a few feet.

When some parts of the body are not moving for long periods of time, avoid making them separate drawings, because you want to see the entire figure's line of action. Of course, there will be a point where this is not feasible, but make it a general rule. Doing cleanups, the assistant will, of course, use held cels, unless it is a matter of making a few tracings.

By 1932, the veteran animators of Fleischer studio had all heard the siren call of the west coast, leaving a group of novices who averaged less than two years of experience. With nobody to teach them, they came up with a number of amateurish concepts that oddly enough continue to plague this group to the present day.

I have already mentioned that some of them thought the mouth closed after every word; they did not use the body to express dialogue. As a group, they were unable to analyze what they were looking at, so in spite of the fact that Disney short subjects were being animated in perfect sync about 1933, the Fleischer animators would have continued with their mistaken theories indefinitely except for the fact that Fleischer hired a number of ex-Disney animators in 1939. Then the others grudgingly learned the new techniques.

## The Use and Misuse of Cel Levels

What they did not rid themselves of was the custom of breaking down a character into as many cel levels as possible. With a cavalier disregard for the principle of the line of action, to this day an ex-Fleischer animator will start by dismembering a character on several cel levels.

Now a certain amount of this approach can be used by the assistant. For example, shoes that should not move can be put on a bottom cel. This is certainly better than tracing them on drawing after drawing, because making tracings of tracings will inevitably make the drawings start to crawl.

But fragmenting characters can be carried to the point of absurdity. Once, I used an ex-Fleischer animator to draw a scene of a lion doing a tap dance, He was manipulating a straw hat in one hand and a bamboo cane in the other. When the resulting mess was brought to my attention, the animator had placed the lion's head on a separate level because he was singing; the body and legs were another level, and each hand had its own level.

He had scarcely started the scene when he inadvertently matched a head to the wrong body, so every head was mismatched right through the rest of the scene. He did the same for both hands. It was such a mass of errors that we junked the whole scene and gave it to an animator who was aware of the principles of the line of action and who drew the complete lion on each drawing.

So don't get into the habit of turning your characters into fragments. You heighten the odds that you will make mistakes in matching, and the opaquer has more opportunity to create further errors in color levels.

Animation studios never take the time to order a positive print of a pencil test, so novice animators have to learn to read their drawings in white line. Bewildering at first, it soon becomes second nature. One must also get adjusted to the fact that linear drawings will look faster than viewing the same action when it is linked and painted. Some of my eight and twelve exposure scenes in a montage have given story people the vapors, because in a pencil test they were little more than a series of flickers.

Since the drawings are usually shot with underneath lighting, it is better to cut down the number of paper levels as much as possible. Where it is feasible, have the assistant ink a held cel, cutting down the paper level by one. If the character resumes animation, I simply accept the difference in density, unlike the final photography, where, if the scenes in the film are predominently five-cel levels, I always have blank cels added to the rest of the scenes so that the entire film has the same number of cel levels throughout.

## Special Effects

As animation developed in the Disney studio during the 1930s, it became necessary to pay more attention to *special effects* such as smoke, fire, water, and shadows. Until then, special effects, considered a nuisance by the average animator, were done very crudely along with the rest of the animation.

Walt Disney recognized that special effects were a complicated speciality. If the effects were going to be equal to the character animation, a whole new approach was called for. So he set up a separate department under Cy Young, who up to that time had been a rather indifferent character animator.

Cy ran his animators with an iron hand. He made them study effects with the same intensity that the other animators were putting into character animation. The result was evident in *Snow White and the*

It is important that special effects follow the drawing style of the picture. In this case, realistic-looking sparks would have been a mistake. *I Know an Old Lady Who Swallowed a Fly,* a film made for the National Film Board of Canada by Derek Lamb and Kaj Pindal.

*Seven Dwarfs.* Before the film was completed, it was necessary to go back to the effects that had been animated at the beginning of work on the picture and do them over. They were too primitive in comparison to the more complex approach the department was developing.

Unless you are willing to spend the rest of your creative life doing special effects to the exclusion of any other form of animation, there is no way to compete with the masterful handling of effects by the Disney staff.

The alternative is to study pictures like *The Old Mill,* a Disney short subject, and features such as *Snow White, Pinocchio,* and *Bambi.* At the same time, start to look at special effects—wind, ripples, rain, smoke, fire, and the like—and try to analyze the shapes you are seeing, as if you were going to draw them. You will have to start thinking in terms other than pencil drawings. Often, effects are drawn or painted directly on cels because there is no other way to delineate some of the rendering. For example, most of the spray and splashing occurring in the scenes of Monstro the Whale in *Pinocchio* were painted in oils right on the cels.

White or light-colored smoke can be done in pastels on black paper and double-exposed in a scene if the area where the smoke appears is a fairly dark value. Another approach would be to airbrush the smoke directly onto cels. You will notice that even in such a simple effect as smoke, there are a myriad of different shapes it can assume, from the simple spiraling in a small fire to the fierce billowing shapes in a big blaze.

Since wind is invisible in itself, one can only assume its presence by its affect on objects such as leaves whirling by, clothes reacting, characters leaning forward to keep in balance, and, of course, sound effects.

Shadows are usually done by painting the areas in black on separate cels. Then a few frames of the scene involved are shot in a test running the gamut between 30-to-75-percent exposure. After the shadows have been exposed in the test at a selected percentage, the shadows are removed and the scene reshot to make the exposure 100 percent. In other words, if the shadows were shot at 70-percent exposure, the reshoot without them would be 30 percent. From this test, the best percentage of shadow exposure is selected. Then the entire scene is photographed using this percentage.

Be very sure that the background artist is aware of the direction that the shadows fall, so that the light source on the background corresponds to the shadows.

The animation of water can range from complex realism to stylized simplicity. Hiroshige and Hokusai, Japanese printmakers, have created some interesting effects; even Rembrandt tried his hand at etching rain. Obviously, rain cannot be animated as a collection of separate drops. To the eye, it looks like a series of diagonal lines. Start with a group of these lines and animate them through the field. When they are halfway through the scene, start another group entering the field. Make several levels of rain in this fashion, using various values of gray, not black. Have the lighter values in the background for a perspective effect.

Fire can be anything from the flickering light of a candle to a ranging

*The Great Wave Off Kanagawa* by Katsushika Hokusai, printed in the 1820s, is an example of Hokusai's preoccupation with various forms of waves.

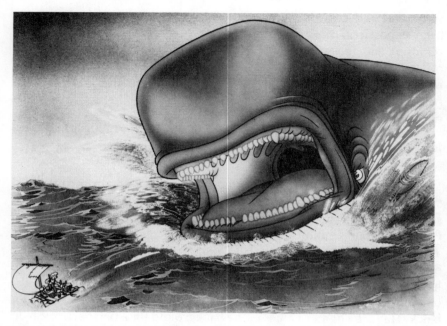

Note the similarity between Hokusai's *Great Wave* and this rendering of foam and water by the special effects department of the Disney Studio in this scene from *Pinocchio.* © 1940 by Walt Disney Productions, Inc.

inferno. The candlelight can be achieved by drawing a number of differently shaped flames and doing very short dissolves between them. Large fires, to the average eye, are just a confusion of shapes; but the trained observer will, after a time, see that there are characteristic shapes in every fire. It depends on what material is burning and the intensity of the blaze.

One approach is to make a series of flame drawings at random. then, taking each drawing separately, add another drawing that brings some of the flames upward. Shooting the two drawing combinations on two exposures apiece, and varying the sequence of each combination, the general effect will be that the flames are going up, but not in obvious pattern.

Lightning can be a distant flash that will animate from a point in the sky to the ground in a few exposures, or it can be animated as a nearby bolt, which makes the entire screen white for several exposures. Remember that the sound effect is not thunder. It is the preceding sheet-tearing sound. The farther away the bolt, the longer the interval between the lightning and the sound of thunder.

*Exercises: Special Effects*

Do the following exercises:

Fatty is on the bank of a pond in a bathing suit. He does a couple of knee bends and dives frog-fashion into the water. There is a big splash; his head bobs up; then he swims to the bank and climbs out very awkwardly. This shot should take five feet.

Tiny crouches at a fireplace in a close-up. He strikes a match and lights the fire. Flames run across the top of the logs as he watches with satisfaction. Suddenly, one flame jumps out of the fireplace and confronts him. Tiny leaps up in alarm; the flame runs at him; and he, in a long shot, runs around frantically with the flame in pursuit. The running action should be a repeated section. The shot should start as a still scene in a close up, then truck back to a twelve field on a pan. Tiny is in a running cycle that is broken up by two leaps as the flame almost burns his backside. The flame should have simulated legs, very short, and be half as tall as Tiny.

Skinny is carrying an umbrella and walking on, sixteen exposures to the step, in a pouring rain. He is leaning forward. Suddenly, a bolt of lightning hits the tip of his umbrella and sizzles there for sixteen exposures; during that time, Skinny is being shocked. When it is over, the umbrella is just a couple of twisted spokes.

## Check Your Storyboard

By this time, your clock-tower story should be beginning to take form. A five-minute film will contain anywhere from 100 to 150 scenes, depending on the graphic style of the story and the storyboard artist's ability to go into detail. The storyboard will have at least 300 to 500 drawings, ranging from detailed key sketches that explain the locale to roughly sketched close-ups of heads.

This is a good time to look over your storyboard very objectively. Have you conceived your film as a series of sequences rather than as a rambling account of the action? Within each sequence is there a high point, a gag that is the reason for the sequence in the first place?

Have you just presented it without preparing the audience with a preliminary action or actions? Just think of the lack of audience reaction if Dopey, getting ready to leave the mine, had just picked up the bag, reared back, and throw it toward the mine door but had forgotten to let go. It might have gotten a mild titter. Instead, it was set up by

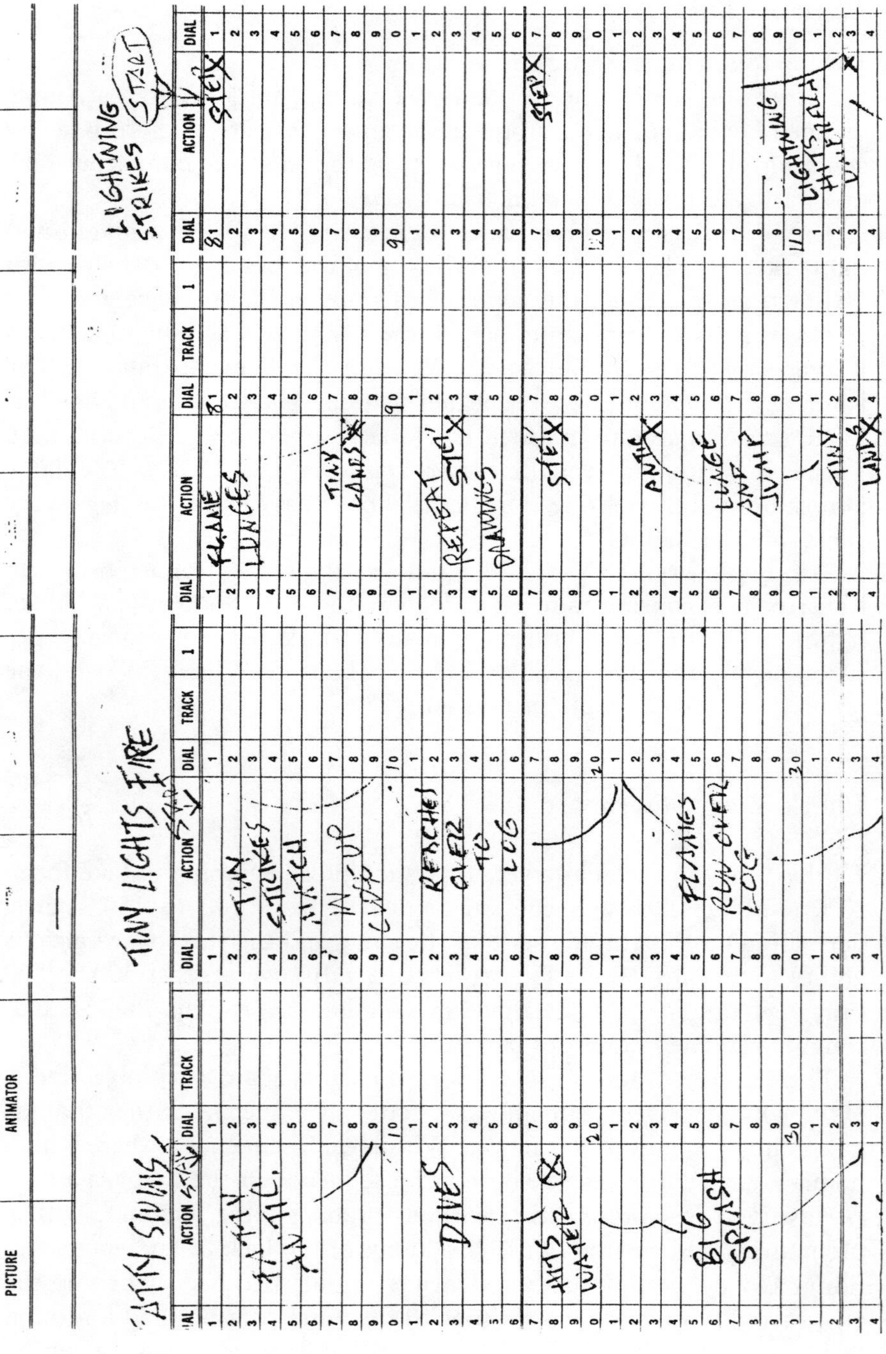
PICTURE
ANIMATOR
ACTION
DIAL
TRACK
DIVES
HITS WATER
BIG SPLASH
TINY LIGHTS FIRE
TINY STRIKES MATCH
REACHES OVER TO LOG
FLAMES RUN OVER LOG
FLAME LUNGES
TINY LANDS
REPEAT STEP
DRAWINGS
LUNGE AND JUMP
LIGHTNING STRIKES
START
STEP

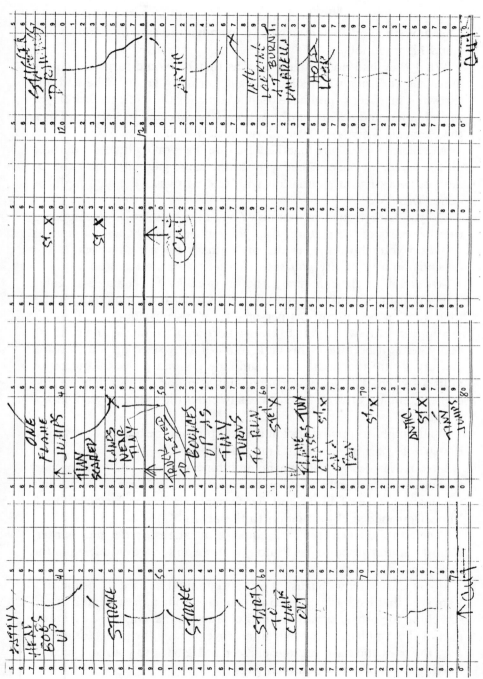

Exposure sheet for the accompanying exercise.

Dopey swinging the bag back and forth a few times before throwing it. This gave the audience a chance to examine the situation and understand his intention.

What they had not anticipated was that he would forget to let go. Since the audience was fooled, the gag got a big laugh. If he had just thrown it in, there would have been no time for the audience to analyze the situation and decide on the action they expected to happen. Thus, the element of surprise would have been missing.

Are the elves working together? Be sure that you really need all three on the screen at once. Could you do the same gag with just two? Or are you working on a situation with one elf, when the gag might be better with two?

Do you have sequences that now seem to be uninteresting compared to other parts of the picture? Can you cut them out? Can you use the situation you now have as the preliminary for a funnier gag? If it depends on a prop, are you sure you are using the right one?

Are you using the character structure of each elf to enhance his gags? Are you using situations where one elf is able to do something better than another because of his personality or his physique?

Suppose Fatty was trying to clean a portion of the clock, and couldn't really get at it because of his bulk. What if Tiny sized up the situation and dived into the gears? One hand emerges and presses a button or pulls a switch. The gears start and Tiny is propelled through the machinery, ending up where he can easily clean the area Fatty could not manage.

What might top this situation if Fatty pressed the button or reversed the switch after he saw that Tiny was finished?

Do not create gags that have no preliminary action, and look for gags that can be topped, maybe more than once, such as Norman Ferguson's famous sequence of Pluto and the flypaper, in which Ferguson took Pluto from one sticky situation to the next.

When an audience sees this sequence, it laughs harder and harder, almost without stopping, as Pluto gets more and more entangled in the flypaper.

If you started off with a list of props that might be used in the picture, I am sure that list has expanded as you have done more research. Keep searching for props, situations, and characters that might be a natural part of this ambience. Let your mind rove over all the possibilities, not only the ones you have yet to use. Keep going back to your storyboard, looking for a clue to additional gags.

This film will be all pantomime, unless there is some very important gag or gags involving dialogue. Remember in a picture such as this, the factor of height should call for some interesting camera angles. If you have little or no experience with perspective, try anyhow. In production, if you just give the layout artist the general idea, it will be enough.

Remember that these elves are people with the ability to think, so use their thinking processes when they are in a precarious situation. This is better than just showing that they are scared.

Don't make drawings with faint gray lines. After the storyboard is finished, the project will be made into the equivalent of an animatic.

# 17

## The Animator's Assistant

There is no better way to learn animation than to become the assistant of an outstanding animator. The standard approach to animation when the business was more stable was to start as an inbetweener, advance to assistant, and then to animator.

These days, the inbetweener is practically a vanished species. The starting position has become assistant animator, but it is not unusual to learn of animators such as Gil Miret, who entered the field as a designer-layoutman at Paramount-Famous studio. When it was closed down by Gulf & Western, Miret decided to teach himself animation. The list of films he has produced and animated in the commercial field show that he succeeded.

### The Assistant's Job

The role of a good assistant is to interpret the animator's rough. This does not mean a slavish rendition of the model sheet. There is a fine line between adjusting the animator's drawings to conform to the model sheet to an extent and losing the individuality of the work in the process.

Of course, the audience does not recognize that there were differences in the handling of star characters. The drawings of Pluto by Norman Ferguson, Freddy Moore and Bill Roberts were all very personal, and none of their assistants tried to make them look like the model sheet. It would have taken a lot of redrawing, ending up in a very sterile rendition of the character.

When the animator first picks up an assignment, there should be a briefing of the assistant, as well. If they are working on a new character, both animator and assistant should go through a period of practice drawings. Both should end up being fully conversant with the structure of the figure. The clean-up period is no time to learn the fine points of a model sheet.

## Analyzing the Exposure Sheet

It is up to the assistant to make an analysis of the animator's exposure sheet to see where the animation can be modified or made simpler for the remainder of the production operations. Held cels should be called for when some portion of the figure does not move for a long time. There is no point in calling for trace backs ad infinitum. Combining cel levels when the exposure sheet shows them to be running in tandem saves shooting time. It also diminishes the possibility of the painter making an error in painting by using the palette for the wrong cel level.

## Pan Moves

The assistant should learn how to compile pan moves. Not only is it a part of the educational process, but it saves the animator's time for more creative work.

## Preparing for Xerox

Cleaning up drawings for Xerox is not the same as working on drawings that are going to be inked. In the first place, for Xerox only the lightest blue pencil, which won't reproduce, can be used to sketch construction lines or make notes for dialogue that explain which areas in a mouth are teeth and which are tongue. Sometimes they are difficult to differentiate on the pencil drawing.

If a color area isn't quite closed on the cleanup, an experienced inker will complete it, but a Xerox machine will only reproduce what is on the drawing. Therefore, the cleanup has to be meticulous if the scene is going to be Xeroxed.

Drawing cleanups is not a matter of omitting extra lines and putting the result on a clean sheet of paper. The final result should not look like a pallid tracing. Very often a drawing is poor because the assistant works very slowly. The line is without snap or strength. On the other hand, working too quickly may result in a slipshod drawing. Every artist has a tempo of drawing that allows for subtle, exact transition from the rough, yet at the same time gives complete control of the pencil so that curves are graceful and the details, such as wrinkles, are in proportion to the rest of the figure.

The assistant should be trying at all times to understand the animator's point of view. Why this particular drawing or action instead of another? Only then can an intelligent cleanup be achieved. Batting out cleanups mechanically will never give the assistant the insight into the emotions of an animator, which in turn should sharpen the perceptions enough to enable the assistant to start doing small bits of animation in a professional way.

## Completing the Exposure Sheet

It is difficult for the average animator to come down from the high that one has when animating roughs to the prosaic task of filling out exposure sheets, writing down the drawing numbers and camera instructions. It is up to the assistant to see to it that the scenes go for the pencil test without errors or omissions.

## Some Common Errors

Certain errors are so common that they should be caught automatically. Animators working on twos will often write down a drawing number on the last exposure of an exposure sheet and forget to add another exposure at the start of the next page.

Instructions for field sizes may be incorrect, as well as the placement of the field. A drawing may be left out of a sequence, and a whole line of drawings will have to be moved down two exposures on the exposure sheet to accommodate it. Notes may have been so scribbled that they are illegible, or they may have been written in such a manner that the camera operator will not understand them. Without bothering the animator about them, these problems should be corrected.

Sometimes, when there have been a lot of sweatbox changes, the exposure sheets have become a shambles of sections crossed out, areas cut, and additional beats inserted. There comes a point when the exposure sheets are too battered to be useful. An efficient assistant does not have to be told to rewrite the whole mess, making sure that the end result is a set of neat, legible exposure sheets that will go through the remainder of production without a hitch.

Be very sure to correct the dial numbers even if only one beat has been removed or added. The numbers will have to be changed throughout the rest of the scene.

## Working Up to Animator

The best way to start the gradual switch from assistant to animator is to take a short scene that has already been animated, and, using the same exposure sheets, draw your own version of the action. Get a critique from your animator, clean it up, and do the inbetweens. Have the pencil test shot and compare the result with your animator's scene.

After a time, you will be allowed to animate very short scenes, then longer ones, until you finally are ready to be promoted to full-fledged animator.

Remember that pushing your endurance to its limits with an all-out burst of energy is the best way to improve your work. A year of learning how to animate five nights a week is certainly a tremendous outlay of exertion, not only physically, but mentally, as well. Yet, at the end of that time, you might become an animator, whereas the same amount of study spread over a couple of years might not get the same happy result.

The reason for this is psychological. Working every day to change your work habits and your thinking processes does not allow your mind to build up a resistance. Working a night here and there will not let you make these changes so readily. In fact, depending on how stubbornly your personality resists change, you may end up getting nowhere.

## Drawing Speed

One final admonition, this about drawing speed: There is one good speed for you when drawing cleanups. Too fast will make for a sloppy drawing. Too slow will end up a dull collection of lines without snap.

Somewhere in the middle is your ideal speed, where you are accurate but your line has dash and verve. Practice cleanups of your roughs until you find what this ideal speed is, until it is your normal speed without thinking about it. This is a most important exercise, not to be ignored or done superficially.

## The Path of Action Drawing

Since the background artist does not have the animation drawings available when rendering the backgrounds, the assistant makes a rough sketch of the layout, and on this drawing indicates the areas where the action occurs.

For example, if a character enters screen left, goes to center screen, delivers a line of dialogue, then exits screen right foreground, the assistant would draw three positions on the layout sketch. One would be the size and position of the character entering, another would indicate where the figure was during the dialogue, a third would show the increase in size during the exit. Thus on one piece of paper the background artist has all the information needed to control the contrast between the animation and the background.

Every scene must have a path-of-action drawing. On a long project, the finished scenes are returned to the camera department and reshot. When they come back from the lab they replace the rough animation in the pencil-test reel.

In television spot production, this step is often omitted, or the animation may have been done originally in the cleaned up mode.

## Tape or Film

While many studios are still photographing pencil tests on film, some studios are taking advantage of shooting on tape.

The greatest gain with tape is the fact that the picture can be seen immediately. Film at best has to be processed overnight in the lab.

Often an animator may be undecided about the speed of an action. With tape the section of animation in question can be seen in a few minutes, and a decision made quickly.

# 18

## Backgrounds

Very often when producing television commercials, there is a need to display the product—a box, can, or jar—in conjunction with the animation. This may involve dozens of cels with a character handling the product. Usually, it is too complicated to attempt a drawn replica, so it must be reproduced by some other process.

One widely used method is by making C prints. These are photographic prints whose main virtue is that they are fairly inexpensive. However, the color often only vaguely resembles the colors used on the product container. There is very little possibility of good color correction. Still, if the commercial has a restricted budget, C prints will have to suffice.

A better method is by the use of silk screen. The colors can be completely controlled with this process. Even very small lettering is sharp. Silk-screen prints are much more expensive than C prints.

### Economizing on Cutouts

In order to keep the cost down, one does not order a print for every drawing of the character. For example, if there are going to be 130

*Mongo Makongo* (1987) was written, designed, animated, and directed by Michael Porsch and narrated by Paul Springle.

artists like to do very detailed layouts, which leave very little leeway for the background department.

## Characters and Action Are Number One

One thing is vital, no matter how interesting the suggestions of the background artist are, they must never in any way steal the scene from the characters. Nor should the palette used for the backgrounds conflict with the colors used for the characters. The values must also enable the audience to see the characters plainly.

If a picture has both day and night scenes, it is usually impossible to use the same bright colors that were used on the characters in the night scenes as on those in the day shots.

If the colors are too bright, the characters will appear to be lit up inside like jack-o'-lanterns. So a second palette with less brilliance must be devised. Sometimes, another method can be used. The whole film is painted in daytime colors. Then for the night shots, a blue translucent paper or colored cel is pasted to the glass of the platen to give a night effect.

*What on Earth?,* a National
Film Board of Canada
production. Story and design
by Kaj Pindal, animation by
Les Drew and Kaj Pindal.

Just as the composition is subservient to the animation, the background artist should also recognize that this area of production must play a secondary role in the filmmaking process. Nothing must be allowed to attract the attention of the audience away from the action.

## Time: A Determining Factor

One of the things placing a restriction on the background artist is the time factor. Without strict attention to the amount of screen time allotted to a given scene, serious mistakes can be made. For example, a three-foot close-up must use a very simple background. It would not do to clutter the scene with so much detail that the audience can't "read" the scene before it is over. Unconsciously, the audience would resent it, and if it happens often enough, there will be a good deal of irritation, whether or not the audience knows why it is feeling frustrated.

Even if the background in a long shot has a lot of detail, when the camera goes to a close-up, it is not necessary to make an exact replica of all the detail in this enlarged scale. The background should be simplified, and even painted slightly out of focus if the style is realistic.

The layout sketch of the background and the drawing showing the path of action should be carefully checked to see whether any part of the composition has been moved or eradicated because its original position proved to be an obstacle to the animator.

A rendering by Gil Miret of the Paris Opera House for *The Opera Caper*. © 1967 by Famous Studio.

## The Whole Picture

When one background is going to be used in several scenes, it is not enough to check the path-of-action drawing for the original scene. All the action charts should be gathered together before painting the background, and the areas where the characters are going to perform carefully considered in the light of the total information.

There should be a set of characters, fully painted in the values for the bottom level. Each character should be on a separate cel so that the background artist will be able to place it on an area of the finished background to see whether the colors are compatible. In addition, blank cels should be put on top of the setup, equal to the other cel levels that will be used in the scene. This is the only accurate way to test the combination of cels and background.

## Creativity with Backgrounds

In spite of having to take all these precautions, it is possible for the background artist to play a highly creative role in the filmmaking process.

For example, Frédéric Bàck, in his film *Crac!,* the vigorous depiction of a French-Canadian country dance, used vignettes instead of painting his scenes right to the strict limits of the screen. The effect is to remind the audience boldly that it is being entertained by the magic of moving drawings, not pseudo-live actors. His medium was colored crayons on frosted cels, with no attempt to delineate the characters with neatly filled-in areas of flat color. This lack of obeisance to edges, in both the screen area and the coloring of the characters, added a freedom, a wildness to the graphics, which echoed the gaiety and sense of abandon in the dancers and the music.

Art Heineman, working with me at the Lantz studio, used cutout bits of colored paper in a manner that would have delighted Matisse. In *The Greatest Man in Siam,* a jazz film, and *Ski for Two,* a Woody Woodpecker cartoon, Heineman used paper instead of paint to construct some dazzlingly brilliant backgrounds whose flat surfaces blended honestly with the flat color areas of the cels.

Gil Miret rendered the backgrounds for *My Daddy the Astronaut* with children's crayons, fully in keeping with the characters he had designed. Instead of the usual ink and paint on cels, the actual animation was colored by crayons, then cut out and mounted on cels. These

A scene from *My Daddy the Astronaut,* drawn by Gil Miret, written by J. Szabor and Shamus Culhane, animated by Al Eugster. © 1967 by Famous Studio.

paper drawings had a feeling of oneness with the backgrounds that could not have been achieved by painted cels.

Cliff Roberts, also working at Famous studio on the same series of films, using the drawing techniques of a small child, chose to make his backgrounds for *The Stuck-Up Wolf* resemble finger painting. The resulting crude backgrounds matched perfectly the childish-looking animation of Red Riding Hood and the Wolf.

While these examples of techniques are unusual, they all have one virtue in common; they are perfectly compatible with the story content in each case. Never use a technique just because it is novel. There should be a valid reason why one approach is better than another.

## Some Cautions

A few precautionary measures are worth mentioning at this point. When using pastels on a background, it is necessary to protect the surface by pasting a blank cel over it. Otherwise, as the camera operator changes cels, the static electricity will remove grains of pastel each time.

It is not necessary to use very heavy paper for the backgrounds, even when applying watercolor in copious washes. However, in order to

Grandma and bedroom design for *The Stuck-Up Wolf* by Cliff Roberts, written and directed by Shamus Culhane. © 1967 by Famous Studio.

prevent buckling or curling, it is best to stretch the paper before beginning to paint.

This is done by thoroughly wetting down the paper, then blotting off the excess, placing it on a flat surface and pasting it down with brown gummed-paper tape along each edge. After it dries, the paper will lie perfectly flat no matter how much water is used in the washes.

Never store finished backgrounds in rolls, even if they are pans five fields long. Keep them flat, preferably in a cabinet similar to an army map chest of drawers.

A final word about color. Avoid a monotonous use of hot or cold color. Do look for an opportunity to play one against the other. The juxtaposition of colors can be just as satisfying to the audience as the radical changes of composition.

# 19

## The Skilled Noncreative Jobs

There are a number of operations in the making of an animated film that are crucial to the final result but that require minimum creativity. They do demand, however, skill, patience, and care.

### The Planner's Role

While the backgrounds are being rendered, the animated drawings go to the planner. Using a very exact tracing of the layout, the planner not only makes a dry run of the entire scene, checking the accuracy of the pan moves, looking for the missing parts of drawings, but also combining characters on one cel where it is feasible. The drawings are matched to the layout to ensure proper registry, and once again the exposure sheet is scanned for errors.

Finally the scene is ready for inking or Xerox.

### Choosing and Preparing the Cels

There is no such thing as a completely transparent cell; they all have a distinct tone. This is why most studios have a limit of five cel levels to a scene. Four is better yet because the gray tone dulls the colors in the backgrounds. It is advisable to buy cels from an art store rather than save money buying directly from a factory. Cels can be purchased already cut to size and punched. Of course, it is cheaper to buy by the roll, cut your own sizes, and punch the holes yourself if you are intent on saving money.

In addition, there are tinted cels for special effects, and frosted cels that the animator can draw on with a litho pencil or colored pencils. This omits the inking process altogether. However, the frosted cels cannot be used for more than one level without a considerable loss of definition in the bottom level unless the frost is cleared off the cel after the drawing. Always order a thickness of .005. Thicker cells will increase the gray tone, and thinner cells will buckle too easily. Also be aware that some cels are more transparent than others. The most satisfactory seem to be the ones with a slightly bluish tint. One-field cels are ten by twelve inches.

A cel may be greasy and refuse the ink. The best cure for that is a pounce made of cheesecloth containing cornstarch. Dab it on the greasy area and carefully wipe it clean with a very soft cloth. Cels scratch easily, so handle them with care and be sure to wear clean white-cotton gloves at all times.

## Xerox Versus Inking

The animation may be Xeroxed onto cels, with the advantage that the result is an exact replica of the drawing. However, Xerox lacks the clean line made by a pen. The animator must be careful to draw enclosed color areas if the drawings are to be Xeroxed, because any roughly drawn lines cannot be cleaned up as they can during inking.

The disadvantage of inking is that it is a tracing, with the inevitable loss of spontaneous feeling in the process. A careless or lackluster inking job can ruin subtle drawing. For example, if the pupil of an eye is not traced very carefully, the axis may shift, changing the expression altogether.

On the other hand, a good inker can make the drawing neater, and, using thick and thin lines, give it a certain flair it may have lacked. In this approach, either a Crow-quill or a Gilliot #290 nib will work very well. When the line is going to be all the same consistency, a mechanical pen is best.

Not every ink will adhere to cels. There are special drawing inks made especially for use on cels. Don't keep a bottle of ink for two years and expect it to be usable. It may seem to be okay but may scale off later. If the cel has already been painted, repairing ink lines is a messy job at best, because the paint, being opaque, will prevent the inker from directly retracing the drawing, and will require a good deal of guessing.

## Inking in Color

Besides inking or Xeroxing in black line, there is a technique called self-line. Any of the Cartoon Color Cel-Vinyl colors can be diluted with water, or Transparent Base can be mixed with small amounts of Cel-Vinyl color, ink, or dyes to outline areas to be painted with opaque color. Since both the ink and the color area match, there appears to be no outline.

Very often, several lines of colored inks are used on the same cel to give a very delicate effect that is impossible to achieve when using an overall black outline.

Another use for diluted color is with Cel-Vinyl Transparent Base. This is a transparent medium. By adding small amounts of Cel-Vinyl, colored or black ink, or dyes to the Base, one can paint a semitransparent area for shadows or special effects. I would not recommend using this mixture on large areas. A more satisfactory large shadow is made using the technique of shooting the shadow and the artwork a certain percentage of exposure, removing the shadow and reshooting to make the combined shot 100-percent exposure.

Various gray and colored inks can be used in Xerox machines. Incidentally, if cels are going to be Xeroxed, the machine requires a special adjustment of the heating element. Normally, it is too hot for cels. If they are run through the machine, they will emerge wrinkled and useless. So do not count on going into a stationery store to use their Xerox machine.

Cel-Vinyl colors are not paint as are poster colors or oil paints. They are a kind of plastic and therefore do not brush on the same way. The best way to paint the back of a cel is to use the biggest brush possible, take up a large brushful of color, and plop it into the middle of the area being colored. Then push the puddle toward the edges, always being sure that there is ample color being moved around. If there is too meager a brushful, the brushstrokes will show up and the area will have to be repainted.

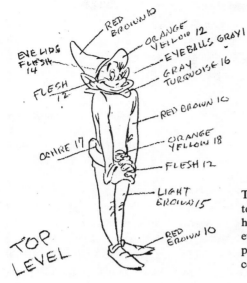

This is a color model for the top-level cels. Each level should have a separate color model for every character, so that the possibility of making a mistake in coloring is minimized.

When painting cels for a matte job, it is most important to make sure that there are no pinholes left because the whole surface hasn't been completely covered. Many studios make sure of good coverage by adding a second coat of white over the original color so that there is no possibility of leaving a pinhole, which would allow the bottom light to shine through.

## Avoid Using the Wrong Colors

One of the most exasperating retakes occurs when the painter confuses the palette of one cel level for another. The end result is a sudden flash as the character becomes too light or too dark. This means that the whole area affected has to be reinked or Xeroxed over again, then painted in the correct color. You can be sure that there will be no profit from this particular section of the picture. It will be eaten up by this absolutely unnecessary retake.

How does one avoid it? The answer is laughably simple. As soon as one level of a character is painted, all the jars of paint involved should have their lids screwed down and the entire batch of paint put into an inactive area. It sounds as if any dolt should be able to accomplish this precaution. Yet this is the most common error in animation production. Why?

For *My Daddy the Astronaut,*
the drawings were colored
with inks, then the characters
cut out and mounted on cels.
Designed by Gil Miret.
© 1967 by Famous Studio.

The answer is that painting is without a doubt the most boring job in an animation studio. People suffer from tedium and get careless. The way to avoid these stupid errors is to inaugurate a system, a ritual of disposal after each level is painted. There should be a space for jars not in use, nowhere near the jars about to be opened for the next cel level. These jars should be opened while reading off the palette list, not unlike a pilot reciting a takeoff ritual. Never use paint-spattered gloves. The spots of dried color become very hard and the paint can scratch the cels.

Cel-Vinyl can turn a good brush into a wreck in a very few minutes. When the color dries, it is almost impossible to dilute it with water and clean off the bristles. If several brushes are in use, they should be in water until it is time to employ them. They should be dried off on a clean rag before they are dipped into a paint jar.

## The High Cost of Errors

While I seem to be going on and on about the least important job in the production process, it is for a good reason. The salary is the lowest on the job scale but the work is fraught with the possibility of making the most expensive retakes, usually at the last minute. This means that the error is often repaired on an overtime basis, losing the company not only the profit on this portion of the picture but a part of the overhead, as well.

The ink and paint supervisor is, of course, held accountable for errors of this nature. The crew has to be really convinced of the importance of ritual and order, coupled with a fanatical devotion to neatness. It is up to the department head to instill these virtues in everybody in the section. Anybody who refuses to conform should be laid off before some horrendous disaster occurs, such as a missed air date and the subsequent loss of an account. It isn't just the financial damage to assay, the loss of integrity and reputation in the business must go into the balance, as well.

It is astonishing that we have so much oil in the skin of our fingers, but even more astonishing is the ease with which it is transferred to cels. If they are not carefully cleaned off, they photograph as a light area. So it is vital that everybody handling cels wears clean white gloves at all times.

After a scene is inked and painted, it must be cleaned—cel by cel—a dull job but very necessary because every scene ends up with several cels spattered by ink or paint. These spots should not be scratched off but cleaned instead by dousing the area with solvent used for cleaning brushes or water.

The best way to polish cels is to cover a board with black velvet. Each cel is placed on this surface and blemishes of any kind will show up. The polishing is done with a very soft cloth. Very vigorous rubbing will cause the cel to build up static electricity, the bane of every camera operator. So the cloth should stroke the cel fairly slowly. This will disperse the dust without causing static.

## Final Checking

The next operation is final checking. In effect, it is a dry run on the function of the camera operator. The checker looks for spots the cel polisher missed; areas that have been painted with an incorrect color; registration, where the art work is matched to some point in the background; the instructions for pans. The sum total of all the moves is recomputed to see that the pan ends up at the stop mark. Also, whether the field sizes are correctly indicated must be checked.

Reading the exposure sheet, the checker puts down each combination of cels that the animator has called for, to make sure that they match up properly. It is a highly responsible job, because if an error gets by the checker, it will be photographed and a negative and print struck off at the lab. All this constitutes a large part of the total production cost of a given scene.

## Camera Work

Being an animation camera operator has none of the excitement inherent in the job of the live-action counterpart. It is true that it's necessary to know a good deal about lenses, and the care and maintenance of the equipment, even to the point of being able to make small repairs. But a large part of the work is almost mechanical—putting down one combination of cels after the other, hour after hour. The camera operator has to know how to prepare tests for the laboratory and must be able to discuss the results with the director.

In all labs, the developer begins to grow weaker after a few days of use, and a booster must be added to restore its strength. This is not always a precise operation, although it should be. Sometimes the developer gets too much booster and many feet of negative can be over-developed; too little, and film is going to be underdeveloped. When either of these mishaps occur, the crew makes a hasty adjustment, but the harm has been done. A wise camera operator will try to find out when booster is going to be added to the developer and hold back some of his film for a day or two.

In many ways, the one behind the camera has to be the most patient person in the studio. Animators scribble illegible numbers on the exposure sheets; checkers stack cels out of sequence; at one in the morning, a cel is found to be missing—the list of possible mishaps is endless.

The scenes to be photographed should be prepared in the following manner:

The drawings should be left between each cel and the entire scene placed in a scene folder. This can be as simple as a piece of wrapping paper, but most studios have folders of light cardboard or buckram with instructions printed on them. Notice that there is the production number, title of the picture, scene number, background number, and a list of drawings used from other scenes, if any.

If there are a number of scenes to be shot, they should be stacked with the first scene on top. If the background is for a still scene, it should be placed on top of the cels for that scene, with the requisite number of blank cels called for.

The exception is pan backgrounds and long cels. These should be neatly wrapped together in one package with a stiff piece of cardboard underneath to support them. Never roll up a pan background or long cels. They will curl and become hard to manage under the camera.

## Color Variations

As the dailies come back from the lab, there will be differences in color from scene to scene. This is because the usual procedure is to make what is called *a one-light print.* It is called that because there is no effort made to balance the color. This will be done later.

However, in a reel of animation footage, these color difference should be slight. If there is a radical difference in the scenes, the camera operator should be told to check the negative to decide whether the color balance can be corrected later. If there is any doubt, it is better to reshoot. Having to reshoot later, after the photography is supposed to be finished, could hold up the printing of the entire film.

A few scenes of questionable exposure in a reel are not unusual. But if there are generally erratic swings in the exposure as the reel begins to fill up, get someone else to operate the camera. There is no excuse for making many improper readings of the light meter, because each scene is shot under the same lighting conditions. With poor meter readings, the picture will be more difficult to color balance than it should be.

While the jobs in this chapter have been labeled *noncreative,* it is not meant to be a pejorative term. Most of the skills involved are not easily learned and they are an integral part of the filmmaking process. Of course, when computerized animation has made the cel system a thing of the past, many of these jobs will vanish.

In comparison to the computer, cels are clumsy and even primitive. There is too much dependence on the human factor, and too many mistakes as a result. The computer process of filmmaking is much less fraught with error.

# 20

# Music Recording and Editing

Music is a natural adjunct to animation but it has its pitfalls. A television commercial, a one-minute or thirty-second film, can have a score from start to finish and no harm done. Try the same wall-to-wall technique on a half-hour special, or worse yet, a feature-length animation cartoon, and you have a disaster.

## Musical Overkill

Possibly the worst example of this kind of misfortune is the score for *Raggedy Ann and Andy.* After seeing this feature, try to walk away whistling one tune from the film. One song blurs into the other because there is no letup. End-to-end songs, after a time, cause the ears to reject any more of this noise.

Not only is the audio area affected, the tempi of the songs tie down the action. It is better in longer films to have long periods where there is no music at all, much less songs.

Have the composer avoid using the same tempo for a song and the music that follows it. In other words, if one song is a waltz, the next piece of music should have a radical change in tempo—a mazurka perhaps, something very different.

Keep in mind that to the composer, the graphics of the film are of no interest—it's the sound track that is all-important. So take the suggestions for the music very seriously, but always remember that although the composer wants the music to stand out, the director wants it to be subordinate to the picture.

## Orchestration

This is especially true of the orchestration. The animation is best embellished by a score that has imaginative orchestration. Composers such as Satie have shown that there is such a thing as comic music. It is the juxtaposition of oddball instruments that best reflect the zany qualities of animation.

Watch out for overorchestration. It does not take four English horns, a tuba, and a bank of violins to accompany a character across a room, unless the character is an elephant.

Find the orchestration that best suits the animation. At the Famous studio, directing *My Daddy The Astronaut,* a film that was drawn in the manner of a five-year-old child, I dismissed the idea of the usual squad of twenty musicians and instead elected to use the finest harmonica player in New York. He almost had a fit when I asked him to blow some clinkers in the score because I wanted the harmonica to sound as if it was being played by a rank amateur. The score was perfect. Nobody even noticed it because it blended in with the story idea.

Darrell Calker, music composer at the Walter Lantz studio during a period when we were turning out very fine jazz films, once told me about a device he had used to get a more tinny effect for boogie-woogie. He put pieces of track from a toy railroad on the strings of a piano. When the keys were struck, the track ties reverberated in a very satisfactory exaggeration of a battered upright piano. That's what I call inspired orchestration.

## Recording the Music

During the recording of the music for a cartoon, the director sits in the control booth next to the sound technician. This recording is only done after all the color dailies have been approved and the last pencil test removed from the reel.

Darrell Calker had a very interesting way of handling his recording.

He put together all the wind and percussion instruments in one session. Then he recorded all the strings and the piano together in a separate recording. Later, this was invaluable to the mixer because he could control each class of instrument without losing the value of the other.

## The Director's Role

While the music director is conducting, the director is reading the action on the bar sheet. It is the first time the director hears the full orchestration. Before this, there has been a piano version of the music, but this does not have the emphasis of a full-scale recording. It is the director's job to judge whether or not the score reflects and interprets the action on the bar sheet.

If, in his or her opinion it does not, there is a quick conference between the director and the conductor/composer. Usually, something can be contrived on the spot: adding more instruments to give more weight to the score; quickening or slowing down the tempi; or making the melodic line more apparent. The conductor is trained to make these modifications there and then.

## Synchronizing Music and Animation

In the beginning of sound films, the biggest problem was to find some way in which to make the musicians play in sync with the completed animation. Walt Disney tried to solve this problem by projecting a piece of blank film with holes punched in the center corresponding to the tempo on the bar sheets. The musicians went crazy trying to read the music, watch the conductor, and look at the screen.

Some genius came up with the idea of the click track. An electronic mechanism called a click box emits a series of clicks that can be quickened or slowed down by the conductor. Each musician is given a headset with one earphone. This way, he can hear both the clicks and the conductor. The conductor selects whichever click is indicated on the bar sheet, and since he also wears an earphone, he conducts the orchestra in perfect sync.

The musical score is not usually recorded in sequence. The conductor chooses the bits and pieces of the score that will be recorded with the full orchestra. When these are finished, as many musicians as possible are dismissed, because there is no reason to keep them when their stint is finished. Everybody, even the conductor, has to keep an eye on the budget at all times.

## What to Avoid

There are some things to avoid in using music in a cartoon. It sounds very mechanical if the music is always cut in exactly at the start of a scene. If the music has a vamp, or grace notes, it is good to have them start in the previous shot and bring in the body of the music in sync with the first frame of the scene.

Often some definite piece of action can be used to cue in a bit of music. It should be a very definite action that brings in a new mood or finishes one off. For example, Skinny is hammering a nail. There are only sound effects in the scene until he finishes. When he walks off in triumph, one could start music.

Songs are usually prerecorded with a simple piano orchestration, so when the music is being recorded, be sure that there are no wild swings in sound levels in the orchestration because they will prove to be a bother during the mix. It is important that the music never obscures the singing. The best examples of beautiful control over singing and orchestration are in the score for *Snow White and the Seven Dwarfs*. However, almost any Disney film will be a masterful example of sound control.

In assembling the music for the mix, always jiggle the sync a few frames, because there is always the possibility, even with the click track, that a better sync can be achieved. As in the relationship of gestures to mouth action, there are no hard-and-fast rules to go by in relating music to action. It is wiser to sync up the music to the dailies, rather than against pencil tests, because the work print may contain changes that were an improvement on the pencil test but possibly were un-recorded on the bar sheet—despite the fact that assistant directors are not supposed to make mistakes!

If you have to use library music, you may find to your astonishment that because you used bar sheets, many accents in the music are in perfect sync to your animation. This is because most library music is recorded to a steady beat and you happened to choose the same tempo for your animation.

If you did not use bar sheets, the chances are that the music will just be general, with an accidental sync here and there.

There is a tendency these days to call the interpretation of the action by the music," Mickey Mousing." It is a term of derision, but I notice that is usually said by a composer who wouldn't know how to go about creating such a score. While doing a whole cartoon with the action matching the music note for note would be mechanical and annoying, if there is a tasteful mix of generalized themes and note-for-note music, the score is bound to be pleasing to the audience.

I consider the score for an animated cartoon very much like the music for ballet, in that some of the dancer's steps and body movements follow the music note for note and others do not. It's the same principle.

## Including Sound Effects

If there are any sound effects that closely follow the action, they have been duly analyzed from the beginning of the track assembly, and cut into the sound track for the pencil-test reel. Now the editor adds the music and the incidental sound effects.

It is important at this point that the director and the editor look for places where the music and sound effects conflict. Sometimes, this can be solved by shifting the music a few exposures or even by cutting out a phrase or a few notes.

## Editing the Music

When music is composed especially for a film, there is a modicum of snipping here and there, or maybe none at all. On the other hand, if you are using library music, the editor may have to do quite a bit of cutting to shape the music into usable form for your film. If the editor isn't really conversant with music, I suggest that, rather than butcher your track, you find a music editor. Editing music is a specialty, and often a very delicate job, where a good ear and a knowledge of the various ways of cutting and butting themes together are an absolute necessity. So if you anticipate having to do a good deal of cutting and matching, use a music editor.

## Mixer's Cue Sheets

After the music and all the sound effects have been cut into various reels, the editor is ready to prepare *cue sheets* for the mixer. Very often the sound at this point consists of two reels of dialogue, two reels of music, and two of sound effects. Sometimes there are loops that are not on reels. For example, there might be a loop of insect sounds, such as locusts, that run through a long section of the picture. Instead of using a great big reel of this sound, it is, in effect, put on a cycle. The sound of a motor running would again be a loop.

The cue sheet is a sheaf of pages diagramming when and where certain sections of the track are going to be recorded. This is so that the mixer can prepare the volume levels to suit this particular material. There should be adequate space around the instructions for the mixer to write notes about certain adjustments to be made on the controls as the picture progresses.

# 21

## Winding Up the Picture:
## The Mix

If supervising a mix is a new experience, or you are having to mix in a strange town, I would advise you to make a tour of the sound facilities before making a decision. A really fanatical sound engineer running a small setup might be very enthusiastic but probably does not have the equipment available in a large studio. Also, there usually would not be a large library of sound effects. Big sound studios keep a large supply on hand. When the director or a client gets a sudden idea that it would be good to add a duck squawk or a tire screech to the track, the mixer can supply the sound effect immediately; that is not a time to think about going out to buy an effect. Most studios supply these additional effects gratis; others charge a small fee.

It is obvious that the editor who assembled the tracks should be at the mix. Don't try to save money by leaving him or her out of the operation. In addition to being ready to quickly splice in an additional sound effect, someone is available if a splice parts during the projection of the work print. The editor also can help if the mixer is puzzled by a notation on the cue sheet. Just as important is to have one more trained ear ready to detect a problem in the mix.

In the early days of sound recording on film, the track had to be recorded perfectly. If a mistake occurred, the whole reel would have to be redone. In addition, the film had to be sent to a lab and several days passed before a print of the track was available. If a mistake was then discovered, either it had to be accepted or the recording done over.

The use of tape dispensed with the delay of having to develop the track. The big advantage, however, is that when a mistake occurs, the mixer can roll back the reels to an appropriate place and do just that part over again.

It is difficult to make a prognostication about the amount of time a recording should take. It depends on whether the director can explain to the mixer exactly what is wanted and on how adept the mixer is at carrying out orders and evaluating the volume of the different tracks. The balance between reels may be very complex, forcing the mixer to do some hasty juggling during a recording.

A client may be present who has ideas to try out, as well. Sometimes these ideas are useful, but all these factors take up time and time costs money.

From my own experience, I believe I can supervise the recording of the mix of a television spot and finish in less than two hours. A five-minute film would take me three hours, and a half-hour special about four to five hours. This scheduling may seem odd to the reader, but long films sometimes have stretches where there is only dialogue or music, whereas short films may have many quick changes of volume.

Whatever amount of time you choose to schedule, ask for another hour to be held in abeyance. Most sound-studio managers are willing to do that, and, if the extra hour is not used, there is no charge.

I am inclined not to invite a composer to a mix. They almost invariably want their music louder. If, for some reason, the director cannot be present, put the recording in the hands of the editor and the mixer. Let them collaborate. Never include the composer!

It is astounding to listen to the number of bad tracks in motion picture theaters and on television. Music is often too loud, obliterating the lyrics; the same thing happens to dialogue in many cases. The director has to be sure not to listen to the mix with a jaded ear. After all, most of the reels have been heard time after time during the course of the work. It is easy to miss some problem because of that. One must try to spend these few hours listening to the track as if it was all new material. Learn to listen like an audience.

Aside from the proper balance between reels, watch for the sudden sharp sound that muffles an important word in a sentence. Also listen for dialogue that lessens in volume near the end of a sentence, then picks up again at the beginning of the next. This should have been caught during the voice recording, but if it wasn't, it certainly should be corrected now.

A mixer must have all the instincts of an orchestra conductor in order to keep a proper balance of dialogue, lyrics, music, and sound effects.

Watching the mixer work, you begin to realize that mixing is really an art requiring a quick mind, a good ear, and very nimble fingers. As in any other job, there are poor mixers, some who are pretty good, and a few who are the leaders in their field. If you are lucky enough to happen upon one of the last, use him or her on every picture.

There is a tendency in American business to keep looking for greener pastures. Superb work is no guarantee of continued employment. In my opinion, this is a sign of insecurity, because many executives hire only people who seem to know less than they do. It may help to bolster up the self-esteem, but it is a stupid way to run a business.

I agree with Walt Disney's policy of hiring the best possible talent in every aspect of filmmaking. This, of course, meant that they were all better at their jobs than he could ever have been. So the continuing improvement of the Disney films was no accident. Walt didn't do it himself but he hired the people who could do it, and many of these people worked at the studio their entire creative lives.

## Room Tone

It is not true that the spaces between sounds are absolutely silent. Each room has its own tone. Never leave a recording without taking several minutes of *room tone*. The editor uses this recording as a filler when extending space between takes. Blank virgin tape or film would cause there to be a perceptible difference between the recorded sound, with its background of room tone, and the blank tape or film.

While you are all intently listening to the tracks, your trusty assistant director is busily taking notes. Each time the recording is stopped, the mixer calls a new take number into the mike before it resumes. In this way, each take is easily identified. The assistant director is making notes on a ruled pad—notes such as, "take 34, good until 375, then cut in latter half of take 32, starting with trumpet in bar 459." There will be notes on every take, some just reading "NG," meaning no good. Others will be starred, meaning the best take in everybody's opinion.

## Editing the Sound Take

When the recording is over, the tape is edited down to the good takes, carefully following the notes. They have to be clear and concise. This is no time to have to read hasty scribbles. The director should *never* try to make notes and listen to the tracks being recorded at the same time. They are two different kinds of functions and it is impossible to do both well simultaneously. If you do not have an assistant present for note taking, use the editor.

Of course, all the outtakes will be carefully labeled and filed by the editor. Nothing is thrown out until the picture is approved, even if some are obviously trash. Some unforeseen catastrophe may happen and suddenly the trash becomes a lifesaver.

My practice is to tell everybody to keep all notes, discarded drawings, exposure sheets, animation that has been the victim of sweatbox changes, and everything that has to do with the film, until the approval of the answer print.

## Titles

Somewhere about this point, your film may need titles. The film business is going through a bad time of title designing right now. At least half of the superimposed lettering over an art or live-action background is unreadable.

Another boner is the scale. Often the screen is cluttered with lettering that is too small, especially if it is a roll-up title working over a live-action background.

Lettering, if the film is going to appear on television, should be sans serif. The screen is still so coarse that a serif seems to disappear, or at best, be seen only vaguely. A serif is supposed to give the end of a stroke of a letter a clean-cut finish. If it can't do that, it ceases to have any function. I believe a good strong modern sans-serif style of lettering is best. Forget Old English, Gothic, and Script. They belong solely on the motion-picture screen. Remember that television has about the same reproduction quality as a newspaper.

As for readability, nothing can beat the stark, clean quality of white lettering over fairly dark backgrounds. This holds for live-action backgrounds, as well, because even on a moving background, if for an instant there is a patch of what seems to be white behind the lettering, the letters will usually show up anyway. There is no true pure white in live action, not as white as white paint.

The timing for a title is loosely about 24 exposures of 35 mm film a word. If the title is used with a musical theme, this timing may have to be adjusted, made longer perhaps, but never shorter. Two or three particles of speech in one sentence may be lumped together and counted as a word.

Of course, these instructions will not hold for those interminable lists of credits that name the gofer, the head trucker's assistant, and the assistant accountant for the client. Give them a cursory swipe at screen time and make no effort to allow the audience to read the names of these noncreative people. Concentrate instead on the names of people who made a creative contribution to the film.

## Opticals

Another job which is often done only at the last minute is the opticals—the special visual effects. In theatrical shorts, they were almost never used because they are expensive and time-consuming. One quickly learns about the myriad possibilities of the optical printer in the field of television commercials. Advertisers know that the audience likes to look at special effects.

One can buy a chart of the different wipes and other effects from a film supply house. An optical printer is really a camera that can do freeze frames, fades and dissolves, various split screens, and skip frames. It can superimpose lettering, slow action down by shooting every frame twice, rotate shots instead of cutting, and create multiexposure scenes.

It can do all these things because it is facing a projector mounted horizontally. The operator can move in to shoot only part of the film that is being projected. With the current interest in fantasy films, an animation house should have a special-effects expert who can create on both the animation camera and the optical printer.

## Matching Work Print and Negative

During the entire process of making the picture, the editor has been receiving negative rolls as well as the positive prints he has been using to supplant scenes in the pencil-test reel. These have been carefully stored away. Now that it is time to match the work-print reel with the negative, it may be that you have to hire another specialist, a *negative matcher.*

Each foot of film has a number for quick identification, and the negative matcher's job is to match the numbers on the positive work reel with negative shots, until the entire film has a complete negative track and picture ready for printing.

Now it may be that your editor announces that he or she can cut negative as well as anybody. Listen with caution and weigh the possibilities. The negative is the sum total of all the studio people's efforts. It must be assembled by an expert so that it not only matches the work reel but has perfect splices and has garnered no scratches in the editing process.

This state of perfection can only be attained by having everything around the cutting equipment spotlessly clean, and with the editor wearing immaculate white-cotton gloves at all times. If the editor isn't working under these strict conditions, take the job away and find a good negative cutter who has made this work a specialty. As the director, you must do this sort of thing without compunction. The editor may have done a superb job right up to the point of negative cutting. Yet if it now looks as if he or she can't handle this next step and is about to butcher your negative, take that editor off the job without hesitation. Don't have false loyalties. The only real one is to the picture. Everybody else comes second, or even gets fired for incompetence. Some of these actions seem cruel or harsh. So be it. In a few months, people will be looking at your picture. It has your name on it as the responsible party. They might wonder why this or that part of the production is poor. Nobody wants to hear that Joe Schmoh's mother was sick and he made sloppy backgrounds because he was worried; or you kept a new animator on longer than you should have. All this does not go down in the history of this particular film. The only thing that remains is that your credits indicate that you condoned bad work. History is remorseless.

Looking back over long years as an executive, and later as a boss, I can see that my worst weakness was being maudlin. I was a bleeding heart. The very first time I fired somebody is a case in point. I hired this middle-aged retouchman to take on a whole television spot by himself. It was for one of our accounts that gave us all their spot work without our having to bid against other studios.

The spot was a series of still photos of an automobile. They all needed lots of airbrushing, reinforcing of highlights, and in some photos, creating of shadows and designing new backgrounds. The retouch man's desk began to look like a hog wallow. It was strewn with tissue-paper masks, bits of cotton, and bottles of various inks and paints. Suddenly, after weeks, he confessed that he couldn't handle the job. He cost us thousands of dollars in overtime to meet the air date, yet it took me three weeks to get up the nerve to fire him. That's a bleeding heart!

Nobody likes the role of disciplinarian but it is one facet of the director's job.

There are two kinds of mistakes in production. One is simply an error of judgment, such as an animator's making a character overact, or a background artist painting a scene too dark. Errors like this are bound to happen because there are no rules to follow; it is a matter of taste. In a case like this, it would be unjust to take disciplinary action.

## Making Sure

The second type of mistake is very different. Every studio has procedures designed to keep errors down to a minimum. And they are not to be flouted without the knowledge and approval of top management. For example, the head of the ink and paint department decides, without consulting the director, to omit final checking on some scenes because of the deadline. The idea that the normal checking procedure would be too time-consuming seems to make this a good move.

Actually, this is a very ill-advised omission. It is a blatant gamble that there will be no mistakes in these scenes, against the possibility that there is one. If a mistake did then appear in the finished film, the studio would certainly miss the delivery date. It would be impossible to complete a retake with photography, developing, printing, editing, and a possible readjustment of the timing of the answer print. None of these factors would have to be coped with if a mistake was found in final checking. Therefore, it is a very unintelligent gamble.

This kind of Hairbreath Harry risk should only lie within the province of the director and producer. At least they will be able to evaluate the gamble properly, weighing every factor and not just being concerned with one procedure.

An independent move of this type rates at the minimum a good chewing out, perhaps even the loss of the job if it risks losing an account.

I might add that nothing is so damaging to the morale of the crew as having to cope with an executive who will not admit to a mistake, looking instead for a scapegoat. On the other hand, freely admitting to an error makes for a good feeling all around.

I have always cheerfully made it a point to explain to my top executives just how I made a particular mistake and how it might have been avoided. Since I believe very strongly in a well-educated staff, we very often would go into a searching discussion of the principles involved. My executives had the same feeling about admitting to errors, so we never had any finger pointing. Instead, we brought down the percentage of errors in our production to an incredible low by devising a set of systematic safety checks, which came about as a result of our lengthy discussions.

The person who has an obsessive need to continue to revise and improve work long after the production money has been spent is fundamentally insecure. There is a confusion between the state of the work and the person's image, which makes it impossible to release the material until it has reached some fancied peak of perfection or has forcibly been taken away.

Insistence on the part of management for the work to be finished within the budget allocated and on the scheduled completion date will often call forth a rebellion against what is interpreted as a Philistine attitude.

The most sensible thing to do in such a case is to look at the neurosis, not the person's talent. Appeals to logic will be fruitless. The most important thing to remember is that such things as profit and overhead have no weight in this situation. Assuaging the obsession is the only thing that matters to the budget buster. Even getting fired will not enable a person with such a fixation to change. The only sensible move is to seek psychiatric care.

It is all very well to be sympathetic and understanding, but budget busters are potential studio wreckers. My advice is to let the person go as soon as the symptoms are recognized, before more damage is done. This in spite of the fact that these people often have a very high degree of creativity. The monetary loss, the irritation at the dislocation of schedules, and the fact that this kind of neurotic has an uncanny ability to foment rebellion against authority, all add up to one thing . . . dismissal.

The only mitigating circumstance would be if the person recognized at last that there was a need for professional help on an ongoing basis several times a week. Even so, do not expect a drastic improvement to occur very quickly.

## Film

Whenever possible, a picture should be photographed in 35 mm, even when the prints are going to be 16 mm. There is much more latitude in balancing color in 35mm, and very few people will assay opticals in a 16mm-animation camera because of the comparative crudity of the sprocket system that advances the film. Added to that, the "checkerboard" technique of editing is a clumsy nuisance compared to 35mm editing. So start with a 35mm negative whenever possible. The additional expense is well worth it in the final result.

Use the best lab you can find, even if it means mailing your film. If possible, establish a line of credit so that you will not have to take cash every time you make a pickup in the shipping room.

Color film is so widely used today that many labs do not develop black-and-white film at all. Those that do often hold all the film until there is a suitable amount to tool up for developing. So if you are shooting in black and white, you may have to wait several days, or even a week, before the lab has acquired sufficient footage to process.

Color film delivered before the end of the workday is usually processed that night, and a negative and print will be ready the next morning. Just as a precaution, never arrange for a client to screen the material the same day it is picked up. There are too many variables.

The lab rarely has a breakdown but when it does, a certain amount of footage is going to be ruined; the camera operator may have made a mistake; the stock may have been defective. So give yourself a day of grace before showing the work to the client. That way, there is time to make small retakes and still present acceptable work on schedule.

## Timing

Understand that all the film in the work print is what is called a one-light print. There has been no attempt to balance the color. Now the negative goes into the hands of a timer, whose job is to evaluate the shots in a negative and decide on the exposure so that the color is consistent. When the work is completed, a print is struck off, showing the result of these computations. For some baffling reason, this is called an "answer print."

It is a good idea to loan the timer a set of cels for comparison with what the original color was, so that the color can be balanced accordingly. However, if the first print does not meet with your approval, say so and make it stick. Of course you must have some solid tangible reasons why the print is being rejected. Theoretically, timing an animated cartoon should be comparatively easy because everything is shot under the same lighting conditions, but for some arcane reason, there are timers who make a big job out of it.

The *Noah* trilogy featured an orange-yellow lion. On one particular picture the color looked fine even in the dailies. It was very consistent. The first answer print was a puzzle. The lion ranged from lemon-yellow to orange-red. When I rejected the print, the timer was incensed. He swore that this was the best he could get out of our negative. He rejected the fact that the work print had excellent balance, with just an inaudible mumble.

The second answer print was no better. When the third print still showed no improvement, I began to question him. Just how was he going about balancing this film? He replied querulously that he was balancing the backgrounds!

The next timer gave me a satisfactory answer print on his first try.

Never use your original material for making a batch of prints. It is enough of a risk to use the precious negative for making answer prints. The actual printing of a print order is made by using a composite negative, which is the graphics plus a synchronized sound track.

## Judicious Cutting

Watch out for oddball problems such as the fact that the three major networks have different specifications for their pictures. Having made one of the *Noah* trilogy specials for Westfall Productions, using NBC guidelines, I was happily waiting for the picture to be scheduled.

Without my being aware of it, Westfall switched to ABC. They were told that the film was a minute too long, but not to be concerned. The ABC film department would edit the picture. Those clods certainly did.

The core of the story was the ending. The lion for most of the picture was just a henpecked Klutz. When Noah announced that there was going to be an election to see who was to become the King of Beasts, the crocodile and the elephant both made impassioned electioneering speeches.

But when the ark caught fire, they both gave way to panic. It was the lion who dashed into the smoke and flame and rescued Noah. Then when he discovered that the crocodile's two kids were trapped in the hold, he returned to the inferno. With a series of gymnastics à la Doug Fairbanks, the lion rescued the babies and came out of the ark safely. He was elected the King by acclamation.

When I saw the picture on television, the idiots had cut out the entire rescue. The Lion just dashed into the smoke and out again, leaving the audience to wonder what all the animals were shouting about. Maybe I'm being paranoic, but an industrial spy could not have done a better job of sabotaging my picture.

We had the same difficulty with our first picture, *Noah's Animals.* In this case, I was told that we had to cut a minute and fifteen seconds out of the film. It was very easy to do. I just sat down with the bar sheets and measured various parts of the film, looking for a big chop. It is hopeless to try to nibble at five feet here and ten there in a situation such as this.

It must have looked like a miracle when I strolled nonchalantly into the cutting room, ran the reel down to a song, marked the start for a cut, and indicated another cut at the finish. Total footage: one minute, fifteen seconds!

Again, let me advise you never to be a termite in a such a predicament. Don't nibble. Be a butcher with a big cleaver. If possible, make one big chop. Surprisingly enough, very often the splice can be made without any further tailoring. Just find the song, the unimportant incident that can be excised without weakening the story.

# 22

## Photographing a Storyboard Reel

When the time comes that you feel that your clock story is finished, I would let it rest for a week. Then look it over to be sure that you have no weak spots. It is your best effort. After that, it's time to put information for the camera on exposure sheets. Be sure to buy half again as many sheets as you think you will need. As you know, you can buy exposure sheets in an animation-supply store. Start as I have taught you with the end sequence. Every drawing should be clearly marked with the sequence letter, scene number, and drawing number. Be sure this information is not in the camera area but that it is in the same place on every drawing. Write so that it is easily read without having to peer. Don't forget that you will be putting dial numbers on the scenes, whether you shoot the film yourself or it is done professionally.

### Timing the Drawings

Your big problem is going to be how to devise a way to find out how long each drawing should be on the screen. One way would be to use a stopwatch, but a better approach might be to find out how long twelve exposures are. Try humming a march and beating time. You will find that march time is two beats of twelve exposures each. You can find out how long eight exposures are by humming a waltz. Three beats in waltz time are eight exposures apiece. Remember that a second is three eight-exposure beats, or two twelves.

If you have a stopwatch, so much the better. You can time the tempo you are humming against the watch. Do it until you can knock off a waltz or march tempo as a veteran conductor would. Every time you begin to work, check your tempo against a watch, just to warm up.

Start by putting the first scene number and the sequence letter in the camera column with an arrow pointing to the first exposure. Obviously, you are going to use only one column through the picture. If the scene has more than one drawing, spread them out and look at them carefully. Take your stopwatch and click it on as you start looking at the drawings, as if you never saw them before. When you have examined the last drawing, stop the watch. Now see how many seconds it took you overall. Are some drawings more complicated than others? Are there drawings that are just transitional? Maybe you will want to time some drawings individually. However you break up the time, it should only add up to the total time that it took you to look at the scene in the first place. If it is a long scene, time the drawings in batches.

## Choosing a Photographer

Before you begin, it would be best to know how this job is going to be photographed: by a professional animation camera operator; by you; or by a crew of willing friends?

If it is a professional, there will be no problems, because you know how to write an exposure sheet properly. Be prepared to spend a sizable bit of money. The rates have been soaring. Right now, you will be hard put to have your film photographed for less than fifty dollars an hour.

Before you agree to start the photography, take some of the story sketches to the shop and get an estimate based on the number of drawings in your story. Most camera operators will allow you to act as assistant, preparing the next scenes as a sequence is being photographed, putting away the drawings that have been shot. All this will serve to cut down your final bill. Acting as assistant has the added advantage of letting you be sure that the camera operator is working on your picture and not not talking to another client on the phone for half an hour. The big advantage of having a professional job is that you can have trucks, wipes, dissolves, and fades, all of which will certainly enhance the appearance of your film.

Remember, if you shoot in 35mm, you will have to order 16mm prints. Most agencies and studios use 16mm projection. Usually in a big ad agency, projection has to be scheduled in advance, so getting an interview and a screening at the same time is not easy. You may be asked to leave your film, which is probably the weakest way to have an interview because you will not be at the screening to answer any questions about your work. At some point, you will want to transfer your film to a video cassette. It is much easier to get an interview and a screening with a cassette.

## Acting as Your Own Photographer

If this is going to be an amateur effort, beg, borrow, or steal a Bolex camera with a cable release to shoot single exposures. If you shoot by hand, you will probably jostle the camera many times, whereas the cable will keep your camera rock-steady. If you are not very familiar with the camera, don't try any technical tricks such as fades, dissolves, or trucks with a *zoom* lens. Keep it simple.

By all means, get a pair of dedicated friends to help you, and you can be sure that the relationship will be sorely tried before the photography is over. It is a boring, tiring job and it will seem interminable, even if you prepare meticulous exposure sheets. I hope you do, because shooting retakes is even more boring.

You will need two floodlights, 150 watts apiece, and some kind of easel to set up the drawings (a child's blackboard might be just right if it is mounted on a table so as to be at a proper height). You will also need a pane of glass larger than the story sketches, which should have the edges covered with Scotch or electrician's tape to protect the worker's hands.

In addition, there should be a back-up board taped down to the easel. The board should be at a slight slant so that the sketches won't fall off. The drill is that the camera operator does nothing but press the plunger one exposure at a time. The camera is mounted on a tripod, which is prevented from moving even slightly by having the legs reinforced by books or other heavy objects. It is aimed slightly downward to match the tilt of the blackboard or whatever you are using to set up the drawings.

One of the assistants does nothing but put the pane of glass down on the sketch every time and take it away after the drawing has been shot. The other assistant picks up the sketch, puts it on a nearby table, and places the next drawing on the easel. The area where the sketch should be placed is indicated by putting a frame of masking tape around the spot.

The camera field should be just inside the black outline around the sketch, so that the line is not being photographed. The camera operator has the exposure sheet and calls out the number of the sketch to the sketch handler. After checking the field, the camera operator starts shooting, counts the exposures from the exposure sheet, and then says, "Cut," at which time the other two assistants dismantle the glass and drawing.

In order to keep an accurate count, I have found it best to have the exposure sheet flat, in a good light, and I actually put a finger marking the exposure being shot, at the same time working the plunger. Cover the ball of your thumb with a strip of tape; otherwise, it will be abraded after a few hours.

Be sure that the whole arrangement of easel, camera, lights, and drawings is not a jerry-built setup so clumsy that it is difficult to move around without knocking into something. Spend some time in devising the proper placement of all the items, and don't start shooting until you know that you have a workable arrangement.

I once worked on a film in an awkward setup and found after a few days that I had burned my ear because I had to stand too near a light when changing drawings. Be sure everybody has working space before you start shooting, and even then look for possible improvements in the setup at the beginning of the shoot.

Try to find a working space where the camera and all the other apparatus can be left untouched until the job is finished, which might be weeks unless the trio can work all day long for perhaps four or five days.

If you can't find help and decide to do the whole job yourself, I can only commiserate. I think St. John the Martyr would back off from this ordeal. But if that's the problem, why, just go ahead and do it.

As a precaution, I would always check the alignment of the drawings in the camera at every new shot, just to be sure that the camera tripod or easel were not inadvertently moved.

To save yourself an editing fee, be sure to have all the scenes shot in their proper order, with no blank exposures in between. That way, when you have completed the photography, you will have a finished picture, except for the *Academy leader,* which you can buy at the lab.

Your clock picture should be shown on a separate reel, with a title and credits. Remember to compute scene length on the basis of 36 exposures per second for 16mm.

On the end title, have your name, address, and telephone number. Then add forty-eight exposures of black leader.

Make another reel of all your walks, runs, and other exercises. Mix them up so that there are animals and elves in an interesting combination, with about 16 black exposures between scenes. Shoot at least 150 exposures of each cycle walk or run. Be sure to have some title such as *Exhibition Reel by . . .* and an end title with name, address, and telephone number. Don't forget the Academy leader.

Buy film cans for your reels and paste your name, address, and telephone number inside on the covers. Also take white tape and put it around the bottoms on the outside. Write your name on them with a heavy Magic Marker. Buy mailing pieces for each can, as well. Reels, cans, and mailing pieces can be purchased at the laboratory.

If you mail a reel, be sure that you check it when it comes back to see that it has been rewound and is in good condition. For that, you will need a pair of rewinds and clamps to secure them to a table. I suggest that you buy a 16mm viewer and a guillotine-type splicer, which uses Mylar tape.

It is also important to have a projector. Possibly you can buy a reconditioned secondhand one. I suggest a self-loading type. If you want to go into making your own sound tracks, you will need a reel-to-reel tape deck, a good microphone, a synchronizer with a sound head for track reading, a tape splicer, and a small viewer. You will need to find a sound studio that transfers quarter-inch tape to optical track.

With this equipment, plus your newly acquired expertise, it will be possible to make animation from script to screen.

# 23

## The Role of the Computer

The word *computer* sends a xenophobic chill through creative workers in cel animation. There is a strong suspicion that computers may take control of the creative process, may even replace it. In the final chapter of my autobiography, *Talking Animals and Other People,* I wrote about my growing presentiment that the computer was going to prove to be the most versatile tool that was ever invented for the artist. Different pictures, more beautiful than we could now imagine, would result.

In rebuttal, I received a chiding letter from one of the foremost directors in the field. How could I, one of the most talented animators in the business, be so misguided as to become enamoured of a machine? It was beyond his understanding. I did not answer this somewhat backhanded compliment. I decided to do that in this book. I think that I can show that I am not a traitor to the Venus Lead Pencil Company, and that computers do not pose a threat to creativity.

While I may do that to my satisfaction, there is no denying the fact that this man, one of our most prestigious directors, is echoing a basic fear that has permeated our profession. There are many creative people who feel that computers are restrictive and stultifying, making the artist the victim rather than the master of sterile, depersonalizing machinery.

Their worries seem to be substantiated by the low level of art that often has been the norm among designers of computer animation. There are too many people involved who, while they may be expert at operating the machinery, have little or no artistic talent. It will be necessary to weed them out and replace them with people who have a special talent in the animation field before the computer can really flourish.

Last year the International Animated Film Society (called ASIFA, an acronym of the international association's French name) put on a screening of art in conjunction with a home-computer group. Each company had an opportunity to show its wares. One after the other, the representatives made drawings appear on their computers' screens. After a while it was obvious that these machines were incapable of creating drawings of professional quality. It was also obvious that none of these people had any talent as draftsmen.

This did not seem to disconcert them in the least. After each drawing was finished, there was a polite but perfunctory round of applause from the bored audience. The worst drawing was made by a young lady who accepted her applause with great pleasure. She beamed as she murmured to another representative, "Just think, six months ago I was teaching Phys Ed."

Is it any wonder that professional people in the cel-animation business eye computers with distrust!

There are only two areas where computers have been readily accepted: One is in making pencil tests. Instead of the camera-film-lab routine, which often takes several days, the computerized pencil test is ready to look at as soon as the last drawing has been stored.

The other area is the animation camera. Practically everybody is now shooting animation with a computerized camera system. I recall that one day when I was visiting Cel Art, Rudy Tomaselli, a veteran cameraman, remarked that while we were talking, one of his computerized cameras was photographing a very intricate truck. We both laughed as we recalled how, in the old days, it was so difficult to compile the data for a truck. Then there was the drudgery of photographing it manually, exposure by exposure, worrying during the entire process about the possibility of making even a small mistake. Now we have reached the point where nobody is even watching the camera perform.

An upheaval like this is going to happen in the ink and paint departments. The rows of desks will be replaced by a few pieces of machinery; gone too, the brushes and jars of paint. The laborious methods used to produce many of the beautiful effects in *Fantasia* will be things of the past.

I am not touting the computer as a kind of artist's panacea. It is just another tool. Complex, yes, but then so are etching, lithography,

*The Adventures of André and Wally B.,* by Alvy Ray Smith, is the first fully animated three-dimensional cartoon ever made entirely on a computer. A P-I-X-A-R Production.

sculpture, watercolor, and oil painting. They all have one thing in common: There is nothing intrinsically creative about any of them. They neither enhance nor detract from an artist's ability to conceive. They all have some quality or qualities not shared by the others. This includes the computer.

I have been fortunate, through my friendship with Dr. Alexander Schure, Chancellor of the New York Institute Of Technology, to have had access to the Computer Graphics Lab. This operation, headed by Dr. Louis Schure, has for many years been involved in improving the means by which character and abstract animation may be created by computer.

In order to better study the role played by the various departments in an animation studio, CGL produced a feature-length cartoon, *Tubby the Tuba,* using traditional cel-animation techniques.

## IMAGE: A Creative Approach to Computer Animation

The result was the creation of an artist-orientated image-manipulation and graphic-enhancement system called IMAGES. Here's how it was shown to me several years ago when I was invited to visit CGL: I was asked whether I cared to try my hand at computer animation. So I drew a downcast Pluto in pencil on paper, and another drawing of Pluto very happy. The two extremes were input to a computer; then I pressed a button, after deciding on a number, and the computer made seven inbetweens! It was explained to me that it could just as easily have been *seventy* inbetweens.

As I watched the Pluto animation, I realized that I was hooked. I was looking at history. When I started in the business in 1924, *Felix the Cat* was still being inked on paper, in the method that predated the

*Nickelodeon Brew* is a computer (3-D solid modeling) animated station ID for Nickelodeon Cable TV by Richard Bakst.

use of cels. Silent motion pictures were still going to be made for five more years!

Then we had music, dialogue, color, and sound effects with which to work. Television animation came after World War II, followed by tape; now the computer, which seems to be a synthesis of all these inventions. In a happy daze, I went on with the rest of my guided tour of the studio.

We came to the equivalent of an ink and paint department, where a completed scene of animation was being put through a scanner, drawing by drawing, As a Xerox machine, the scanner only took a few seconds.

Then I watched the coloring process with astonishment. The average output of cels in my opaquing department was 25 cels a day, or about 15 minutes apiece. Here a veteran cel painter, who had been retrained, was coloring that many drawings in a few minutes, easily turning out 250 in a day.

She was quickly whisking each finished character off the screen and replacing it with another replica of a pencil drawing. Along the bottom of the screen was a row of small rectangles of different colors. The operator was using an electronic stylus to guide a small patch of light on the screen, causing it to dip into one of the colors. She brought it up swiftly to the character she was working on, and in one deft move an entire area was instantly colored. The ritual was repeated time after time until the character was completely colored. It didn't matter a jot how intricate the shape of the area, it was filled in with the speed of light.

Gone was the necessity to compensate for the various cel levels by arranging for a different palette for each one. These colors would not be grayed down by the lack of true transparency that plagues cel animation; nor would there be any more color flashes, which are often caused by the opaquer using the wrong set of colors for a given cel level.

While this performance was astonishing, it was even more amazing to watch Paul Xander at work. He is CGL's designer, background artist, and creator of storyboards. Paul has had a long career as an artist. He started out as a painter, working out of a gallery on the west coast. Later he went to Hollywood and became interested in animation. He worked in the major cartoon studios as a background artist.

Eventually Xander drifted east, and now has worked for many years at CGL—so many, in fact, that using the IMAGES is as easy and automatic for him as driving a car.

In giving me a sample of what could be done on a background, Xander flashed a menu on the screen. It listed a number of "brushes" of different widths, as well as effects that created facsimiles of water-color, acryilic paint, pencil, and charcoal, as well as "brushes" that could apply several colors on each stroke.

Selecting a "brush," Paul quickly sketched in a desert scene, and began to block in the color. At one point, he zoomed up a very small section of the field to full screen and painted in some details that would have been extremely difficult to do in their actual size. Suddenly, Xander changed the shot from daytime to a moonlit night. After that, he proceeded to change the entire palette of the scene from fairly naturalistic colors to exotic combinations. The marvel was not only that it happened in the twinkling of an eye but that Xander stated there were literally thousands of possible combinations. The whole thing from start to finish was a stunning performance by a maestro.

At no point in this tour did I see any indication of a restriction, some obstacle to creativity. Rather, I kept seeing features in the system that seemed to open new vistas for the creative mind.

Of course, I am focusing on one computer system, and there are many other kinds, but my intention is to tell you about the result that can be achieved, rather than go into an explanation of how it is done.

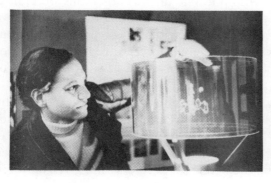

Holography and animation go hand in hand to increase the magic of David Ehrlich's holograph movie *Oedipus at Colonus,* 1978.

*Phallacy,* an award-winning 360° animated integral hologram, was made by David Ehrlich. It was done with clay, shot with a 16mm camera, then transferred to holographic film to create a 3-D moving image.

Dr. Louis Schure, head of the Computer Graphics Laboratories, kindly loaned me the company's flowchart. One can see that several initial efforts are the same as the processes used in cel animation, that is, the director's functions, layout, animation, assistant animation, and inbetweening. In some cases, it is possible to do the inbetweens by means of the computer; otherwise, the animation and layout are drawn with paper and pencil exactly as in cel animation.

In addition, I borrowed a list of the various features of the Computer Assisted Animation System.

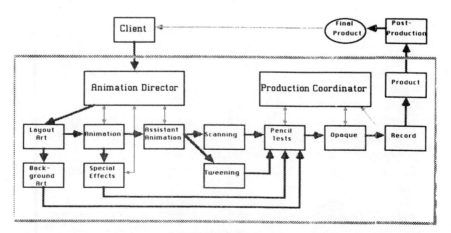

A computer-based flowchart outlining the various production stages. Courtesy of the Computer Graphics Laboratories, Inc.

### IMAGES II—The background painting system features:

a.  Big 'N Fast offers high resolution backgrounds.
b.  Real time color adjustments on color models, backgrounds, etc.
c.  Ability to extract overlays from painted backgrounds.
d.  Ability to create and save "brushes."
e.  Ability to duplicate painted backgrounds, then modify elements and/or color composition for reuse in different scenes.

### SCAN—The digital image processing system includes:

a.  Digitizes drawings.
b.  Color scanning of conventionally painted backgrounds
c.  Background layout scanning for use on the IMAGES II system.
d.  Animation scanning.

### TWEEP—The program for opaquing drawings features:

a.  Automatic filling of color areas in one touch.
b.  "Seed fill," which is the ability to fill in key frames (like extremes) and call for the frames inbetween to be automatically colored.
c.  No concern for color compensation caused by multiple levels as in cel animation. There is no limit to the number of levels that can be used.
d.  Ability to paint color lines in delineating areas.
e.  Can duplicate and combine drawings.
f.  Re-use of daytime animation in a night scene need not be repainted.
g.  "Quick check" displays consecutive drawings for color checking.

### TWEEN—Animation assistant inbetween system features:

a.  Accomplishes checking of line drawings by instant pencil tests. Excellent tool for the animator to review the animation and make adjustments in animation and/or timing.
b.  Zoom from a small area to a full field allows the animator to draw in extreme detail, then zoom area back to its original position.
c.  The animator can draw extreme frames and the program can then interpolate the inbetween frames.
d.  The line width used in drawing can be changed at a later stage of production.

### MIC—The recording system (the equivalent of the camera) features:

a.  The ability to change size and colors.

b.  Animation may be output to film and/or video.
c.  Multiple uses for animation. For example if one bird flying is
    animated, it can be duplicated in different sizes and positions on
    the screen. Also it can be elongated or compacted to change its
    shape. Each bird could be a different color. There is no limit to the
    number of birds which could be generated from the original anima-
    tion, and no limit to the number of levels exposed.
d.  Instant pencil tests on video.
e.  Ability to do simple single frame editing.
f.  Airbrushing to give dimension to traditionally flat animation.
g.  Can generate partially transparent glows and shadows.
h.  Ability to do ease-in, ease-out zooms, pans, trucks, on individual
    levels at specified frames.
i.  Can make color dissolves.

An electronic mail system makes it possible to provide better communi-
cation among the staff. For example, if on one shift there is a change
in the color of a character's head, a memo to that effect can be sent to
all personnel in the next shift by sending one message, which goes to
all stations.

Those are the main features of the system. Of course, there are many
small details, such as Paul Xander's new ability to actually mix colors
on his screen just like wet paint, but the list of features pretty much
covers the ability of each facet of the system.

## Learning the Computer

In preparation for writing this chapter, I bought several books about
computers but find myself sunk without a trace in a morass of jargon.
I am reminded of the time a year ago when I bought a word processor.
It came with eight or nine books, which gave me great satisfaction. I
enjoy learning at my own speed from books. However, when I opened
these up, I found that the instructions for assembling and working the
processor and printer were crouched in the most tortured collection of
words imaginable. Most of the time, I could barely distinguish the
parts of speech.

Stubborn as I am, I embarked on several months of solitary experiment. I refused to go to a class in computer operation. Finally, I
painfully worked out all the various commands you need in order to
write a book. I can only tell you that a perfectly good electric typewriter
is gathering dust in a corner, but then so are the books full of engineer's

Animation Control's AC 112 system. Upper left is the camera. It has 550 lines of resolution. In the lower left is the recorder, a standard half-inch VHS modified for single-frame recording. In the center is the controller. It features a LED frame counter, reset button, one- or two-frame recording synced to 24 FPS. The monitor displays a black-and-white picture on a twelve-inch diagonal screen. Up to 700 lines of resolution for clarity of image. Photo courtesy of John Lamb.

jargon. CGL's material is the first information I have discovered on the subject of computers that was not crammed with gobbledygook.

So, while I have recommended *Computer Graphics* by Kerlow and Rosebush, it is still much too arcane for the average artist to wade through. The problem is that the technical words are not in the dictionary.

The only solution is to find somebody with a computer system set up for use with line drawings and computerized color, and practice.

An artist does not have to know about pixels, bytes, and algorithms, any more than he or she has to be an automotive engineer in order to drive a car.

As I stated in *Talking Animals and Other People,* computerized animation is going to give us films of such complexity and beauty that cel animation will become a thing of the past. Would you believe Walt Disney was a primitive? I do.

# 24

## Survival as an Artist

Anybody who studies the history of American motion pictures is struck by the intensity of the savage war that has been waged between the business world and the creative people in the field. This is especially true after 1929, when the banks moved in and couldn't understand why making pictures could not be run exactly as any other manufacturing business.

As I have shown, animated cartoons have been constricted in subject matter and production methods in order to make the optimum amount of profit. This stony indifference to the creative needs of the artists in the field will continue to be damaging. Actually, the condition may worsen.

Looking back to the era of theatrical animation, some people did carp about the fact that there were so few distribution companies, making the prospects of owning your own studio limited.

But even the most pessimistic never dreamed that absolute control of production, from a one-page outline to the finished film, was going to be taken out of the hands of the producers and seized by a covey of amateurs in advertising agencies and networks. How long this nightmare is going to go on is unforeseeable.

Whether you are an employer or an employee, it affects you and will continue to control your creative life, probably to the end of your career.

There are not many ways to survive as an artist under those conditions, but there are some. In the first place, one should not think of oneself solely as a cartoonist, because if the responsibilities of raising a family, or even the fact that it's the only game in town, forces you to work on schlock animation, you have resources in other creative directions.

Let me tell you how I handled a similar situation. I went broke in 1959 and found that I had become a pariah. None of my former lucrative accounts would give me work. I found myself having to work for other people to support my family.

Most of the work was animation, terrible stuff, at scale. As I drew it, I writhed in my chair in anguish and boredom. My wife understood my plight completely and began to alleviate it, first by playing records of music by Vivaldi, with whose work I was unfamiliar, then by introducing me to the beauty of string quartets. I had been avoiding them for years because I found them incomprehensible during the years I studied violin.

In addition, she took to reading aloud from D. H. Lawrence, and over many months finished his entire works. This was followed by Sean O'Casey, Thomas Hardy, and many others.

After work, I began again to study ancient Greek, and to draw, either my cat or my wife from life. In effect, there was never a dull moment. Now, I could have groused about my lot and sunk out of sight in the depths of self-pity. Instead, I not only survived this miserable experience but actually gained a lot of ground as a creative person.

Just think, if I had thought myself just a cartoonist, I would have wasted eight years out of my life. Maybe this is the most important lesson I present in this book.

Circumstances may force you to work on junk, but that doesn't mean that you have to succumb to it.

If you are young, be adventurous. The whole world is opening up to animation. Because the United States is expected to contribute a solid half of the income from a motion picture, most producers and investors worldwide like to see Americans in many of the key jobs in an animation studio. It's a form of insurance that the film only contains art and animation that is understandable and acceptable to an American audience.

This is how I once ended up spending almost six months in Milan directing a marvelous, skillful, rollicking group of Italian animation people at a studio called Erredia 70.

Remember, if at the moment the only work available is pretty poor stuff, better to be doing it in a foreign country then having a dreary time at home. A Saturday afternoon at the Pitti Palace or a Shinto shrine is a pretty good reward for a week of working on crud. Not that one can be actually happy with such a woeful waste of time, but it is the time after work that in this case is all-important.

The psyche of a creative person is particularly fragile. Guard it well and keep it nourished.

For my readers who have finished this book and the exercises I have laid out, I can only say that you have been exposed to professional thinking and methodology. In some cases, information that you may not have gotten for several years as a beginner is now a part of your equipment.

I wish you well.

# 25

## Schools

For those of my readers who elect to acquire a more formal education, there are a number of animation schools in North America.

In Canada, I believe that Sheridan College probably is the only school of any size that teaches animation. It has an excellent staff; several of the teachers have international reputations in the field. Most of the animation studios in Canada are staffed, to a large extent, by graduates of Sheridan College. In existence for many years, the school has always maintained a very high standard of excellence.

The University of California at Los Angeles Animation Workshop is one of the finest animation schools in the United States. The Workshop, a part of the Department of Theatre, Film, and Television, was started by William Shull, who left Walt Disney Productions at the time of a strike. His production approach, one person to a film, still applies, although he has retired. In order to acquire a Masters of Fine Arts degree, the student has to complete three films in their entirety.

To quote Professor Dan MacLaughlin, now head of the Workshop, "This philosophy allows each filmmaker complete control over the film, its content, idea, viewpoint, style, purpose, audience, form, process, and value. The filmmaker learns the complete process by doing it."

In addition to having its own computer apparatus, the Workshop keeps students abreast of the latest advances in laser, computer, and other new areas of animation by having internships in some of the high-tech houses in Hollywood.

Films range from conceptual to cartoon, from object animation to computer, from entertainment to experimental in diverse materials, and from traditional to new animation.

California Institute of the Arts is headed by Jules Engels, a former Disney artist. Teaching ranges from experimental animation using diverse materials to traditional full animation specifically aimed at the qualifications for working at Walt Disney Productions. The school attracts students with great talent, and the instructors are some of the outstanding artists in the field.

Walt Disney Productions itself submits its workers to a great deal of personalized instruction. It is, of course, possible to submit an outstanding portfolio or exhibition reel to the studio, and get a job without having gone to Cal Arts.

In Chicago, Columbia College maintains a very good animation curriculum, as well as courses in live-action, film history and criticism.

The Rhode Island School of Design turns out graduates with an impressive amount of ability. Yvonne Anderson, a noted filmmaker, teaches with remarkable skill and sensitivity, which is reflected in her group's skillful use of the principles of filmmaking.

The School of Visual Arts, Pratt Institute, and New York University are all New York City schools with a sound approach to animation. The major difference between them and the California schools is that their teachers do not have as impressive a background as the California instructors.

Hanna-Barbera Animation College is devoted to teaching the methods used in producing the Saturday morning television shows for which the studio is famous. This is probably the quickest way to grasp the principles of limited animation, and the bookkeeping techniques that are a part of using morgues properly.

If I were going to go to school, I would certainly try to enter either UCLA Workshop or Cal Arts, and split my time between learning traditional animation techniques and the latest computer methods. The reason for the division is that a youngster skilled in full animation would probably find that there are more jobs for cel animation artists than computer animators at this time. This condition is bound to be reversed eventually.

If neither UCLA or Cal Arts were available, I believe that I would concentrate on the animation schools of the West Coast anyhow. That's really where the action is in the cel animation studios, as well as a very healthy share of the computerized animation business. Remember that there is a very good relationship between the California schools and the animation studios, which, if it exists in New York, is imperceptable.

But before taking a step in any direction, I suggest that the reader take a long look at the field from the standpoint of its history and its restrictions.

It is only after seeing twenty or more animated films from the so-called Golden Age in one evening that one begins to understand that American theatrical animation, at its best, had a very narrow scope from a literary point of view.

This may be lèse majesté, but as a writer I find very little difference between Mighty Mouse and Mickey Mouse. A pratfall by either rodent is still just a pratfall, even if the Disney version is far better written and animated. To make the constriction even more disturbing, all the studios of the period, without exception, used the cel system.

Can the humor in these cartoons compare in diversity with the writings of Aristophanes, Mark Twain, Will Rogers, and Anatole France? The answer is a resounding *no!*

Is it restrictive to the creativity of an artist to have to draw and think as everybody else in a group in order to be a useful filmmaker? The answer is a resounding *yes!*

Just think of the impact on Western art if artists such as Picasso, Braque, Miró, and Matisse all had had to work within a group; had had to paint in oil; and their subjects could only have been baskets of fruit. Van Gogh would not have been the only one to commit suicide. It is shocking to realize that this simile is not as farfetched as it might seem at first glance.

The reason that I bring up this doleful subject is that you may elect to work in one of the studios but at the same time begin to make independent films, as well. In the television business on the west coast, there is usually a period of several months when there is no work. This time might be used to produce a film of your own, or perhaps work on a co-op venture.

The only place on this continent where filmmakers working on staff can make pictures using any technique that suits their fancy, and produce any type of story they choose, is the National Film Board of Canada.

The Montreal branch is divided between English-speaking and French-speaking filmmakers. There are additional branches in Toronto, Winnipeg, Halifax, Edmonton, and Vancouver.

The National Film Board was created in Ottawa in 1939, and Norman McLaren was asked to head the animation department in 1946. There could not have been a better choice to lead a group of filmmakers. During his long career in animation, scarcely a year went by in which McLaren did not explore new ground, and he encouraged the staff to do the same.

They made films for information, education, and entertainment, and in the doing, broke with the traditional ink-and-paint-on-cel approach whenever it suited their purpose. Pictures were made using underlit sand; colored pencil on frosted cels; underlit cutout silhouettes; pixillation (which is moving live people exposure by exposure); scratching images into black leader; drawing on clear leader with a pen; animating beads and building blocks; painting on glass; puppets; pastel; watercolors; and combinations of these techniques.

I suggest that every person interested in animation do the following experiment: Screen a dozen or more animated cartoons from all of the studios that were operating in the 1940s and 1950s, or record them from television. Arrange a screening of all of them in one long session. As soon as possible after that, attend a screening session made up solely of National Film Board pictures.

It is only by this juxtaposition that one can realize how narrow the scope of the former and how diverse the approach of the latter. The following is a suggested list of NFB pictures to see:

*Hors d'Oeuvre*
*I Know an Old Lady Who Swallowed a Fly*
*Walking*
*Cat's Cradle*
*Hen Hop*
*What on Earth?*
*Why Me?*
*Bead Game*
*Hot Stuff*
*The Street*
*Big Snit*
*Every Child*
*Sandcastle*
*Special Delivery*
*The Great Toy Robbery*
*The Sweater*

*Getting Started*
*The Owl Who Married a Goose*

It is only after one has made this direct comparison that the enormity of the deprivation becomes apparent. The wealth of ideas, techniques, and styles in the Canadian animation compared to the sameness of technique and style in the so-called Golden Age films makes the loss incalculable.

The real Golden Age started in 1941 with the National Film Board of Canada, when the studio was based in Montreal. Now that the NFB has been split into branches, the policy seems to be to hire local artists rather than accept animators from all over the world. Caroline Leaf was the last American artist to be hired by the Board and that was in the middle 1970s.

At its apogee, the NFB turned out a spate of prestigious writers, directors, and animators, probably more than any other studio in the field, not excluding the Disney studio.

It isn't only that there was artistic freedom; there was a mingling of talents. Everybody who worked at Disney's during the thirties and forties agrees that it was the interchange of ideas that enabled the quality of the pictures to improve so dramatically within the space of a few short years.

This same conjoining of talents was begun by Norman McLaren when he accepted the job as head of the National Film Board. However, he carried the principle much further than Walt Disney did. Instead of fixed jobs as writer, director, background artist, or whatever, McLaren allowed his artists to write on one picture and direct or animate on the next.

Disney, whether he knew it or not, was using the methodology of the Machine Age to produce his films. Therefore, the accent was on specialization. Each department worked on the animation, not unlike workers on the production line in an automobile-assembly plant. Each artist had a niche and never was permitted to stray out of it.

McLaren had a much more humanitarian approach. He recognized that specialization is a form of restriction and never allowed it to develop in his staff.

With McLaren dead, the policies he instigated may become somewhat modified, but for Canadians the National Film Board still remains the best workplace for the talented filmmaker.

Working in the United States poses a question of quality. There is no doubt that an artist looking for a chance to work on full-animation feature films will turn to the Walt Disney Studio, which is still turning out the most manicured animation in the business. Feature film production, because of the length of the picture, supplies a writer, director, or animator with a unique opportunity to work with complex plot material and highly complicated forms of timing and acting, which are not available in any other animation format.

There are other U.S. feature films being done, but more and more, the work is being done outside of the country. However, producers such as Dick Williams, who has a studio in London; Jimmy Murakami, who has a group of transplanted Americans in Dublin; and Don Bluth, who has also opened a studio in Ireland, all produce animated films of very high quality. From time to time other feature film projects come up, especially in Japan, often with Americans occupying key positions on the staff.

At the other end of the spectrum are the Saturday-morning shows. They are usually nothing but long commercials for the products of toy factories.

For artists whose goal is to make a lot of money, these studios pay the best wages in the business. However, there is the least artistic gratification in these films because the direction and animation are kept to a minimum effort and the writing is to match.

I believe that it would be disastrous for a newcomer in any area of production to start a career by working in one of these film factories.

If one is looking for diversity of drawing styles, a knowledge of special effects, as well as various animation techniques, a studio specializing in television spots is the best place to learn. The drawback is that studio writers are rarely used, even on a free-lance basis, and because each spot is so short, the animator has very little opportunity to explore the nuances of pantomime, and a director is reduced to making very simple decisions for the same reason.

The advantages are that the wages are good; learning how to pack a lot of information into a short amount of screen time is good experience; and one learns a great deal about special effects. I would say that, after the possibility of working on a feature film, being on the staff of a studio specializing in television-spot production would be the best start for a beginner.

There are a few independent filmmakers, such as Faith Hubley, John Canemaker, and Michael Sporn, but their output is limited, so there is no way to make a steady income working on their films.

Those are the main areas of job opportunities. There are some manufacturing plants that use in-house film units, including animators, but the output is limited and so is the subject matter. There are also firms that produce medical pictures, but they are usually highly professional and very technical. There are a few companies producing educational films, but again, the job opportunities are few.

The reader may wonder why I have not mentioned computerized animation. I would consider it a mistake to start working on a computer before acquiring a sound knowledge of the traditional field. There are many people now doing computerized animation who are little better than engineers. In fact, the artistic aspect of computer animation has been stalled because the equipment has not been readily available to the amateur with animation talent, except in a few schools.

It is only when all of the foremost people in every aspect of the field have become expert in both cel and computer animation that the combined techniques will start to produce important pictures.

I predict that the beginners astute enough to follow my advice and learn traditional full animation before looking for a job in computer animation are going to be the leaders in the great upheaval which is slowly but surely going to radically change the course of the art of animation.

# Animation Schools

## California

Computer Arts Institute
5627 F Paradise Drive
Corte Madera, CA 94925

De Anza College
21250 Stevens Creek Blvd.
Cupertino, CA 95014

Los Angeles City College
855 N. Vermont Ave.
Los Angeles, CA 90029

UCLA Animation Workshop
405 Hildgard Ave.
Los Angeles, CA 90024

University of Southern California
University Park
Los Angeles, CA 90007

American Animation Institute
4729 Lankershim Blvd.
N. Hollywood, CA 91602–1864

California College of Arts and Crafts
5212 Broadway
Oakland, CA 94618

Art Center School of Design
1700 Lida St.
Pasadena, CA 91103

Center for Computer Art
329 Bryant St.
San Francisco, CA 94107

San Francisco Art Institute
800 Chestnut Street
San Francisco, CA 94133

San Francisco State University
1600 Holloway Drive
San Francisco, CA 94132

California Institute of the Arts
24700 McBean Parkway
Valencia, CA 91355

## Illinois

Columbia College
600 S. Michigan Blvd.
Chicago, IL 60605

School of the Art Institute of Chicago
Columbus Drive and Jackson Blvd.
Chicago, IL 60603

University of Illinois
Box 4348
Chicago, IL 60680

## Massachusetts

Harvard University
24 Quincy St.
Cambridge, MA 02138

## Michigan

Wayne State University
906 West Warren
585 Manoogian Hall
Detroit, MI 48202

W. Ford Vocational Center
36455 Marquette
Westland, MI 48135

## New Jersey

Joe Kubel School of Cartoon Art
37 Myrtle Ave.
Dover, NJ 07801

## New York

Brooklyn College
Bedford Ave. and Ave. H
Brooklyn, NY 11210

Pratt Institute
200 Willoughby Ave.
Brooklyn, NY 11205

Adelphi University
Blodgett 113
Garden City, NY 11530

New York University
65 S. Bldg.
Washington Square
New York, NY 10003

School of Visual Arts
209 E. 23 St.
New York City, NY 10010

Rochester Institute of Technology
One Lomb Memorial Drive
Rochester, NY 14623

**Ohio**

Ohio State University
156 W. 19 Ave.
Columbus, OH 43210

**Pennsylvania**

Edinboro State College
School of Arts and Humanities
Edinboro, PA 16444

University of the Arts
Pine and Broad Sts.
Philadelphia, PA 19102

**Rhode Island**

Rhode Island School of Design
2 College St.
Providence, RI 02903

**Canada**

Concordia University
1395, boul. Dorchester ouest
Montréal, Québec H3J 2MS

Université de Montréal
3150 Jean Brillant
Montréal, Québec H3C 3J7

Université du Québec à Montréal
2094, rue Kimberly
Montréal, Québec H2X 2M1

Sheridan College of Applied Arts
Trafalgar Rd.
Oakville, Ontario L6H 2L1

Université Laval
Pavillon Casault
Ste-Foy, Québec G1K 7P4

Emily Carr College of Art
1299 Johnston St.
Vancouver, British Columbia V6H 2R9

# Appendices ～～～～～～～～～

## 1
## Information

Join the International Animated Film Society. There are branches in New York, Chicago, Los Angeles, San Francisco, Washington, Montreal, Vancouver, and Toronto. These groups are a part of ASIFA International. (ASIFA stands for *Association Internationale du Film D'Animation,* the French-language name for the International Animated Film Association.) The membership is composed of professionals, students, and interested nonprofessionals. Membership fee includes a subscription to AnimaFilm, an animation magazine.

*Animation News* sells for $9.95 for six issues. The address is *Animation News,* P.O. Box 25547, Los Angeles, CA 90025. It has general animation news, but its chief value is in the Home Video Directory. It lists dozens of short subjects and animated feature films, with a short synopsis and the price. It is a must for animation students.

*Get Animated! Update* is a monthly news letter, featuring news from around the world for people in the animation industry. Also has a yearly international directory featuring studio listings, magazines and publications, organizations and clubs, supplies and equipment, voice talent agencies, art-work and collectables. Editor is John Cawley, P.O. Box 1582, Burbank, CA 91507.

*Animatrix* is published annually. Rates are $5.00 a copy, plus $2.50 mailing charge. It is a magazine published by the UCLA Animation Workshop, Dept. of Theatre, Film, and Television, 405 Hilgard Ave., Los Angeles, CA 90024.

*Cartoonist Profiles* is a magazine for both comic-strip artists and animators. Rates are $25 a year. P.O. Box 325, Fairfield, CT 06430.

*Graffiti* is a publication of ASIFA-Hollywood. It is a bimonthly review of film and video animation. Rates are $12 for six issues. 5301 Laurle Canyon Blvd., no. 219, N. Hollywood, CA 91607.

The International Tournee of Animation is an annual screening in art houses and repertory theaters, of a feature-length compilation of prize-winning short subjects. They have been selected from major film festivals worldwide.

*Millimeter* is a trade magazine that has news about the various trends in the commercial animation field. Rates are $45 a year. The address is 826 Broadway, New York, NY 10003.

## 2
## Suppliers

Cartoon Color Co.
9024 Lindblade St.
Culver City, CA 90203

the best paint for cels

Animation Controls
1856 Wilstone Ave.
Leucadia, CA 92024

AC 112 video animation pencil-test system

Fax Co.
374 S. Fair Oaks Ave.
Pasadena, CA 01105

animation disks, stands, cameras, paper punch

Behrends, Inc.
161 E. Grand Ave.
Chicago, IL 60611

animation supplies

Victor Duncan, Inc.
200 E. Ontario St.
Chicago, IL 60611

animation equipment and supplies

Oxberry
180 Broad St.
Carlstadt, NJ 07072

cameras, stands, peg bars, other equipment

Arthur Brown and Bros.
2 W. 46 St.
New York, NY 10036

animation art supplies
212-575-5555

Eastman Kodak Co.
1133 Ave. of the Americas
New York, NY 10036

film, technical books

F and B. Ceco, Inc.
315 W. 43 St.
New York, NY 10036

cameras, film, paper, peg bars,
disks, etc. 212-206-8280

General Analine and Film Corp.
140 W. 51 St.
New York, NY 10020

film

George Millar Co.
161 Ave. of the Americas
New York, NY 10013

cels and art supplies

# 3
# Animation Photography

Boyington Film Productions, Inc.
1290 Sixth St.
Berkeley, CA 94701

Aninagic Computerized Animation, Inc.
1309 W. Magnolia Blvd.
Burbank, CA 91502

James Byfield Animation
417 Tenth Ave.
San Francisco, CA 94118

Animart FX
812 South Weber St.
Colorado Springs, CO 80903

Celluloid Animation Studios
2422 Delgany
Denver, CO 90202

Animation Station
406 W. 65 St.
Minneapolis, MN 55423

Bandalier, Inc.
3815 Osuna Ave.
Albuquerque, NM 87109

Animators, Inc.
849 Delaware Ave.
Buffalo, NY 14209

Al Stahl Animated
1600 Broadway
New York, NY 10019

Animation Camera Workshop
153 W. 27 St.
New York, NY 10001

Cel Art
20 E. 49 St.
New York, NY 10017

Granato Animation Photography
15 W. 46 St.
New York, NY 10036

Leo Animation Camera Service
25 W. 43 St.
New York, NY 10036

Mavericks Motion Graphics
45 W. 45 St.
New York, NY 10036
    Also does photocopy on cels

R. J. Backle Productions, Inc.
321 W. 44 St.
New York, NY 10036

Animated Arts
5963 Curry Rd. Extension
Schenectady, NY 12303

Anivision
981 Walnut St.
Pittsburgh, PA 15234

**Canada**

Les Animations Drouin, Inc.
19 Leyorer
Montréal, Québec

Atkinson Film Arts
19 Fairmont Ave.
Ottowa, Ontario J1Y 1X4

Animation Group.
312 Adelaide St., W.
Toronto, Ontario M5V 1R2

Mammoth Pictures
67 Mowat
Toronto, Ontario M6K 3E3

MS Art Services
410 Adelaide St., W.
Toronto, Ontario M5V 1S8

Delaney and Friends Productions
206–1000 Beach Ave.
Vancouver, British Columbia V6E 1T7

Marmalade Animation, Ltd.
2040 W. 12 St.
Vancouver, British Columbia V6J 2O2

Credo Group
120 Sherbrook
Winnipeg, Manitoba

**4**
**Film Editors**

Connecticut Editing Services, Inc.
297 Dunbar Hill Rd.
Hamden, CT 06514

Kesser Post Production
21 S. W. 15 Rd.
Miami, FL 33129

Szabo/Tohtz Editing, Inc.
301 E. Erie
Chicago, IL 60611

Flite Three Recordings
1130 E. Cold Spring La.
Baltimore, MD 21239

Production Consultants
5480 Wisconsin
Chevy Chase, MD 20815

Searchlight Films
Fox Hill Rd.
Bernardston, MA 01337

Cutters
138 Newbury St.
Boston, MA 02116

Image Express, Inc.
15565 Northland Drive
Southfield, MI 48075

Imageworks
660 Lankland L. Drive
Jackson, MS 39208

Jim Young
279 E. 44 St.
New York, NY 10018

Sandpiper Editorial Services, Inc.
50 W. 40 St.
New York, NY 10018

World Cinevision Services, Inc.
321 W. 44 St.
New York, NY 10036

DuPertuis Creed Productions
355 Valley Rd.
Merion, PA 19066

Kinotex
1505 Southmore Blvd.
Houston, TX 77004

**5**
**Laboratories**

CFI
959 Seward St.
Hollywood, CA 90038

Cineservice, Inc.
6518½ Santa Monica Blvd.
Hollywood, CA 90038

Technicolor
4050 Lankershim Blvd.
N. Hollywood, CA 91608

Highland Labs
840 Battery St.
San Francisco, CA 94111

Alexander Film Services
3200 N. Nevada Ave.
Colorado Springs, CO 80907

Bono Film Services
1042 Wisconsin Ave., NW
Washington, DC 20007

CineFilm
2156 Faulkner Rd., NE
Atlanta, GA 30324

Allied Film and Video
1322 W. Belmont
Chicago, IL 60657

Filmcraft Labs
5216 N. Keystone
Indianapolis, IN 46220

Pan American Films
822 N. Rampart St.
New Orleans, LA 70116

Quality Films
5800 York Rd.
Baltimore, MD 21212

Film Service Lab
58–62 Berkely St.
Boston, MA 02116

Allied Film and Video
7375 Woodward Ave.
Detroit, MI 48202

Academy Film Lab
60 Euclid Ave. Rd.
Fort Lee, NJ 07024

Cinema Services, Inc.
118 N. Ave.
Park Ridge, NJ 07656

Du Art Film Laboratories
245 W. 56 St.
New York, NY 10019

Guffanti Film Labs
630 Ninth Ave.
New York, NY 10036

Jan Film Lab
302 W. 37 St.
New York, NY 10018

Kin-o-lux
17 W. 45 St.
New York, NY 10036

Precision Labs
630 Ninth Ave.
New York, NY 10036

Reverse-o-Lab
333 W. 39 St.
New York, NY 10018

**Canada**

Capital Film Lab, Ltd.
4828 93 Ave.
Edmonton, Alberta T6B 2P8

Mid-Can Labs
500 Century St.
Winnepeg, Manitoba R3H 0L8

Graphic Films, Ltd.
19 Fairmont Ave.
Ottawa, Ontario K1Y 1X4

The Filmhouse Group
380 Adelaide West
Toronto, Ontario M5V 1R7

Bellevue Pathé Quebec, Inc.
2000 Northcliff Ave.
Montréal, Québec H4A 3K5

Laboratoire Mount-Royal Film Corp.
1240 W. St. Antoine St.
Montréal, Québec, H3C 189

**6
Music and Sound Effects**

Don Great Music
7155 Santa Monica Blvd.
Hollywood, CA 90046

Arcal Productions
2732 Bay Rd.
Redwood City, CA 94063

Corelli-Jacobs
25 W. 45 St.
New York, NY 10036

Pisces Music
12 E. 46 St.
New York, NY 10017

Ross-Gaffney
21 W. 46 St.
New York, NY 10036

The Sound Patrol
342 Madison Ave.
New York, NY 10017

Musifex
2420 Wilson Blvd.
Arlington, VA 22209

# 7
# Recording

B and B Sound Studio
3610 West Magnolia
Burbank, CA 91505

Glen Glenn
6624 Romaine
Hollywood, CA 90038

Orion
17 Palmetto Drive
Miami Springs, FL 33166

Du Art Laboratories, Inc.
39 Chapel St.
Newton, MA 02158

Recorded Pubs Labs
1558 Pierce Ave.
Camden, NJ 08105

Aquarius Transfer
12 E. 46 St.
New York, NY 10017

The Audio Department, Inc.
110 W. 57 St.
New York, NY 10019

CC Sound Shop
304 E. 44 St.
New York, NY 10017

CP Sound
200 Madison Ave.
New York, NY 10016

Electro-Nova Productions
342 Madison Ave.
New York, NY 10017

Magno Sound
212 W. 48 St.
New York, NY 10036

The Mix Place
663 Fifth Ave.
New York, NY 10022

Soundone
1619 Broadway
New York, NY 10019

Tape Tracks, Ltd.
16 W. 46 St.
New York, NY 10036

IIIdb Sound Specialists
121 E. 24 St.
New York, NY 10010

## Canada

CFRN-TV
Box 5030, Station E
Edmonton, Alberta T5P 4C2

Atray Ltd.
P. O. Box 4700
Vancouver, British Columbia V6B 4A3

ABS Productions Ltd.
Dartmouth, Nova Scotia B3B 1N4

Atkinson Film-Arts Ltd.
19 Fairmont Ave.
Ottawa, Ontario K1Y 1X4

Aldon Group Productions, Ltd.
111 Queen St. E., Suite E
Toronto, Ontario M5C 1S2

Mars Studio
96 Spadina Ave., 9th Flr.
Toronto, Ontario M5V 2J6

Great Lakes Riverton Television, Ltd.
1130 Crawford Ave.
Windsor, Ontario H9H 5C9

Champlain Productions
405 Ogilvy Ave.
Montreal, Quebec H3N 1M4

CKCK Television
Box 2000
Regina, Saskatchewan S4P 3E5

# 8
# Rentals

### Independent Filmmakers

Creative Film Society
7237 Canby Ave.
Reseda, CA 91335
Knowlton, Russett, Stenhura,
J. and J. Whitney, Oskar Fischinger

International Film Bureau
332 S. Michigan Ave.
Chicago, IL 60604
McLaren, Coderre, others

Trans-World Films
332 S. Michigan Ave.
Chicago, IL, 60604
Reels of National Film Board of
Canada films

American Federation of Art
41 E. 65 St.
New York, NY 10021.
Films by Beckett, Nelson, Conrad,
Mouris, Noyes, Pies, Russett,
Schwartz, Sharita, Smith, Spinello,
James and John Whitney

Contemporary/McGraw Films
1221 Ave. of the Americas
New York, NY 10020
Trinka, Noyes, Starevitch

Cecil Starr
50 W. 96 St.
New York, NY 10025
Alexieff, Richter, Batosch, others

Film Images
17 W. 60 St.
New York, NY 10023
Cohl, Starevitch

Learning Co. of America
711 Fifth Ave.
New York, NY 10022
Foldes, McLaren,
Noyes, others

Museum of Modern Art Film Dept.
11 W. 53 St.
New York, NY 10019
Fischinger, Lye,
John Whitney,
Jordan, Breer, others

National Film Board of Canada
1251 Ave. of the Americas
New York, NY 10020
McLaren, Leaf, others

Ed Emshwiller
43 Red Maple Drive
Wantagh, NY 11793

### Theatrical Film Rentals

Kit Parker Films
Carmel Valley, CA 93924
Max Fleischer, Van Beuren

Columbia Pictures
711 Fifth Ave.
New York, NY 10022
UPA

Ivy Films
165 W. 46 St.
New York, NY 10036
Max Fleischer

United Artists
729 Seventh Ave.
New York, NY 10019
Warner Bros. films

Universal
445 Park Ave.
New York, NY 10022
Walter Lantz

**Send for Catalogues**

Budget Films
4590 Santa Monica Blvd.
Los Angeles, CA 90029

Cinema Concepts
91 Main St.
Chester, CT 06412

Reel Images
456 Monroe Turnpike
Monroe, CT 06468

Blackhawk Films
1235 W. 5 St.
Davenport, IA 52808

National Cinema Service
333 W. 57 St.
New York, NY 10019

# 9
# Running the Business

Anyone embarking on a career as a studio owner had best be aware that it is a risky venture, even if the business starts with a good supply of capital and some fine talent. My accountant once called running a studio a form of Russian roulette, because there has to be a steady outgo of cash, even if it is just for the basics such as rent, light, heat, and telephone; but no steady income whatsoever.

It is a sobering thought that even the most successful animation studios, if they concentrate on television spots, have an average lifespan of about twelve years. The mortality among new studios is horrendous the first year.

## Why Studios Fail

The most common items that lead to their demise are:

1.  Not enough capital to keep the studio going until a significant amount of work starts rolling in.
2.  Using up the basic capital in buying equipment too soon and investing in things that are used infrequently, instead of renting.
3.  Failure to go into business with a good sample reel.
4.  Inept or inexperienced salesmanship.
5.  Hiring an accountant who knows nothing about the business.
6.  Hiring a lawyer who may not know enough about the business to set up a proper corporate structure.
7.  Ignorance about the real talent of the artists on the staff.

8. Inability to prepare a budget that will bring in a good profit and overhead.
9. Inability to calculate the production time on each job in all departments.

It is worth studying this formidable list at some length. The first item seems fairly obvious, but I think it reflects one weakness in the temperament of the average entrepenuer—optimism. It seems to be a characteristic of the breed. Before actually investing money, it is wise to go to the Small Business Administration or a similar service for advice. (Some people are psychologically unable to accept advice. What they are really doing is looking for someone who will agree with what they have already decided upon.)

Also, talk to other people who are already in the field, not only successful ones but some who have failed as studio owners. Listen carefully.

## Some Advice

For a start, such things as office furniture and typewriters can be rented; ink and paint services can be hired; Xerox and camera services are also available. Ask around and pick a good editor, one who has his or her own equipment. Don't blow money on a flashy-looking studio. You may need that money to survive six months from now. Just see that the studio is clean and neat.

Without a good sample reel, your business doesn't have a prayer. A few good samples are better than a dozen uninspired spots. Have your reel neatly spliced with a minimum of leader in between pictures.

Even a good sample reel is useless without a fine sales pitch to go with it. Somebody has to be good at it, whether it is the studio owner, a partner, or a salesman working on a draw plus commission.

Your accountant must know at least the rudiments of your business so that he can help you with monetary problems.

You need a lawyer who knows about corporate law, and can be called upon to evaluate a client's contract, if the client won't use yours.

Do not hire your staff until you actually have a signed contract. In fact, never start a dollar's worth of work until you have the contract in your hands, the lawyer has approved of it, and you are ready to go. Always ask for at least three references from a prospective employee, and make sure that you are inquiring about the same kind of work for which the person is being hired.

A budget is not just a set of figures that can be applied to all jobs. Every picture is a little different and needs special handling. Be sure to check prices for services, and be sure you understand the fine print in a union contract.

Get advice from everybody involved in figuring out production time. When it is available, settle for paying a lump sum. It may be more money than paying by the hour or cel, but it is a form of insurance.

Never work without a contract! Never!! Even if it is just a letter of intent (checked by your lawyer, of course); in any case, no oral contracts.

## Should You Work on Spec?

You will be asked to do work on spec. This poses a dilemma. To do it costs you money. Believe me, it is absolutely no guarantee of future work. I have usually avoided working for nothing by pointing out that there is some money involved that will raise my overhead, and people who are giving me work have to pay it. So I must respectfully decline, since I do small favors only for steady clients. This may definitely end your relationship with this particular client.

On the other hand, if the account has been the source of steady work, do the job, then hang the expense on the next picture you do for them.

If you are losing money on a project, and it is your own fault, never try to get extra money from your client. In the first place, it is difficult for the client to get more money once a job has been assigned and a contract signed. Second, it makes you look like a klutz. Better to swallow the loss and learn from it.

If a client wants more work than is indicated in the contract, point this out and tell him or her that you will be able to give an exact figure on the addition the next day. Never give the price on the spot. Give yourself time to think over just how much work is involved. Maybe you need to get an estimate from one of your people. Don't forget overhead and profit! Then send it in the form of a memo and keep a copy. You may need it at the end of the job.

## The Basic Contract

Probably every studio feels better with its own contract, but if you have never needed one before, this one has been my basic contract for television commercials for forty years:

SAMPLE CONTRACT

Date

(1) The following shall constitute the agreement between Shamus Culhane Productions, Inc. (hereinafter called the Producer) and Producers Finding Corporation, Inc. (hereinafter called the Client) under which we agree to produce, deliver and sell to the Client, which agrees to purchase an animated main title 25 seconds in length, and an end title 15 seconds long.

(2)    Client will supply a quarter inch tape and a 35mm magnetic track, on which the dialogue, lyrics, and music are already mixed. Producer agrees to deliver answer print 6 weeks from delivery of track.

(3)    Producer will supply the following:
   1. Direction
   2. Personnel
   3. Materials
   4. Full animation
   5. Color photography
   6. Laboratory processing
   7. A 35mm negative and print synchronized to Client's sound track.

(4) Client approval is necessary for:
   1. Character design
   2. Storyboard
   3. Color keys
   4. Finished layouts
   5. Rough animation
   6. Completed animation
   7. Backgrounds
   8. Dailies
   9. Answer print
  10. Changes or additions to production.

(5) If, during the course of production, Producer shall consider it

advisable or necessary to make changes in, or variations from, the storyboard, for the intended purpose of enhancing the quality of the film, Producer may make such changes or variations provided the Client agrees in writing.

(6) If, during the course of production, Client desires to make any changes or variations from the storyboard, or the work in progress, heretofore approved by Client, Producer agrees to make such changes or variations on request. If such a request involves additional costs, or adds to the length of the schedule, Producer agrees to so notify Client before proceeding with said changes or variations.

(7) If, for any reason, such as strikes, war, acts of God, labor troubles, riots, restraints of public authority, or for any reason beyond the Producer's control, excluding financial reasons, Producer shall be unable to produce and deliver the film within the time period set forth in this contract, the same shall not be deemed a breach of this agreement by the Producer; nor shall the Client be entitled to receive damages of any kind therefore; but the date mentioned in this agreement shall be correspondingly postponed, and when such reason no longer exists, Producer shall produce and deliver the film herein provided.

(8) Since the schedule in this agreement is based on the production of a motion picture in a continuous process, any delay in production caused by the Client, may result in a similar delay in the delivery date.

(9) Shamus Culhane Productions, Inc., does agree to and hereby sells, assigns, transfers, and delivers to Producers Finding Corporation, Inc., with no reservation, any and all rights to the above mentioned titles, the negative and print thereof, to make such use as Client deems appropriate, to copyright in whole or in part, as Client sees fit.

(10) As compensation for our performance hereunder, we agree to accept in payment for all obligations owing to us hereunder, the sum of $65,000 to be paid in the following manner:
$25,000 immediately on signing this document.
$20,000 three weeks after the date of first payment
$20,000 within one week after the delivery of the negative and print.

(11) In respect to any controversies between the parties to this agreement, such controversies are to be submitted to an arbitration board appointed by the American Arbitration Association. All decisions by the board are to be binding on both parties, and any and all costs incidental to this arbitration are to be paid by the loser in this action.

(12) Both Client and Producer agree that this contract constitutes the entire agreement between the parties, and there are no oral understandings of any kind which would modify or change this contract, in whole or in part.

Will you kindly indicate your acceptance of these terms by signing below at the place indicated, and returning to us two (2) copies of this letter contract.

Producers Finding           Shamus Culhane
Corporation, Inc.            Productions, Inc.
By _____ By _____

That contract with slight modifications has been used for twenty-minute live-action films, and five-minute educational pictures, as well as television commercials.


## Get It in Writing

A word of caution. Never make changes or take an order to start production by an oral order unless you have been working with the person involved for a long time and he or she has proven to be highly ethical.

The lessons can be bitter. I once faced an account executive who had phoned me to make a series of storyboards for Volkswagon. Pale-faced and trembling, he denied that he had ever talked to me about the account, in spite of the fact that I had taken to the agency three one-minute storyboards that we had labored over for two weeks.

I finally recognized the problem. The agency had lost the account several days before. Since it was my word against his, the agency was happy to save the money. In the vivid parlance of Madison Avenue, I had to eat the storyboards.

### Payola

Very soon after you open your studio, you will be faced with the problem of payola. My advice is not to do it. If you give an advertising executive a bribe, it is the client who is paying, not you, because it is a part of your estimate. So you are stealing money. You will probably be pressured by the boyos who are on the take, and, if you don't mind being a thief, give in. You join a small but very smelly group of people in the advertising business.

Others do not take money but they do take favors, such as $100-an-hour call girls. I still submit that any money that is not spent on production has been stolen from the client. Be sure that the salespeople that you hire understand your policy, whichever way your ethics go, and act accordingly. One of my salesmen was fired, even though he had hired a whore for a client with his own money. He just couldn't see why he was fired.

### Memos

Train all your people to write memoranda whenever a situation arises where there is a possible expense. A talk on the phone between the head of the ink and paint department and an art director should be followed up by a memo in the mail the next day—with a copy for your book-keeper, to be included in the file on the picture.

The memo should contain an estimate for changes signed by the director, and if it will involve extra time on the production, that should be included. As Sam Goldwyn once said, "A verbal contract isn't worth the paper it's written on."

### Selling

The best way to solve the problem of sales is to hire a person who has already worked in the market for some time and has a good track record. First, find out why he or she is looking for a new job. Don't take the person's word for it; check the story with the former employer. During your first interview, mention that you are going to check. If it is a woman applicant, don't be chivalrous; the role of salesperson is too important to the very life of your studio to take anyone's word.

The first few times the salesperson makes a pitch, go along to watch the performance. Also, it pays to make an appearance at various times, just to remind the agency people that you are running the show. Psychologically, it is important that the client understands that the smiling, cajoling, salesman is neither the boss nor responsible for the good work the studio is doing.

Looking back on my own career, I made the mistake of being too removed from my customers: rarely taking anybody to lunch or going to a client with not only a bid but a suggestion that might improve the picture. Too often, I would have the sales rep make the suggestion. Knowing sales people as I now do, I doubt that the client would be corrected if he thought the good idea was the salesperson's.

If you are taking on a sales rep who has never been in the business before, make sure that the résumé contains some reference to sales experience, then find out why this job was given up. If it was due to incompetency, look for somebody else. There are salesmen who are door openers, who could manage to see the Pope if it were useful. Very often they prove to be unable to close a deal, so you are continually being dazzled by the number of agencies being exposed to your exhibition reel, quite forgetting that no opportunities for making bids are forthcoming.

Make sure that the deal is a weekly draw against a commission, usually 10 percent. Never hire a sales rep on a straight salary, and never allow the draw to be such an amount as to ensure a comfortable living without the commission.

The expense account should be fairly modest, and a fixed amount, otherwise, in the name of generating goodwill, you will be getting a list of expensive lunchs and dinners so large, it will look as if Diamond Jim Brady had attended every meal.

Keep a record of the number of times an agency has asked for a bid and then some other studio got the job. There are agencies who like to use a stalking-horse technique. They ask for bids from many studios, assemble the bids of the most expensive ones, as well as the very lowest bid, and show these figures to the advertiser in the fond hope that it will look as if they have managed to find a huge bargain. If you find that you have submitted a dozen bids without a result, you may be sure that you are being used.

Don't let your sales rep talk you into putting in such a low bid that there will be little or no profit. The argument will be that this is the best way to get a foot in the door. It isn't. If you do such a job, and the next time put in a normal bid with proper overhead and profit, you will be suspected of being overpriced, trying to recoup your profit on the first job.

Agency people have been playing one studio against the other for about forty years, and they are expert at it. Bid an honest amount. Many studios work on 25 or 30 percent overhead and 10 to 12 percent profit. These figures are quite reasonable.

Try for long-range relationships based on good work and promptness in meeting delivery dates, rather than looking for a killing on one project.

Handling a sales rep is about as chancy as a marriage. It has to be a mixture of commiseration, enthusiasm, and pressure to go out there and hustle. How much of each ingredient will make for a good relationship depends on the intuition of the employer and the objectivity of the salesperson.

## The Bid

Do have a very complete form to use in preparing for a bid. Don't make calculations on the back of an old envelope. Bidding ad lib can be a disaster. Never make an off-the-cuff estimate just because a customer wants one. Avoid what they laughingly call "ball-park" figures, because when you do have the time to make a proper estimate, if it's a larger number than your guesstimate, there will be a chill in the air.

The following is a sample form:

> Date
> Name of Agency
> Number of spots
> Length
> Storyboard
> Director
> Recording
> Editor
> Art materials
> Layouts
> Backgrounds
> Animators
> Assistant animators
> Inbetweeners

Pencil-test photography
Lettering
Planning
Checking
C prints or silk screen
Inking
Xerox
Painting
Still photography
Opticals
Color photography
Retakes
Answer print
Composite negative
Commission
Overhead
Profit
Total

Approved by_____

If you take my advice and use an ink and paint service, hire an editor by the job, and take your picture to a camera service; you should be able to get fairly solid estimates from them for each of their operations. However, do not add all of your overhead on these figures. They already have one overhead and profit; to add yours, too, might price you out of the bidding. Maybe use 10 percent on those processes that are farmed out.

## Watch the Cash

For some months after your studio has gotten off the ground, do not buy equipment; farm out as much work as possible and rent equipment. You need to know what your base income is going to be before making investments. Remember that every dollar spent on a piece of equipment is tied up until you sell it.

The most common reason for losing a business is running out of cash before the studio has a chance to start an ongoing relationship with several advertising agencies or other sources of business. For that reason, one must conserve cash.

Of course, limping along this way is not a spectacular start for a business, but it is a lot safer than trying to make a big splash. When you hire people, keep in mind how much profit it takes to pay for even one day's work, and be prepared to lay off any employee who runs out of work. Do not wait a few days or a week to see whether new work is forthcoming. Do it *now!*

Find the best talent available and be prepared to pay high wages. Later you may find that you pay the highest wages in town, but you also have the most successful studio.

Always meet a contractual commitment even if you lose money in the process. If you present an image of a completely reliable studio, you are already halfway to being a success. It is worth protecting this image at any cost.

# 10
# A Feature-Picture Budget

Nobody is more optimistic than a filmmaker who has just been given a chance to bid for a feature-length cartoon. The idea of handling millions of dollars conjures up visions of completing the picture and retiring with a huge amount in the bank. The realist dourly reminds himself that the bigger the budget, the larger the possible loss.

In the first stages of bidding, the prospective client and/or investors may be content with a blanket sum. But the time will come when the producer will be asked for an estimate based on every detail of production.

Don't think that because you have had experience in budgeting thirty-second spots for television, you are prepared to bat out the whole thing in a few days. It took me two weeks, glued to an adding machine, to prepare a budget of $2 million for the *Raggedy Ann and Andy* feature film.

The following is a sample budget for a cartoon one and a half hours long with an original story. The figures include all state, federal, and city taxes, as well as health, pension, and holiday and vacation payments where they apply.

The production flow would be based on fifteen to eighteen feet per week per animator of full animation. Obviously, this means that the film will be of fine quality. Since some artists will be getting more money than others, at this stage we can only estimate what the total sum for a department will be.

We will start with the above-the-line costs.

### Producer, directors, writer

| | |
|---|---|
| Producer/director. . . . . . . . . . . . . . . . . . . . . . . . . . . . . | $370,000 |
| Scriptwriter(s). . . . . . . . . . . . . . . . . . . . . . . . . . . . . | $60,000 |
| Sequence directors (2) . . . . . . . . . . . . . . . . . . . . . . . | $260,000 |
| Dialogue talent. . . . . . . . . . . . . . . . . . . . . . . . . . . . | $100,000 |
| | $790,000   total |

### Production management staff

| | | |
|---|---|---|
| Production manager . . . . . . . | 106 weeks. . . . . . . . . . . | $84,800 |
| Assistant director . . . . . . . . . | 106 weeks. . . . . . . . . . . | $37,100 |
| Head of ink and paint . . . . . . | 80 weeks. . . . . . . . . . . | $60,000 |
| Producer's secretary . . . . . . . | 106 weeks. . . . . . . . . . . | $37,100 |
| Errand boy . . . . . . . . . . . . . | 106 weeks. . . . . . . . . . . | $21,200 |
| Stenographer . . . . . . . . . . . . | 106 weeks. . . . . . . . . . . | $21,200 |
| | | $261,400   total |

### Animation

| | | |
|---|---|---|
| Animators . . . . . . . . . . . . . . | 60 weeks. . . . . . . . . . | $450,000 |
| Assistant animators. . . . . . . . | 60 weeks. . . . . . . . . . | $270,000 |
| | | $720,000   total |

| | | |
|---|---|---|
| Head Layout artist . . . . . . . . | 100 weeks. . . . . . . . . . . | $65,000 |
| Layout artists (2) . . . . . . . . . | 60 weeks. . . . . . . . . . . | $84,000 |
| Storyboard artist. . . . . . . . . . | 15 weeks. . . . . . . . . . . | $11,250 |
| | | $160,250   total |

| | | |
|---|---|---|
| Head Background artist. . . . . | 64 weeks. . . . . . . . . . . | $48,000 |
| Background artists (2) . . . . . . | 64 weeks. . . . . . . . . . . | $76,800 |
| Character designer . . . . . . . . | 10 weeks. . . . . . . . . . . | $15,000 |
| | | $139,800   total |

### Xerox, ink, and paint

| | | |
|---|---|---|
| Xerox operator . . . . . . . . . . . | 75 weeks. . . . . . . . . . . | $41,250 |

Inkers (8). . . . . . . . . . . . . . . . 52 weeks. . . . . . . . . . $188,700
Painters (30) . . . . . . . . . . . . . 52 weeks. . . . . . . . . . $561,600
Paint dispenser . . . . . . . . . . . 52 weeks. . . . . . . . . . . $20,800

                                                    $812,350   total

## Checking

Head checker. . . . . . . . . . . . . 70 weeks. . . . . . . . . . . $30,000
Checkers (4) . . . . . . . . . . . . . 65 weeks. . . . . . . . . . . $97,500

                                                    $127,500   total

## Photography

Head camera operator . . . . . 100 weeks. . . . . . . . . . . $60,000
Camera operators (2) . . . . . . . 60 weeks. . . . . . . . . . . $60,000

                                                    $120,000   total

## Editing

Supervising editor . . . . . . . . . 100 weeks. . . . . . . . . . . $75,000
Assistant editors (2) . . . . . . . . 75 weeks. . . . . . . . . . . $45,000
Music editor . . . . . . . . . . . . . 10 weeks. . . . . . . . . . . . $7,500
Trainee. . . . . . . . . . . . . . . . . 100 weeks. . . . . . . . . . . $20,000

                                                    $147,500   total

## Bookkeeping

Production accountant . . . . . 104 weeks. . . . . . . . . . . $52,000
Audit. . . . . . . . . . . . . . . . . . . . . . . . . . . . . . . . . . . . . $5,000
Assistant bookkeeper . . . . . . 104 weeks. . . . . . . . . . . $31,260

                                                     $88,260   total

## Dialogue recording and dubbing

Dialogue recording. . . . . . . . . . . . . . . . . . . . . . . . . . . $4,000
Dubbing . . . . . . . . . . . . . . . . . . . . . . . . . . . . . . . . . . . $1,500

                                                      $5,500   total

## Music recording and mix

| | | |
|---|---|---|
| Recording | $6,000 | |
| Mix | $2,000 | |
| | $8,000 | total |

## Music fees

| | | |
|---|---|---|
| Composer | $25,000 | |
| Conductor | $10,000 | |
| Arranger | $5,000 | |
| Copier | $3,000 | |
| Musicians (25) | $20,000 | |
| Booking fees | $3,000 | |
| Special instruments | $500 | |
| | $66,500 | total |

## Legal fees and contingencies

| | | |
|---|---|---|
| Production company | $50,000 | |
| Client/investors | $50,000 | |
| Other fees or commissions | $20,000 | |
| Contingency fund | $80,000 | |
| | $200,000 | total |

## Publicity

| | |
|---|---|
| Stills, radio, television, newspapers. | $100,000 |

## Supplies

| | | |
|---|---|---|
| Cutting room | $6,000 | |
| Ink and paint | $90,000 | |
| Office | $5,000 | |
| Equipment maintenance and repair | $5,000 | |
| | $106,000 | total |

## Film and laboratory charges

| | |
|---|---|
| Black-and-white stock | $5,000 |

Color stock . . . . . . . . . . . . . . . . . . . . . . . . . . . . . . . . . $12,000
Optical sound negative . . . . . . . . . . . . . . . . . . . . . . . $700
Postsync leader. . . . . . . . . . . . . . . . . . . . . . . . . . . . . . . $800
Full coat mag. . . . . . . . . . . . . . . . . . . . . . . . . . . . . . . $6,000
Quarter-inch tape. . . . . . . . . . . . . . . . . . . . . . . . . . . . $700
35mm Mag. tape transfers. . . . . . . . . . . . . . . . . . . . $2,500
35mm M&E Mag transfers. . . . . . . . . . . . . . . . . . . $1,000
35mm Library EFX. . . . . . . . . . . . . . . . . . . . . . . . . . $2,500
Sound EFX royalties . . . . . . . . . . . . . . . . . . . . . . . . . $1,000
$32,200   total

**Insurance**

Film Producers Indemnity
Negative and Daily takes
Employees Liability
Public Liability
Equipment
Loss of film or tape in transit
Fire
Completed negative picture
Completed sound masters

$35,000   total

**Miscellaneous**

Postproduction script. . . . . . . . . . . . . . . . . . . . . . . . $2,500
Printing and stationery . . . . . . . . . . . . . . . . . . . . . . $10,000
Entertaining and gratuities . . . . . . . . . . . . . . . . . . . $25,000
Petty cash . . . . . . . . . . . . . . . . . . . . . . . . . . . . . . . . . $7,050
Special production screenings . . . . . . . . . . . . . . . . . $3,000
$47,550   total

**Overhead**

Rent, light, heat, telephone, maintenance . . . . . . . . $100,000

The sum total of this sample film is $3,967,810. It sounds like a lot
of money, but just look at some of these figures. Of course, rates keep

changing all the time, but I believe this will enable you to construct a budget yourself, and it should be fairly close to the mark. Once again, you will have to check up on rates and get estimates where it is possible.

The salary figures are not high but they are good given the fact that it is a long schedule. Do not think that I have overdone the contingency money; I am just a cautious producer. Usually, any remaining money in this fund is returned to the client, but this can be a debatable point in setting up the contract conditions.

Obviously, the big factor is how the profit is going to be split. Make every effort to have your share of the income come from the gross. This is a nice clean deal. If it comes after expenses, you may very well find that you have worked for nothing, and I mean *nothing!*

If in the course of bargaining the opposition gives you the "What's the matter? Don't you trust me?" routine, look them in the eye very innocently and assure them that you trust them as if they were Jesuits. Maybe more. But one never knows, a heart attack, an auto accident, a drowning, and one may be facing a very different person for a partner. So it is best to make everything very legal and watertight.

This is a very difficult ploy to discount because it is so reasonable. Stick to it. In fact, start to worry if the opposition is becoming too hard-nosed. The worst thing you can do is to accept the contract because it is a lot of money. Nobody ever went broke walking away from a bad contract. Let your lawyer do all the initial dueling.

Listen to his or her advice and stay away from the meetings until the lawyers are getting down to the short strokes. This is because your lawyer needs the leverage to say at some difficult point that it's necessary to consult with you. This gives you a chance to talk things over and maybe plan some changes in your strategy.

Never go to a meeting without your lawyer, even when you are assured that it is going to be a casual get-together. When you are jockeying over a contract, there are no casual meetings—*never!* Don't drink at meetings, not even a beer. Mention a delicate digestive problem or some such excuse, but no drinking. Urge the other party to drink if they want to, so that you don't look like a puritan.

If, to your dismay, you find yourself making a picture with people who have proven to be untrustworthy, be sure that you keep a detailed production diary. Always send them memos and avoid oral agreements about anything. You might need this material in court. Nothing disconcerts the opposition more than to see that you have arrived in court with a sheaf of detailed notes. In fact, keeping a diary and using memos a lot is always a good idea, even if things look very bright.

Try to make the contract as equitable as possible. In the long run, this is better business than trying to take advantage of something the other party has done that fails to protect their interests. If the picture is good and well distributed, there is plenty of profit for everybody; so be fair.

# Glossary ――――〜〜〜〜〜〜〜〜――

**Academy leader:** a preliminary length of film, standardized by the Society of Motion Picture and Television Engineers, designed to allow the projectionist time to focus the picture properly

**acetate:** a sheet of plastic the size of an animation drawing, with peg holes. Used by inkers or Xerox operators to transfer animation drawings from paper.

**answer print:** an approved print, in which the color has been properly balanced, scene by scene, by the timer

**action axis:** an imaginary horizontal line drawn through the center of an action. A sequence of scenes can only be shot on one side of the line; otherwise the audience's point of view will be disorientated.

**background:** a piece of artwork that is placed under the cels during photography

**bar sheet:** a diagramatic form used by the director to make a blueprint of the action, music, dialogue and sound effects for an entire animated picture

**body English:** the involuntary movements people make as they are talking

**camera field:** the area being photographed by the camera

**cel levels:** the number of cels that have been combined to make one complete frame of the action

**cels:** trade jargon for *celluloids*. There is a mistaken belief that the acetate sheets are made of celluloid.

**checker:** one who makes a dry run of a scene that is ready for the camera. The purpose is to detect and correct errors.

**clean up:** a detailed drawing made from a rough sketch

**click track:** a series of clicks that go into earphones worn by musicians during a recording session. The intervals between clicks control the tempo of the music being recorded. The conductor selects the tempo by means of a dial on an electronic box that emits the clicks.

**commercials:** jargon for television advertisement that are usually one minute or less in length

**cue sheet:** a form that shows the mixer where various sounds on a track stop and start. It is used when combining the tracks of a picture into one master track.

**cut:** The end of one scene is followed by the beginning of the next scene.

**cutting room:** the editor's work area

**dailies:** the footage that has been developed and printed overnight by the laboratory

**dial numbers:** The camera operator can determine whether a given exposure has been shot by consulting the dial numbers on his camera stand against those on the exposure sheet.

**dialogue:** any speech, even if only one actor is talking

**dissolve:** an effect made by making one scene go gradually to black, then reversing the film to the beginning of the fadeout. Starting with black, the following scene is double-exposed over the same footage, ending with full exposure. The effect is that one scene has dissolved into the next.

**editor:** one who deletes or adds scenes to a picture by following the instructions of the director, and who keeps the sound tracks in sync

**exposure:** one frame of film that has been exposed

**exposure sheet:**  a form filled out by the animator. It has detailed camera instructions for every frame in a scene.

**fade in:**  a scene that starts as black and gradually is brought, frame by frame, to full exposure

**fade out:**  The scene goes from full exposure to black towards the end. Fades can be any length the director chooses, but in most animated films, fades are short, perhaps sixteen to twenty-four exposures.

**field guide:**  a diagram of the various field sizes, used to determine the position of the camera at a given time in the scene

**footage:**  film that has been exposed by the camera operator

**FPS:**  frames per second

**frame:**  an area of film equal to one exposure

**gag:**  trade jargon for a funny situation in a story

**good take:**  a scene that has been approved by the director

**inbetweener:**  a person whose function it is to draw inbetween drawings. Usually a novice.

**inbetweens:**  drawings that the assistant animator has left for the inbetweener to do. So-called because they come between the drawing of one phase of an action and that of a phase several steps later

**inker:**  the person who traces animation drawings onto cels

**iris out:**  a special effect in which a series of masks containing circles of diminishing sizes obliterate the action

**layouts:**  drawings of backgrounds for each scene, which will later be rendered by the background artist.

**matte:**  a mask. There are two kinds: the female mask, which is the character or object photographed over a black background; the male mask, which is a silhouette of a character or object shot on a white background.

**mix:** a recording session during which all the tracks for dialogue, music and sound effects are combined

**model sheet:** a group of drawings showing various views of a character, designed to show the animators and assistants how the character is constructed

**morgue:** a collection of graphic material, classified by a large number of different subjects, that might be useful to a layout and background artist

**mouth action:** the numerous shapes the mouth must take when speaking

**music editor:** an editor whose specialty is editing music tracks

**negative matcher:** an editor who specializes in assembling a negative reel by matching the scenes against the shots in the work reel

**one-light print:** prints from dailies are usually made by using one exposure for all the scenes, as opposed to employing a timer to balance the color by different exposures where it seems necessary. One-light printing saves a lot of money. The work reel does not need scenes with balanced color.

**optical printer:** a machine that is a combination of a projector and a camera. Used to combine live action and animation, and also to make fades, dissolves and wipes, or to make closer shots from scenes that were shot too long—from too far away.

**opticals:** special effects made on an optical printer

**out of sync:** The sound track is running either ahead or behind the picture.

**outtake:** a scene that has been rejected by the director.

"Good take" and "outtake" have nothing to do with "take" meaning a start of surprise or fear.

**overlay:**    art that is mounted on a cel and works in front of the animation

**pan:**    trade jargon for *panorama.* A scene where the camera sweeps across a given area.

**peg bar:**    a metal or plastic bar to which the registration pegs are attached

**pencil test:**    The animator's drawings are photographed, and the resulting negative is cut into the work reel. No print is ever made, because the staff is trained to evaluate the drawing as white lines.

**pencil test reel:**    a reel of pencil tests assembled according to the instructions on the bar sheets

**platen:**    a hinged frame containing a glass plate which the operator presses down on the cels in order to iron out wrinkles

**production chart:**    a form that shows the status of every scene in the picture during the various stages of production

**retake:**    a corrected scene or scenes

**room tone:**    the natural sound of any location, including outdoors. Room tone is used instead of blank film or tape for spaces in between sound takes, because every location has a sound, whereas blank film and tape do not.

**rotoscope:**    a machine made to project filmed images frame by frame onto the surface of a drawing board. The image is traced onto animation paper, and used by the animator to achieve lifelike movement.

**rough:**    a drawing made by the animator, usually lacking details such as buttons, wrinkles, etc. If the rough animation is approved in sweatbox, the scene is turned over to the assistant animator for cleanup.

**rushes:** another word for dailies

**scene:** a shot from the picture

**sequence:** a series of scenes that make up a definite episode in a story

**shot on twos:** jargon for photographing each set of cels two exposures. Only very fast action is shot on ones.

**special effects:** a department entirely devoted to animating special effects such as rain, snow, lightning, waves, shadows, ripples, wind and reflections. Disney's studio was the only one in the business to have one.

**sprocket holes:** holes in the film that engage the sprockets on the gears as the film is projected. They prevent the film from jiggling from side to side.

**still shot:** a scene in which the camera is immobile

**storyboard:** a large piece of beaverboard or other panel material that is used to fasten a number of story sketches in such a way that they can be viewed by a group. Also used as the name of the story itself when it is not written, but drawn by a storyboard artist.

**sweatbox:** When Disney began to show animators their rough animation and make corrections, the group was jammed into a small niche in the hall. The original studio had no space for a proper projection room. What with the close body contact and the heat coming from the projector, the name "sweatbox" was very appropriate. Later, when a projection room was built, and Disney's demands for perfection had multiplied, the term "sweatbox" had a more sinister meaning.

**sync:**  trade jargon for "synchronize. "In sync" means that the picture and sound are running in unison.

**take:**  A start of surprise or fear is a take. A double take is when a character looks at something, has no reaction and turns away. After an interval, the character reacts to what it has seen. The reaction can range from mild to violent.

**thumbnail sketch:**  a drawing about an inch and a half high, usually rendered very roughly

**timer:**  a laboratory worker who examines every scene in a picture and decides on the amount of exposure the print will need to balance the color so that it is compatible with the other scenes.

**track analysis:**  an examination of a sound track by the editor to determine exactly where various sounds occur

**transfer:**  to record from quarter-inch tape to magnetic 16 mm or 35 mm, or from magnetic to film

**trucking:**  a movement of the camera toward or away from the scene. "Trucking in" means that the camera is being moved closer. "Trucking back" means that the camera is being moved farther away.

**underlay:**  a section of the background mounted on a cel that works with the animation cels

**wipe:**  an optical effect in which one scene supercedes the other by using mattes. There are so many kinds of mattes that optical companies issue charts to enable the customer to select the appropriate effect.

**zoom:**  a very fast truck in or out

# Index

**330**